THE LAST ADIEU OF LOUIS XVI. AND MARIE ANTOINETTE

Photogravure after a painting by Meisel.

SECRET MEMOIRS OF PRINCESS LAMBALLE

BEING

HER JOURNALS, LETTERS, AND CONVERSATIONS DURING HER CONFIDENTIAL RELATIONS WITH

MARIE ANTOINETTE

WITH ORIGINAL AND AUTHENTIC ANECDOTES OF THE
ROYAL FAMILY AND OTHER DISTINGUISHED
PERSONAGES DURING THE REVOLUTION

EDITED AND ANNOTATED BY
CATHERINE HYDE

MARQUISE DE GOUVION BROGLIE SCOLARI
IN THE CONFIDENTIAL SERVICE
OF THE UNFORTUNATE PRINCESS

WITH A SPECIAL INTRODUCTION BY
OLIVER H. G. LEIGH

AUTHOR OF
"FRENCH LITERATURE OF THE XIXth CENTURY," etc.

University Press of the Pacific
Honolulu, Hawaii

Secret Memoirs of Princess Lamballe:
Her Confidential Relations with Marie Antoniette

by
Princess Lamballe

Edited and Annotated by
Catherine Hyde

ISBN: 1-4102-0412-X

Reprinted from the 1901 edition

University Press of the Pacific
Honolulu, Hawaii
http://www.universitypressofthepacific.com

ILLUSTRATIONS

SPECIAL INTRODUCTION

M ARIE THÉRÈSE LOUISE DE SAVOIE-CARIGNAN, Princess
de Lamballe, was fated to be not only an eyewitness but a victim of the Reign of Terror. She
was born in Turin in 1749, was married in 1767 to Stanislaus, Prince of Lamballe and son of the Duke of
Penthièvre, which brought her into the relationship of
sister-in-law to the Duke of Orléans. Her husband died
within a year, leaving her, as she expresses it, "a bride
when an infant, a widow before I was a mother or had a
prospect of becoming one." A marriage was proposed
between the Princess and Louis XV., but it fell through.
In her retirement she gained the friendship of Marie
Antoinette, who appointed her superintendent of the royal
household on the accession of Louis XVI. This official
connection grew into a sisterly intimacy of the most cordial kind. Their youth of brilliant promise was soon
overshadowed with ominous troubles. The lighter tem-
perament of the Queen was happily balanced by the
philosophic gravity of the Princess, who foresaw the bitter fruits of the conditions in which her royal mistress
had been reared and would not radically change. This
journal-record of experiences and reflections is as pathetic
a tale as has ever been told. Lit up as it is with gleams
of the merriment supposed to be the normal atmosphere
of court life, it progresses with the doleful tread of a
funeral march, each step lessening the too short space
that separates the palace from the dungeon, the glamor
of hollow sovereignty from the bloody tyranny of an ir-
responsible populace.

The Princess Lamballe, as will be seen, was as loyal
to her own conscience as to her less clear-sighted mistress. When the catastrophe was impending the Queen

and King implored her to leave France and so save her life. The beauty and purity of her character was equaled by her devotion to duty and her courage. She scorned to leave her friends in the hour of peril, "faithful among the faithless" titular nobility who scampered away to safe hiding-places until they might creep back in the returning sunshine. She was harassed with repeated attempts at bodily injury, and when arrested, calmly refused to forswear her principle of fealty to the monarchy, while cheerfully willing to accept the mandate of the nation. Thereupon the gentle and brave woman was stabbed to death by the fiends who invaded her cell, and who added an exquisite pang to the sufferings of the Queen by parading the head of the Princess, on the point of a pike, before the window where her mistress was expected to see it.

How the Princess's journal came to light is narrated in the following pages. It is edited and annotated, in a liberal sense of those terms, by the lady who, in her youth, was the confidential secretary and messenger, in fact a diplomatic maid-of-all-work, of the Princess. From the copious diary of the latter, supplemented by the graphic and elaborate additions and comments of the brillantly gifted editor, to whose care the diary was intrusted, we get a most impressive realization of the life endured by Louis XVI. and Marie Antoinette in those appalling years of doom.

The portraiture of these unconsciously fatalistic royalties is eloquently painted in many offhand touches, the force of which has been made clearer by lapse of years. The young Queen owed more grudges than gratitude to her imperial mother for her bringing-up. Conspicuous lack of common sense may more justly be blamed for the failure of her life than any of the faults charged against her. The Princess avers that Marie Antoinette was an unsophisticated country girl at heart, with a natural dislike for fine dress and jewel display. The artifice and pomposity of the court were alien to her artless nature She loved genuine jollity, unhampered by stilted conventionalities, and preferred the society of pleasure-loving youth to that of the elderly aunts of the King, who sought to rule her as they dominated him. Add to this wholesome rebelliousness an unfortunate hereditary and exaggerated superstition as to the divinity of royalty, and we have the elements of the hopeless deadlock which culminated in the Revolution.

Marie Antoinette is here shown as developing an unexpected solidity of character as the need for it became more insistent. In the beginning she made light of national susceptibilities, a fatal folly in ordinary circumstances, much more serious in those times. As the King's weakness and her own unpopularity increased, she rose to the situation with somewhat of her mother's masterful spirit, unwise, but compelling a qualified admiration. When the Princess Lamballe was the transmitter of outside opinion and counsel to the King through the Queen she backed it up by candid advice of her own, with the usual result of offending, without influencing, the object of her solicitude. For a time this intercourse, or at least this faithful remonstrance, ceased, to be resumed when its wisdom had struck home. But it was then too late to undo past follies, and a few lingering stupidities were never given up. The old nobility felt their order had been humiliated by the persistently alien Queen. The common people were incensed against a monarchy that reveled, as they were assured, in wanton luxury while famine threatened the land. The resurrected States General were regarded as an audacious attempt to set up the vulgar human against the Lord's anointed. Marie Antoinette made no politic effort to veil her sovereign contempt for the masses when massed. As individuals no one was at heart more of a "friend of the people." She proudly disdained to exchange thoughts with our Franklin or the sages of France on the social convulsions raging around. "I was the only silent individual among millions of infatuated enthusiasts at La Fayette's return to Paris," at the head of the throng he so half-heartedly led. There is a queenly grandeur in this attitude despite its perversity. Of all infatuated enthusiasts she herself was at that supreme moment the queen, and did not know it. Weakness was behind that show of strength, for she was even then dallying with Mirabeau, the man of the people, the man of the hour; friend of republicans, friend of the monarchy. Disguised in monkish robe and cowl he crept into the palace and negotiated for terms as between the dissolving view of the throne and the coming people, and his impecunious but statesmanlike and doubtless honest self. When he was cut off in the critical phase of the struggle, (by disease, or, as here suggested, by poison), the cord was snapped that held up the curtain on the last act but one of the tragedy of a make-believe reign. Then it fell, and in the black gloom of the background was played out the final tableau of horrors on which this book throws so painful a light.

The sympathies of both the writers are openly expressed. We know where they stand and which view they will take of characters and events. The fact that they are women, with feminine instincts, tastes and literary style, gives special interest to their admirably composed pages, whether of narrative or comment. From any point of view this book cannot but win its way among students of history, character, and the strange inner life of the Revolution period.

Oliver H. V. Leigh.

CONTENTS

SECRET MEMOIRS

OF THE

ROYAL FAMILY OF FRANCE

———

AUTHOR'S INTRODUCTION

I SHOULD consider it great presumption to intrude upon the public anything respecting myself, were there any other way of establishing the authenticity of the facts and papers I am about to present. To the history of my own peculiar situation, amid the great events I record, which made me the depositary of information and documents so important, I proceed, therefore, though reluctantly, without further preamble.

In the title page of this work I have stated that I was for many years in the confidential service of the Princess Lamballe, and that the most important materials, which form my history, have been derived not only from the conversations, but the private papers of my lamented patroness. It remains for me to show how I became acquainted with Her Highness, and by what means the papers I allude to came into my possession.

Though, from my birth, and the rank of those who were the cause of it (had it not been from political motives kept from my knowledge), in point of interest I ought to have been very independent, I was indebted for my resources in early life to His Grace the late Duke of Norfolk and Lady Mary Duncan. By them I was placed for education in the Irish convent, Rue du Bacq, Fauxbourg St. Germain, at Paris, where the immortal Sacchini, the instructor of the Queen, gave me lessons in music. Pleased with my progress, the celebrated composer, when one day teaching Maria Antoinette, so highly overrated to that illustrious lady my infant natural talents and acquired science in his art, in the presence of her very shadow, the Princess Lamballe, as to excite in Her Majesty an eager desire for the opportunity of hearing me, which the Princess volunteered to obtain by going herself to the convent next morning with Sacchini. It was enjoined upon the composer, as I afterward learned, that he was neither to apprise me who Her Highness was, nor to what motive I was indebted for her visit. To this Sacchini readily agreed, adding, after disclosing to them my connections and situation, "Your Majesty will be, perhaps, still more surprised, when I, as an Italian, and her German master, who is a German, declare that she speaks both these languages like a native, though born in England; and is as well disposed to the Catholic faith, and as well versed in it, as if she had been a member of that Church all her life."

This last observation decided my future good fortune: there was no interest in the minds of the Queen and Princess paramount to that of making proselytes to their creed.

The Princess, faithful to her promise, accompanied Sacchini. Whether it was chance, ability, or good fortune, let me not attempt to conjecture; but from that moment, I became the *protégé* of this ever-regretted angel. Political circumstances presently facilitated her introduction of me to the Queen. My combining a readiness in the Italian and German languages, with my knowledge of English and French, greatly promoted my power of being useful at that crisis, which, with some claims to their confidence of a higher order, made this august, lamented, injured pair, more like mothers to me than mistresses, till we were parted by their murder.

The circumstances I have just mentioned show that to mere curiosity, the characteristic passion of our sex and so often its ruin, I am to ascribe the introduction, which was only prevented by events unparalleled in history from proving the most fortunate in my life as it is the most cherished in my recollection.

It will be seen in the course of the following pages, how often I was employed on confidential missions, frequently by myself, and, in some instances, as the attendant of the Princess. The nature of my situation, the trust reposed in me, the commissions with which I was honored, and the affecting charges of which I was the bearer, flattered my pride and determined me to make myself an exception to the rule that "no woman can keep a secret." Few ever knew exactly where I was, what I was doing, and much less the importance of my occupation. I had passed from England to France, made two journeys to Italy and Germany, three to the Archduchess Marie Christiana, Governess of the Low Countries, and returned back to France, before any of my friends in England were aware of my retreat, or of my ever having accompanied the Princess. Though my letters were written and dated at Paris, they were all forwarded to England by way of Holland or Germany, that no clue should be given for annoyances from idle curiosity. It is to this discreetness, to this inviolable secrecy, firmness, and fidelity, which I so early in life displayed to the august personages who stood in need of such a person, that I owe the unlimited confidence of my illustrious benefactress, through which I was furnished with the valuable materials I am now submitting to the public.

I was repeatedly a witness, by the side of the Princess Lamballe, of the appalling scenes of the *bonnet rouge*, of murders *à la lanterne*, and of numberless criminal insults to the unfortunate royal family of Louis XVI., when the Queen was generally selected as the most marked victim of malicious indignity. Having had the honor of so often beholding this much-injured Queen, and never without remarking how amiable in her manners, how condescendingly kind in her deportment toward everyone about her, how charitably generous, and withal, how beautiful she was; I looked upon her as a model of perfection. But when I found the public feeling so much at variance with my own, the difference became utterly unaccountable. I longed for some explanation of the mystery. One day I was insulted in the Tuileries, because I had alighted from my horse to walk there without wearing the national ribbon. On this I met the Princess: the conversation which grew out of my adventure emboldened me to question her on a theme to me inexplicable.

"What," asked I, "can it be, which makes the people so outrageous against the Queen?"

Her Highness condescended to reply in the complimentary terms which I am about to relate, but without answering my question.

"My dear friend!" exclaimed she, "for from this moment I beg you will consider me in that light,—never having been blessed with children of my own, I feel there is no way of acquitting myself of the obligations you have heaped upon me, by the fidelity with which you have executed the various commissions intrusted to your charge, but by adopting you as one of my own family. I am satisfied with you, yes, highly satisfied with you, on the score of your religious principles;* and as soon as the troubles subside, and we have a little calm after them, my father-in-law and myself will be present at the ceremony of your confirmation."

The goodness of my benefactress silenced me; gratitude would not allow me to persevere for the moment. But from what I had already seen of Her Majesty the Queen, I was too much interested to lose sight of my object,— not, let me be believed, from idle womanish curiosity, but from that real, strong, personal interest which I, in common with all who ever had the honor of being in her presence, felt for that much-injured, most engaging sovereign.

A propitious circumstance unexpectedly occurred, which gave me an opportunity, without any appearance of

---

* I was at that time, by her orders, under examination by Monsieur de Brienne, for being confirmed to receive the sacrament.

officious earnestness, to renew the attempt to gain the end I had in view.

I was riding in the carriage with the Princess Lamballe, when a lady drove by, who saluted my benefactress with marked attention and respect. There was something in the manner of the Princess, after receiving the salute, which impelled me, spite of myself, to ask who the lady was.

"Madame de Genlis," exclaimed Her Highness, with a shudder of disgust, "that lamb's face with a wolf's heart, and a fox's cunning." Or, to quote her own Italian phrase which I have here translated, "*colla faccia d'agnello, il cuore d'un lupo, e la dritura della volpe.*"

In the course of these pages the cause of this strong feeling against Madame de Genlis will be explained. To dwell on it now would only turn me aside from my narrative. To pursue my story, therefore:

When we arrived at my lodgings (which were then, for private reasons, at the Irish convent, where Sacchini and other masters attended to further me in the accomplishments of the fine arts), "Sing me something," said the Princess, "*Cantate mi qualche cosa*, for I never see that woman" (meaning Madame de Genlis) "but I feel ill and out of humor. I wish it may not be the foreboding of some great evil!"

I sang a little rondo, in which Her Highness and the Queen always delighted, and which they would never set me free without making me sing, though I had given them twenty before it.* Her Highness honored me with even more than usual praise. I kissed the hand which had so generously applauded my infant talents, and said, "Now, my dearest Princess, as you are so kind and good-humored, tell me something about the Queen!"

She looked at me with her eyes full of tears. For an instant they stood in their sockets as if petrified: and then, after a pause, "I cannot," answered she in Italian,

---

* The rondo I allude to was written by Sarti for the celebrated Marchesi, *Lungi da te ben mio*, and is the same in which he was so successful in England, when he introduced it in London in the opera of "*Giulo Sabino.*"

as she usually did, "I cannot refuse you anything. *Non posso negarti niente.*" It would take me an age to tell you the many causes which have conspired against this much-injured Queen! I fear none who are near her person will escape the threatening storm that hovers over our heads. The leading causes of the clamor against her have been, if you must know, Nature; her beauty; her power of pleasing; her birth; her rank; her marriage; the King himself; her mother; her imperfect education; and, above all, her unfortunate partialities for the Abbé Vermond; for the Duchess de Polignac; for myself, perhaps; and last, but not least, the thorough unsuspecting goodness of her heart!

"But, since you seem to be so much concerned for her exalted, persecuted Majesty, you shall have a Journal I myself began on my first coming to France and which I have continued ever since I have been honored with the confidence of Her Majesty, in graciously giving me that unlooked-for situation at the head of her household, which honor and justice prevent my renouncing under any difficulties, and which I never will quit but with my life!"

She wept as she spoke, and her last words were almost choked with sobs.

Seeing her so much affected, I humbly begged pardon for having unintentionally caused her tears, and begged permission to accompany her to the Tuileries.

"No," said she, "you have hitherto conducted yourself with a profound prudence, which has insured you my confidence. Do not let your curiosity change your system. You shall have the Journal. But be careful. Read it only by yourself, and do not show it to anyone. On these conditions you shall have it."

I was in the act of promising, when Her Highness stopped me.

"I want no particular promises. I have sufficient proofs of your adherence to truth. Only answer me simply in the affirmative."

I said I would certainly obey her injunctions most religiously.

She then left me, and directed that I should walk in a particular part of the private alleys of the Tuileries, between three and four o'clock in the afternoon. I did so; and from her own hand I there received her private Journal.

In the following September of this same year (1792) she was murdered!

Journalizing copiously, for the purpose of amassing authentic materials for the future historian, was always a favorite practice of the French, and seems to have been particularly in vogue in the age I mention. The press has sent forth whole libraries of these records since the Revolution, and it is notorious that Louis XV. left Secret Memoirs, written by his own hand, of what passed before this convulsion; and had not the papers of the Tuileries shared in the wreck of royalty, it would have been seen that Louis XVI. had made some progress in the memoirs of his time; and even his beautiful and unfortunate Queen had herself made extensive notes and collections for the record of her own disastrous career. Hence it must be obvious how one so nearly connected in situation and suffering with her much-injured mistress, as the Princess Lamballe, would naturally fall into a similar habit had she even no stronger temptation than fashion and example. But self-communion, by means of the pen, is invariably the consolation of strong, feeling, and reflecting minds under great calamities, especially when their intercourse with the world has been checked or poisoned by its malice.

The editor of these pages herself fell into the habit of which she speaks; and it being usual with her benefactress to converse with all the unreserve which every honest mind shows when it feels it can confide, her humble attendant, not to lose facts of such importance, commonly made notes of what she heard. In any other person's hands the Journal of the Princess would have been incomplete, especially as it was written in a rambling manner, and was never intended for publication. But connected by her confidential conversations with me, and the recital of the events to which I personally bear testimony, I trust it will be found the basis of a satisfactory record, which I pledge myself to be a true one.

I do not know, however, that, at my time of life, and after a lapse of thirty years, I should have been roused to the arrangement of the papers which I have combined to form this narrative, had I not met with the work of Madame Campan upon the same subject.

This lady has said much that is true respecting the Queen; but she has omitted much, and much she has misrepresented: not, I dare say, purposely; but from ignorance, and being wrongly informed. She was often absent from the service, and on such occasions must have been compelled to obtain her knowledge at second-hand. She herself told me, in 1803, at Ecouen, that at a very important epoch the peril of her life forced her from the seat of action. With the Princess Lamballe, who was so much about the Queen, she never had any particular connection. The Princess certainly esteemed her for her devotedness to the Queen: but there was a natural reserve in the Princess's character, and a mistrust resulting from circumstances of all those who saw much company as Madame Campan did. Hence no intimacy was encouraged. Madame Campan never came to the Princess without being sent for.

An attempt has been made since the Revolution utterly to destroy faith in the alleged attachment of Madame Campan to the Queen, by the fact of her having received the daughters of many of the regicides for education into her establishment at Ecouen. Far be it from me to sanction so unjust a censure. Although what I mention hurt her character very much in the estimation of her former friends, and constituted one of the grounds of the dissolution of her establishment at Ecouen, on the restoration of the Bourbons, and may possibly in some degree have deprived her of such aids from their adherents, as might have made her work unquestionable, yet what else, let me ask, could have been done by one dependent upon her exertions for support, and in the power of Napoleon's family and his emissaries? On the contrary, I would give my public testimony in favor of the fidelity of her feelings, though in many instances I must withhold it from the fidelity of her narrative. Her being utterly isolated from the illustrious individual nearest to the Queen must necessarily leave much to be desired in her record. During the whole term of the Princess Lamballe's superintendence of the Queen's household, Madame Campan never had any special communication with my benefactress, excepting once, about the things which were to go to Brussels, before the journey to Varennes; and once again, relative to a person of the Queen's household, who had received the visits of Petion, the Mayor of Paris, at her private lodgings. This last communication I myself particularly remember, because on that occasion the Princess, addressing me in her own native language, Madame Campan, observing it, considered me as an Italian, till, by a circumstance I shall presently relate, she was undeceived.

I should anticipate the order of events, and incur the necessity of speaking twice of the same things, were I here to specify the express errors in the work of Madame Campan. Suffice it now that I observe generally her want of knowledge of the Princess Lamballe; her omission of many of the most interesting circumstances of the Revolution; her silence upon important anecdotes of the King, the Queen, and several members of the first assembly; her mistakes concerning the Princess Lamballe's relations with the Duchess de Polignac, Count de Fersen, Mirabeau, the Cardinal de Rohan, and others; her great miscalculation of the time when the Queen's confidence in Barnave began, and when that of the Empress-mother in Rohan ended; her misrepresentation of particulars relating to Joseph II ; and her blunders concerning the affair of the necklace, and regarding the libel Madame Lamotte published in England with the connivance of Calonne: all these will be considered, with numberless other statements equally requiring correction in their turn. What she has omitted I trust I shall supply; and where she has gone astray I hope to set her right; that, between the two, the future biographer of my august benefactresses may be in no want of authentic materials to do full justice to their honored memories.

I said in a preceding paragraph that I should relate a circumstance about Madame Campan, which happened after she had taken me for an Italian and before she was aware of my being in the service of the Princess.

Madame Campan, though she had seen me not only at the time I mention but before and after, had always passed me without notice. One Sunday, when in the gallery of the Tuileries with Madame de Staël, the Queen, with her usual suite, of which Madame Campan formed one, was going according to custom to hear mass, her Majesty perceived me and most graciously addressed me in German. Madame Campan appeared greatly surprised at this, but walked on and said nothing. Ever afterward, however, she treated me whenever we met with marked civility.

Another edition of Boswell to those who got a nod from Dr. Johnson!

The reader will find in the course of this work that on the 2d of August, 1792, from the kindness and humanity of my august benefactresses, I was compelled to accept a mission to Italy, devised merely to send me from the sanguinary scenes of which they foresaw they and theirs must presently become victims. Early in the following month the Princess Lamballe was murdered. As my history extends beyond the period I have mentioned, it is fitting I should explain the indisputable authorities whence I derived such particulars as I did not see.

A person, high in the confidence of the Princess, through the means of the honest coachman of whom I shall have occasion to speak, supplied me with regular details of whatever took place, till she herself, with the rest of the ladies and other attendants, being separated from the Royal Family, was immured in the prison of La Force. When I returned to Paris after this dire tempest, Madame Clery and her friend, Madame de Beaumont, a natural daughter of Louis XV., with Monsieur Chambon of Rheims, who never left Paris during the time, confirmed the correctness of my papers. The Madame Clery I mention is the same who assisted her husband in his faithful attendance upon the Royal Family in the Temple; and this exemplary man added his testimony to the rest, in presence of the Duchess de Guiche Grammont, at Pyrmont in Germany, when I there met him in the suite of the late sovereign of France, Louis XVIII., at a concert. After the 10th of August, I had also a continued correspondence with many persons at Paris, who supplied me with thorough accounts of the succeeding horrors, in letters directed to Sir William Hamilton, at Naples, and by him forwarded to me. And in addition to all these high sources, many particular circumstances have been disclosed to me by individuals, whose authority, when I have used it, I have generally affixed to the facts they have enabled me to communicate.

It now only remains for me to mention that I have endeavored to arrange everything, derived either from the papers of the Princess Lamballe, or from her remarks, my own observation, or the intelligence of others, in chronological order. It will readily be seen by the reader where the Princess herself speaks, as I have invariably set apart my own recollections and remarks in paragraphs and notes, which are not only indicated by the heading of each chapter, but by the context of the passages themselves. I have also begun and ended what the Princess says with inverted commas. All the earlier part of the work preceding her personal introduction proceeds principally from her pen or her lips: I have done little more than changed it from Italian into English, and embodied thoughts and sentiments that were often disjointed and detached. And throughout, whether she or others speak, I may safely say this work will be found the most circumstantial, and assuredly the most authentic, upon the subject of which it treats, of any that has yet been presented to the public of Great Britain. The press has been prolific in fabulous writ-

ings upon these times, which have been devoured with
avidity. I hope John Bull is not so devoted to gilded
foreign fictions as to spurn the unadorned truth from
one of his downright countrywomen: and let me advise
him *en passant*, not to treat us beauties of native growth
with indifference at home; for we readily find compensation in the regard, patronage, and admiration of every
nation in Europe.* I am old now, and may speak freely.

I have no interest whatever in the work I submit but
that of endeavoring to redeem the character of so many
injured victims. Would to Heaven my memory were less
acute, and that I could obliterate from the knowledge of

---

*I wish it were in my power to include a certain lady in these
kingdoms, who has recently written upon Italy, in my contrast between British accuracy and foreign fable. This lady seems quite
unincumbered by the fetters of truth. She has either been deceived,
or would herself be the deceiver, respecting the replacing of the famous
horses at Venice. I was present at that ceremony, and when I cast
my eyes over the fiction of Lady Morgan upon the subject, it made
me grieve to see the account of a country so very interesting and to
me endeared by a residence of nearly thirty years, among real friends
of humanity and general good faith, drawn by a hand so unhesitatingly
inaccurate.

As for her account of the Emperor of Austria and Maria Louisa —
Maria Louisa had never been at Venice at the time she mentions.
When she did come there it was merely to condole with her imperial
father for the loss of her cousin and mother-in-law, the Empress Lodo-
vica, daughter of the Archduke of Milan, the third wife of the Emperor.
This happened a considerable time after the restoration of the Golden
Steeds of Lysippus. Besides, it was the Holy Week, *Settimnonæ
Santa*, when there are never theatrical performances in any part of
Italy. The Court, too, from the event I have stated, was in deep
mourning. Sometimes I myself may be misled, and papers which have
been thirty years undisturbed, may retain inaccuracies. Still, whenever
I assert from hearsay I have been careful — at least, I have endeavored
so to do — to save my credit under the shield, beneath which all writers
have it in their power to take shelter, the never failing *salva con dotta*,
the *on dit*. But neither the Count nor the Countess Cicognara, whatever their private reasons may be to be dissatisfied with the conduct of
the Austrian government relative to themselves, could ever have
asserted such flagrant falsehoods to Lady Morgan; the circumstances
being too notorious even to the Ciceroni of the Piazza, whose ignorance
has spoiled the books of so many of her ladyship's predecessors.

the world and posterity the names of their infamous destroyers; I mean not the executioners who terminated their mortal existence — for in their miserable situation that early martyrdom was an act of grace — but I mean some, perhaps still living, who with foul cowardice, stabbing like assassins in the dark, undermined their fair fame and morally murdered them, long before their deaths, by daily traducing virtues the slanderers never possessed from mere jealousy of the glory they knew themselves incapable of deserving.

Montesquieu says, "If there be a God, he must be just!" That divine justice, after centuries, has been fully established on the descendants of the cruel, sanguinary conquerors of South America and its butchered harmless Emperor Montezuma and his innocent offspring, who are now teaching Spain a moral lesson in freeing themselves from its insatiable thirst for blood and wealth, while God himself has refused that blessing to the Spaniards which they denied to the Americans!* Oh, France! what hast thou not already suffered, and what hast thou not yet to suffer, when to thee, like Spain, it shall visit their descendants even unto the fourth generation?

To my insignificant losses in so mighty a ruin perhaps I ought not to allude. I should not presume even to mention that the fatal convulsion which shook all Europe and has since left the nations in that state of agitated undulation which succeeds a tempest upon the ocean, were it not for the opportunity it gives me to declare the bounty of my benefactresses. All my own property went down in the wreck; and the mariner who escapes only with his life can never recur to the scene of

* The constitutional members, who were gloriously fighting in the field of liberty to rescue a rising generation from tyranny and superstitious bigotry (an operation commenced on the foundation of the law of the land, delegated to the nation by its chosen representatives and sacredly guaranteed through the sanction of a constitutional king, who now, with the rest of the Spanish nation, is in jeopardy, a prisoner, and dependent on a foreign sovereign), now expiate in turn the bloody crimes of their ancestors on the nations so long held by them in savage and unnatural bondage!

his escape without a shudder. Many persons are still living, of the first respectability, who well remember my quitting this country, though very young, on the budding of a brilliant career. Had those prospects been followed up they would have placed me beyond the caprice of fickle fortune. But the dazzling luster of crown favors and princely patronage outweighed the slow, though more solid hopes of self-achieved independence. I certainly was then almost a child, and my vanity, perhaps, of the honor of being useful to two such illustrious personages got the better of every other sentiment. But now when I reflect, I look back with consternation on the many risks I ran, on the many times I stared death in the face with no fear but that of being obstructed in my efforts to serve, even with my life, the interests dearest to my heart — that of implicit obedience to these truly benevolent and generous Princesses, who only wanted the means to render me as happy and independent as their cruel destiny has since made me wretched and miserable! Had not death deprived me of their patronage I should have had no reason to have regretted any sacrifice I could have made for them, for through the Princess, Her Majesty, unasked, had done me the honor to promise me the reversion of a most lucrative as well as highly respectable post in her employ. In these august personages I lost my best friends; I lost everything — except the tears, which bathe the paper as I write — tears of gratitude, which will never cease to flow to the memory of their martyrdom.

CHAPTER I.

"THE character of Maria Theresa, the Empress-mother of Maria Antoinette, is sufficiently known. The same spirit of ambition and enterprise which had already animated her contentions with France in the latter part of her career impelled her to wish for its alliance. In addition to other hopes, she had been encouraged to imagine that Louis XV. might one day aid her in recovering the provinces which the King of Prussia had violently wrested from her ancient dominions. She felt the many advantages to be derived from an union with her ancient enemy, and she looked for its accomplishment by the marriage of her daughter.

" Policy, in sovereigns, is paramount to every other consideration. They regard beauty as a source of profit, like managers of theaters, who, when a female candidate is offered, ask whether she is young and handsome ? — not whether she has talent. Maria Theresa believed that her daughter's beauty would have proved more powerful over France than her own armies. Like Catharine II., her envied contemporary, she consulted no ties of nature in the disposal of her children; a system more in char-

acter where the knout is the logician than among nations
boasting higher civilization: indeed her rivalry with
Catharine even made her grossly neglect their education.
Jealous of the rising power of the North, she saw that
it was the purpose of Russia to counteract her views in
Poland and Turkey through France, and so totally forgot her domestic duties in the desire to thwart the as-
cendency of Catharine that she often suffered eight or
ten days to go by without even seeing her children, allowing
even the essential sources of instruction to remain un-
provided.   Her very caresses were scarcely given but for
display, when the children were admitted to be shown to
some great personage; and if they were overwhelmed
with kindness, it was merely to excite a belief that they
were the constant care and companions of her leisure
hours.   When they grew up they became the mere instruments of her ambition.   The fate of one of them will
show how their mother's worldliness was rewarded.*

"A leading object of Maria Theresa's policy was the
attainment of influence over Italy.   For this purpose she
first married one of the archduchesses to the imbecile
Duke of Parma.   Her second maneuver was to contrive
that Charles III. should seek the Archduchess Josepha
for his younger son, the King of Naples.   When everything had been settled, and the ceremony by proxy had
taken place, it was thought proper to sound the Princess as to how far she felt inclined to aid her mother's
designs in the Court of Naples.   'Scripture says,' was
her reply, 'that when a woman is married she belongs to
the country of her husband.'

"'But the policy of State?' exclaimed Maria Theresa.

"'Is that above religion?' cried the Princess.

"'This unexpected answer of the Archduchess was so
totally opposite to the views of the Empress that she was
for a considerable time undecided whether she would
allow her daughter to depart, till, worn out by perplexi-

* The Princess, could she have looked into the book of Fate, might
have said the fate of TWO; but the most persecuted victim was not at
that time sacrificed.

ties, she at last consented, but bade the Archduchess, previous to setting off for this much-desired country of her new husband, to go down to the tombs, and in the vaults of her ancestors offer up to Heaven a fervent prayer for the departed souls of those she was about to leave.

"Only a few days before that, a princess had been buried in the vaults — I think Joseph the Second's second wife, who had died of the smallpox.

"The Archduchess Josepha obeyed her imperial mother's cruel commands, took leave of all her friends and relatives, as if conscious of the result, caught the same disease, and in a few days died!

"The Archduchess Carolina was now tutored to become her sister's substitute, and when deemed adequately qualified was sent to Naples, where she certainly never forgot she was an Austrian nor the interest of the Court of Vienna. One circumstance concerning her and her mother fully illustrates the character of both. On the marriage, the Archduchess found that Spanish etiquette did not allow the Queen to have the honor of dining at the same table as the King. She apprised her mother. Maria Theresa instantly wrote to the Marchese Tenucei, then Prime Minister at the Court of Naples, to say, that if her daughter, now Queen of Naples, was to be considered less than the King her husband, she would send an army to fetch her back to Vienna, and the King might purchase a Georgian slave, for an Austrian Princess should not be thus humbled. Maria Theresa need not have given herself all this trouble, for before the letter arrived the Queen of Naples had dismissed all the ministry, upset the cabinet of Naples, and turned out even the King himself from her bedchamber! So much for the overthrow of Spanish etiquette by Austrian policy. The King of Spain became outrageous at the influence of Maria Theresa, but there was no alternative.

"The other daughter of the Empress was married, as I have observed already, to the Duke of Parma for the purpose of promoting the Austrian strength in Italy

2

against that of France, to which the Court of Parma, as well as that of Modena, had been long attached.

"The fourth Archduchess, Maria Antoinette, being the youngest and most beautiful of the family, was destined for France. There were three older than Maria Antoinette; but she, being much lovelier than her sisters, was selected on account of her charms. Her husband was never considered by the contrivers of the scheme: he was known to have no sway whatever, not even in the choice of his own wife! But the character of Louis XV. was recollected, and calculations drawn from it, upon the probable power which youth and beauty might obtain over such a King and Court.

"It was during the time when Madame Pompadour directed, not only the King, but all France with most despotic sway, that the union of the Archduchess Maria Antoinette with the grandson of Louis XV. was proposed. The plan received the warmest support of Choiseul, then Minister, and the ardent co-operation of Pompadour. Indeed it was to her, the Duke de Choiseul, and the Count de Mercy, the whole affair may be ascribed. So highly was she flattered by the attention with which Maria Theresa distinguished her, in consequence of her zeal, by presents and by the title, 'dear cousin,' which she used in writing to her, that she left no stone unturned till the proxy of the Dauphin was sent to Vienna, to marry Maria Antoinette in his name.

"All the interest by which this union was supported could not, however, subdue a prejudice against it, not only among many of the Court, the cabinet, and the nation, but in the Royal Family itself. France has never looked with complacency upon alliances with the House of Austria: enemies to this one avowed themselves as soon as it was declared. The daughters of Louis XV. openly expressed their aversion; but the stronger influence prevailed, and Maria Antoinette became the Dauphiness.

"Brienne, Archbishop of Toulouse, and afterward of Sens, suggested the appointment of the Librarian of the College des Quatre Nations, the Abbé Vermond, as instructor to the Dauphiness in French. The Abbé Vermond was accordingly dispatched by Louis XV. to Vienna. The consequences of this appointment will be seen in the sequel. Perhaps not the least fatal of them arose from his gratitude to the Archbishop, who recommended him. In some years afterward, influencing his pupil, when Queen, to help Brienne to the ministry, he did her and her kingdom more injury than their worst foes. Of the Abbé's power over Maria Antoinette there are various opinions; of his capacity, there is but one — he was superficial and cunning. On his arrival at Vienna he became the tool of Maria Theresa. While there, he received a salary as the daughter's tutor, and when he returned to France, a much larger one as the mother's spy. He was more ambitious to be thought a great man, in his power over his pupil, than a rich one. He was too jesuitical to wish to be deemed rich. He knew that superfluous emoluments would soon have overthrown the authority he derived from conferring, rather than receiving favors; and hence he never soared to any higher post. He was generally considered to be disinterested. How far his private fortunes benefited by his station, has never appeared; nor is it known, whether by the elevation of his friend and patron to the ministry in the time of Louis XVI., he gained anything beyond the gratification of vanity, from having been the cause: it is probable he did not, for if he had, from the general odium against that promotion, no doubt it would have been exposed, unless the influence of the Queen was his protection, as it proved in so many cases where he grossly erred. From the first he was an evil to Maria Antoinette; and ultimately habit rendered him a necessary evil.*

"The education of the Dauphiness was circumscribed; though very free in her manners, she was very deficient in other respects; and hence it was she so much avoided all society of females who were better informed than herself, courting in preference the lively tittle-tattle of

* Upon these points more will be said hereafter.

the other sex, who were in turn, better pleased with the gayeties of the youth and beauty than the more substantial logical witticisms of antiquated Court dowagers. To this may be ascribed her ungovernable passion for great societies, balls, masquerades, and all kinds of public and private amusements, as well as her subsequent attachment to the Duchess de Polignac, who so much encouraged them for the pastime of her friend and sovereign. Though naturally averse to everything requiring study or application, Maria Antoinette was very assiduous in preparing herself for the parts she performed in the various comedies, farces, and *cantatas* given at her private theater; and their acquirement seemed to cost her no trouble. These innocent diversions became a source of calumny against her; yet they formed almost the only part of her German education, about which Maria Theresa had been particular : the Empress-mother deemed them so valuable to her children that she ordered the celebrated Metastasio to write some of his most sublime *cantatas* for the evening recreations of her sisters and herself. And what can more conduce to elegant literary knowledge, or be less dangerous to the morals of the young, than domestic recitation of the finest flights of the intellect ? Certain it is that Maria Antoinette never forgot her idolatry of her master Metastasio; and it would have been well for her had all concerned in her education done her equal justice. The Abbé Vermond encouraged these studies; and the King himself afterward sanctioned the translation of the works of his Queen's revered instructor, and their publication at her own expense, in a superb edition, that she might gratify her fondness the more conveniently by reciting them in French.* When Maria Antoinette herself became

* Happy, thrice happy, had it been for Maria Antoinette, happy for France, happy, perhaps, for all Europe, had this taste never been thwarted The mind, once firmly occupied in any particular pursuit, is guarded against the danger arising from volatility and *ennui*. The mind, in want of an object of occupation congenial to its youth and tendencies often rushes unconsciously into errors, fatal to its peace, its reputation and its existence.

a mother, and oppressed from the change of circumstances, she regretted much that she had not in early life cultivated her mind more extensively. 'What a resource,' would she exclaim, 'is a mind well stored against human casualties!' She determined to avoid in her own offspring the error, of which she felt herself the victim, committed by her imperial mother, for whose fault, though she suffered, she would invent excuses. 'The Empress,' she would say, 'was left a young widow with ten or twelve children; she had been accustomed, even during the Emperor's life, to head her vast empire, and she thought it would be unjust to sacrifice to her own children the welfare of the numerous family which afterward devolved upon her exclusive government and protection.'

" Most unfortunately for Maria Antoinette, her great supporter, Madame de Pompadour, died before the Archduchess came to France. The pilot who was to steer the young mariner safe into port, was no more, when she arrived at it. The Austrian interest had sunk with its patroness. The intriguers of the Court no sooner saw the King without an avowed favorite than they sought to give him one who should further their own views and crush the Choiseul party, which had been sustained by Pompadour. The licentious Duke de Richelieu was the pander on this occasion. The low, vulgar Du Barry was by him introduced to the King, and Richelieu had the honor of enthroning a successor to Pompadour, and supplying Louis XV. with the last of his mistresses. Madame de Grammont, who had been the royal confidante during the interregnum, gave up to the rising star. The effect of a new power was presently seen in new events. All the ministers known to be attached to the Austrian interest were dismissed; and the time for the arrival of the young bride, the Archduchess of Austria, who was about to be installed Dauphiness of France, was at hand, and she came to meet scarcely a friend, and many foes: — of which even her beauty, her gentleness, and her simplicity, were doomed to swell the phalanx."

NOTE.

THE preceding pages of the Princess Lamballe excite reflections, which, as editor, I cannot suffer to pass without a commentary of my own. My reflections are grounded upon what I know to have been in some degree the apprehensions of Her Highness; but she did not live to see the fearful prophecies accomplished. I have often heard her utter many of the following sentiments, of which I may be deemed in part, therefore, only the transcriber; and the awful result has been a thorough illustration of the precision with which she judged. Some of my observations, it will be apparent, she could not have uttered; but I have every reason to believe that she foresaw, as distinctly as mortal vision can look into futurity, those parts of what I am about to state, which, though her thoughts dwelt upon, her discretion would not let her name. It is this which gives to her unwavering devotedness to the Queen, amid a consciousness of the inevitable *dénouement*, all the grace of martyrdom.

Maria Theresa was greatly deceived in the speculations she had formed in her private cabinet at Vienna upon her daughter's marriage, and the influence she hoped to gain from that event over the cabinet of France. To imagine for a moment that she acted from any view to her daughter's happiness or aggrandisement would be absurd Her real views were built on error. The hostile feeling against Austria was too strong in France to be overcome by State policy, and she was only preparing a scaffold for her child where she meditated a triumph for herself. She sacrificed everything to her ambition, and in her ambition she was punished. Had Maria Theresa been less cruel after the battle of Prague, perhaps the French nation would have been kinder to her child. There may be no rule without an exception; but there is one inculcated by the mystery of religion, instituted by the word of the Supreme Himself. by that primitive food wherewith our intellects are nourished, by that school and guide of our infancy, by that conductor of our youth, by that pilot which steers us with rectitude into the harbor of maturity — that Holy Book declares without reserve, DO AS YOU WOULD BE DONE BY, OR YOU SHALL BE VISITED TO THE THIRD AND FOURTH GENERATION! How scrupulously just, then, ought the head of a family to be in dealing with others! Not but I conceive it the duty of every individual to act righteously; but of parents it is a SPECIAL duty. And if more awful the responsibility upon parents, how tremendous must it be upon rulers! Look at the example Maria Theresa set her children! What lessons has she

given them as a mother? What as a monarch? The violent usurpation of Mantua from the princely family of the Gonzagas and the
partition of Poland form the answer. But there is a madness in power
which prevails even over nature, and often over interest itself, when
it seeks the attainment of any specific end. Silesia, in the consideration of Maria Theresa, outweighed all others. Of the same stamp
was the headlong pertinacity of Louis XIV. He waged war against
almost all Europe to destroy the Austrian influence in Spain, and with
his own to place Philip V. his grandson on the throne of Iberia.
From State policy he as readily agreed to subsidize Great Britain, in
order to tear asunder the very crown, which he himself had cemented
with the blood and treasures of his subjects; and tried his utmost to
hurl from the throne a prince seated on it, at the risk of losing his
own! It was for political intrigue Maria Antoinette was sent to
France — or rather, a family compact, under which title the true purpose is disguised in royal marriages, and by political intrigue she fell
into snares fatal to her peace.

CHAPTER II.

B EFORE I return to the Journal of the Princess Lamballe, as it falls into the regular chronological
arrangement, let me give a passing moment to the
more recent biographer of Maria Antoinette, Madame
Campan. Her description of the first appearance of Her
Majesty at Kehl, where the change took place from the
Austrian wardrobe to the French, according to the prescribed etiquette on those occasions, is so strikingly
characteristic of that unfortunate Princess that I cannot
avoid referring to it, though I much doubt the authenticity of some of its details. The reader, however, will
see a glimmer of the bewitching simplicity of its subject
through all the errors of the narrative; whence it will

be evident how inestimable a gem this Princess would have proved had she been left in her rough German artlessness.

In page 45, chapter 3, Madame Campan says: "WHEN THE DAUPHINESS HAD BEEN ENTIRELY UNDRESSED, EVEN TO HER BODY LINEN AND STOCKINGS, IN ORDER THAT SHE MIGHT RETAIN NOTHING BELONGING TO A FOREIGN COURT, THE DOORS WERE OPENED": — mark, in a state no less than that of the Lady Godiva, — "THE YOUNG PRINCESS CAME FORWARD" — not even *en chemise* — as the horse jockeys do at Newmarket, I suppose, in order to be weighed before they mount the steed! But let us go on, — "CAME FORWARD," — coolly, she should have said, — "LOOKING ROUND FOR THE COUNTESS DE NOAILLES."

Now among Hottentots, or some of those Egyptian females * who conceive the face to be the most sacred part of the human frame, and who, when surprised drawing water at the well or fountain to fill their jars do, in order to prevent the men from seeing them, actually throw up their clothing, even to the body linen, to hide their faces! Among these I say such an exhibition might be possible; but that an Austrian princess should, like a maniac, have been thus exposed to the contemplation of some forty or fifty idle gazers! — can such a thing be credited?

"THEN," — continues Madame Campan, — " RUSHING INTO HER ARMS," — which I dare say she did, if it was cold, — "SHE IMPLORED HER" — "implored!" a word that is very seldom in the mouth of princesses, and much less in that of the high-mettled race of an Austrian archduchess like Maria Antoinette. But once more to the text: "IM-PLORED HER, WITH TEARS IN HER EYES, AND WITH A HEART-

---

*General Menou, when Governor of Venice, told me among other circumstances that the great hatred of the Egyptians against the French arose from their having violated many Egyptian females on the exhibition of what other nations generally conceal, and several innocent and respectable persons were thus sacrificed to the brutality of the soldiers. He said he could not pronounce whether the custom was universal, but in some villages he had witnessed it himself.

FELT SINCERITY, TO DIRECT HER, TO ADVISE HER, AND TO BE, IN EVERY RESPECT, HER FUTURE GUIDE AND SUPPORT!"

Upon this, Madame Campan observes, "IT WAS IMPOSSIBLE TO REFRAIN FROM ADMIRING HER AËRIAL DEPORTMENT; HER SMILE WAS SUFFICIENT TO WIN THE HEART; AND IN THIS ENCHANTING BEING THE SPLENDOR OF FRENCH GAYETY SHONE FORTH!"

I have often heard splendor and dignity coupled together, but I do not remember the union of gayety and splendor. No doubt it is correct, however, as a French woman, who has been the instructress of princesses, has written it.

To proceed with Madame Campan: "AN INDESCRIBABLE BUT AUGUST SERENITY, PERHAPS ALSO THE SOMEWHAT PROUD POSITION OF HER HEAD AND SHOULDERS, BETRAYED THE DAUGHTER OF THE CÆSARS."

However, the word "betrayed" is here misapplied (and I myself should have used PORTRAYED, UNFOLDED, or DEMONSTRATED, which I think, with all due submission to the compiler or composer of Madame Campan's work, would have been more appropriate than the word "betrayed"), the remark is thoroughly correct. Such were indeed the head and shoulders of Maria Antoinette. Their beauty was the envy of the one sex, and the source of much abominable detraction in those who might not approach it of the other.

There are no doubt many inconveniencies inseparable from the etiquette of royal marriages, and many more which spring from chance. I have read somewhere of a proxy, who came so near the bride, as to prick her with his spur; which certainly was not the intention of the royal spouse. But I am much disposed to believe, comparing the forms on the marriage of Maria Antoinette with those observed with others of her husband's family at the same period, as well as with her own excessive modesty, that in this instance, as in many others, she has been misrepresented. I should rather conceive the etiquette to have been similar to that adopted when the Princess Clotilda, the sister of Louis XVI., was consigned

over to the Piedmontese ladies of the Court of Turin.
A large wardrobe of different dresses of every kind met
her at the last frontier town of France.   There she put
on the clothes provided for the purpose, returning those
she brought to the persons who saw her out of France.
No public dressing or undressing was thought of ; and
she was by far too fat to run, *in puris naturalibus*, into
the arms of any lady of honor who might not be of the
most uncourtly dimensions.   Such, also, was the mode
pursued when Madame and her sister, the Countess
d'Artois, both Princesses of Piedmont, were married to
the two brothers of Louis XVI.   No indelicate display
like that which Madame Campan describes as having
taken place under the Countess de Noailles was exacted
from either of the brides.   And why should such an exception have been made in the case of the young Austrian ?
Indeed (and I speak here from the authority of my papers), so scrupulous was Maria Antoinette in her observance of modesty and decorum, that she was laughed at
by the young princes and nobles, for withdrawing with
her tire-woman to have her hair arranged in private ; because her toilet being the usual morning rendezvous of
all belonging to the Court, she could not reconcile it to
her feelings, to follow the precedent of all former dau-
phinesses and queens, by allowing even this slight ceremony
to be performed about her person, *pro bono publico*.   Is
it at all likely, then, that she could have consented under
any circumstances to the exposure Madame Campan has
described ?   But enough of this : I resume my editorial
functions, and return to the more agreeable narrative of
the Princess of Lamballe.

"On the marriage night, Louis XV. said gayly to the
Dauphin who was supping with his usual heartiness,—
'Don't overcharge your stomach to-night.'

"'Why, I always sleep best after a hearty supper,' replied the Dauphin, with the greatest coolness.

"The supper being ended, he accompanied his Dauphiness to her chamber, and at the door, with the greatest

politeness, wished her a good night. Next morning, upon his saying, when he met her at breakfast, that he hoped she had slept well, Maria Antoinette replied, 'Excellently well, for I had no one to disturb me!'

"The Princess de Guèmenèe, who was then at the head of the household, on hearing the Dauphiness moving very early in her apartment, ventured to enter it, and not seeing the Dauphin, exclaimed, 'Bless me! he is risen as usual!' 'Whom do you mean?' asked Maria Antoinette. The Princess misconstruing the interrogation, was going to retire, when the Dauphiness said, 'I have heard a great deal of French politeness, but I think I am married to the most polite of the nation!' 'What, then, he is risen?' 'No, no, no!' exclaimed the Dauphiness, 'there has been no rising; he has never lain down here. He left me at the door of my apartment with his hat in his hand, and hastened from me as if embarrassed with my person!'

"After Maria Antoinette became a mother, she would often laugh and tell Louis XVI. of his bridal politeness, and ask him if in the interim between that and the consummation he had studied his maiden aunts or his tutor on the subject. On this he would laugh most excessively.

"Scarcely was Maria Antoinette seated in her new country before the virulence of Court intrigue against her became active. She was beset on all sides by enemies open and concealed, who never slackened their persecutions. All the family of Louis XV. consisting of those maiden aunts of the Dauphin just adverted to (among whom Madame Adelaide was specially implacable) were incensed at the marriage, not only from their hatred to Austria, but because it had accomplished the ambition of an obnoxious favorite to give a wife to the Dauphin of their kingdom. On the credulous and timid mind of the Prince, then in the leading strings of this pious sisterhood, they impressed the misfortunes to his country and to the interest of the Bourbon family, which must spring from the Austrian influence through the medium

[margin note: good marriage]

[margin note: Austria]

of his bride. No means were left unessayed to steel him against her sway. I remembered once to have heard Her Majesty remark to Louis XVI. in answer to some particular observations he made, 'These, sire, are the sentiments of our aunts, I am sure.' And indeed great must have been their ascendancy over him in youth, for up to a late date he entertained a very high respect for their capacity and judgment. Great indeed must it have been to have prevailed against all the seducing allurements of a beautiful and fascinating young bride, whose amiableness, vivacity, and wit became the universal admiration, and whose graceful manner of address few ever equaled and none ever surpassed; nay, even so to have prevailed as to form one of the great sources of his aversion to consummate the marriage! Since the death of the late Queen, their mother, these four Princesses (who, it was said, if old MAIDS, were not so from choice) had received and performed the exclusive honors of the Court. It could not have diminished their dislike for the young and lovely newcomer to see themselves under the necessity of abandoning their dignities and giving up their station. So eager were they to contrive themes of complaint against her, that when she visited them in the simple attire in which she so much delighted, *sans cérémonie*, unaccompanied by a troop of horse and a squadron of footguards, they complained to their father, who hinted to Maria Antoinette that such a relaxation of the royal dignity would be attended with considerable injury to French manufactures, to trade, and to the respect due to her rank. 'My State and Court dresses,' replied she, 'shall not be less brilliant than those of any former Dauphiness or Queen of France, if such be the pleasure of the King,— but to my grandpapa I appeal for some indulgence with respect to my undress private costume of the morning.'*

"It was dangerous for one in whose conduct so many prying eyes were seeking for sources of accusation to

* Trifling, however, as Maria Antoinette deemed these cavils about dress and etiquette, they contained the elements of her future fall.

gratify herself even by the overthrow of an absurdity,
when that overthrow might incur the stigma of innovation.   The Court of Versailles was jealous of its Spanish
inquisitorial etiquette.   It had been strictly wedded to
its pageantries since the time of the great Anne of Austria.   The sagacious and prudent provisions of this illustrious contriver were deemed the *ne plus ultra* of royal
female policy.   A cargo of whalebone was yearly obtained
by her to construct such stays for the maids of honor
as might adequately conceal the Court accidents which
generally — poor ladies! — befell them in rotation every
nine months.

"But Maria Antoinette could not sacrifice her predilection for a simplicity quite English, to prudential considerations.   Indeed she was too young to conceive it
even desirable.   So much did she delight in being unshackled by finery that she would hurry from Court to
fling off her royal robes and ornaments, exclaiming, when
freed from them, 'Thank Heaven, I am out of harness!'

"But she had natural advantages, which gave her enemies a pretext for ascribing this antipathy to the established fashion to mere vanity.   It is not impossible that
she might have derived some pleasure from displaying a
figure so beautiful, with no adornment except its native
gracefulness; but how great must have been the chagrin
of the Princesses, of many of the Court ladies, indeed of
all in any way ungainly or deformed, when called to
exhibit themselves by the side of a bewitching person
like hers, unaided by the whalebone and horsehair pad-
dings with which they had hitherto been made up, and
which placed the best form on a level with the worst?
The prudes who practiced illicitly, and felt the convenience of a guise which so well concealed the effect of
their frailties, were neither the least formidable nor the
least numerous of the enemies created by this revolution
of costume; and the Dauphiness was voted by common
consent — for what greater crime could there be in
France? — the heretic Martin Luther of female fashions!
The four Princesses, her aunts, were as bitter against

[margin note: dress]

[margin note: heretic of dress]

the disrespect with which the Dauphiness treated the armor, which they called dress, as if they themselves had benefited by the immunities it could confer.

"Indeed, most of the old Court ladies embattled themselves against Maria Antoinette's encroachments upon their HABITS. The leader of them was a real medallion, whose costume, character and notions, spoke a genealogy perfectly antediluvian; who even to the latter days of Louis XV., amid a Court so irregular, persisted in her precision. So systematic a supporter of the antique could be no other than the declared foe of any change, and, of course, deemed the desertion of large sack gowns, monstrous Court hoops, and the old notions of appendages attached to them, for tight waists and short petticoats, an awful demonstration of the depravity of the time!*

"This lady had been first lady to the sole Queen of Louis XV. She was retained in the same station for Maria Antoinette. Her motions were regulated like clockwork. So methodical was she in all her operations of mind and body, that, from the beginning of the year to its end, she never deviated a moment. Every hour had its peculiar occupation. Her element was etiquette, but the etiquette of ages before the flood. She had her rules even for the width of petticoats that the queens and princesses might have no temptation to straddle over a rivulet, or crossing, of unroyal size.

"The Queen of Louis XV., having been totally subservient in her movements night and day to the wishes of the Countess de Noailles, it will be readily conceived, how great a shock this lady must have sustained on being informed one morning, that the Dauphiness had actually risen in the night, and her ladyship not by to witness a ceremony from which most ladies would have felt no little pleasure in being spared, but which, on this occasion, admitted of no delay! Notwithstanding the Dauphiness excused herself by the assurance of the

* The editor needs scarcely add, that the allusion of the Princess is to Madame de Noailles.

urgency allowing no time to call the Countess, she nearly
fainted at not having been present at that, which others
sometimes faint at, if too near! This unaccustomed
watchfulness so annoyed Maria Antoinette, that, determined to laugh her out of it, she ordered an immense
bottle of hartshorn to be placed upon her toilet. Being
asked what use was to be made of the hartshorn, she
said it was to prevent her first lady of honor from falling into hysterics when the calls of nature were uncivil
enough to exclude her from being of the party. This,
as may be presumed, had its desired effect, and Maria
Antoinette was ever afterward allowed free access at
least to one of her apartments, and leave to perform
that in private which few individuals except princesses
do with parade and publicity.

"These things, however, planted the seeds of rancor
against Maria Antoinette, which Madame de Noailles
carried with her to the grave. It will be seen that she
declared against her at a crisis of great importance. The
laughable title of Madame Etiquette, which the Dauphiness gave her, clung to her through life; and, though
conferred only in merriment, it never was forgiven.

"The Dauphiness seemed to be under a sort of fatality
with regard to all those who had any power of doing her
mischief, either with her husband or the Court. The
Duke de Vauguyon, the Dauphin's tutor, who, both from
principle and interest, hated everything Austrian, and
anything whatever which threatened to lessen his despotic influence so long exercised over the mind of his
pupil, which he foresaw would be endangered were the
Prince once out of his leading-strings and swayed by a
young wife, made use of all the influence which old
courtiers can command over the minds they have formed
(more generally for their own ends than those of uprightness), to poison that of the young Prince against
his bride.

"Never were there more intrigues among the female
slaves in the Seraglio of Constantinople for the Grand
Signior's handkerchief than were continually harassing

one party against the other at the Court of Versailles. The Dauphiness was even attacked through her own tutor, the Abbé Vermond. A cabal was got up between the Abbé and Madame Marsan, instructress of the sisters of Louis XVI. (the Princesses Clotilda and Elizabeth) upon the subject of education. Nothing grew out of this affair excepting a new stimulus to the party spirit against the Austrian influence, or, in other words, the Austrian Princess; and such was probably its purpose. Of course every trifle becomes Court tattle. This was made a mighty business of, for want of a worse. The royal aunts naturally took the part of Madame Marsan. They maintained that their royal nieces, the French Princesses, were much better educated than the German Archduchesses had been by the Austrian Empress. They attempted to found their assertion upon the *embonpoint* of the French Princesses. They said that their nieces, by the exercise of religious principles, obtained the advantage of solid flesh, while the Austrian Archduchesses, by wasting themselves in idleness and profane pursuits, grew thin and meager, and were equally exhausted in their minds and bodies! At this the Abbé Vermond, as the tutor of Maria Antoinette, felt himself highly offended, and called on Count de Mercy, then the Imperial Ambassador, to apprise him of the insult the Empire had received over the shoulders of the Dauphiness's tutor. The Ambassador gravely replied that he should certainly send off a courier immediately to Vienna to inform the Empress that the only fault the French Court could find with Maria Antoinette was her being not so unwieldy as their own Princesses, and bringing charms with her to a bridegroom, on whom even charms so transcendent could make no impression! Thus the matter was laughed off, but it left, ridiculous as it was, new bitter enemies to the cause of the illustrious stranger.

"The new favorite, Madame du Barry, whose sway was now supreme, was of course joined by the whole vitiated intriguing Court of Versailles. The King's favorite is always that of his parasites, however degraded. The

politics of the Pompadour party were still feared, though
Pompadour herself was no more, for Choiseul had friends
who were still active in his behalf.   The power which
had been raised to crush the power that was still strug-
gling, formed a rallying point for those who hated Austria,
which the deposed ministry had supported; and even the
King's daughters, much as they abhorred the vulgarity
of Du Barry, were led, by dislike for the Dauphiness, to
pay their devotions to their father's mistress.   The influence of the rising sun, Maria Antoinette, whose beau-
teous rays of blooming youth warmed every heart in her
favor, was feared by the new favorite as well as by the
old maidens.   Louis XV. had already expressed a sufficient interest for the friendless royal stranger to awaken
the jealousy of Du Barry, and she was as little disposed
to share the King's affections with another, as his
daughters were to welcome a future Queen from Austria
in their palace.   Mortified at the attachment the King
daily evinced, she strained every nerve to raise a party
to destroy his predilections.   She called to her aid the
strength of ridicule, than which no weapon is more false
or deadly.   She laughed at qualities she could not com-
prehend, and underrated what she could not imitate.
The Duke de Richelieu, who had been instrumental to
her good fortune, and for whom (remembering the old
adage: WHEN ONE HAND WASHES THE OTHER BOTH ARE
MADE CLEAN), she procured the command of the army—
this duke, the triumphant general of Mahon and one of
the most distinguished noblemen of France, did not blush
to become the secret agent of a depraved meretrix in
the conspiracy to blacken the character of her victim!
The Princesses, of course, joined the jealous Phryne
against their niece, the daughter of the Cæsars, whose
only faults were those of nature, for at that time she
COULD have no other excepting those personal perfections
—which were the main source of all their malice.   By
one considered as an usurper, by the others as an intruder, both were in consequence industrious in the quiet
work of ruin by whispers and detraction.

"To an impolitic act of the Dauphiness herself may be in part ascribed the unwonted virulence of the jealousy and resentment of Du Barry. The old dotard, Louis XV., was so indelicate as to have her present at the first supper of the Dauphiness at Versailles. Madame la Mareschale de Beaumond, the Duchess de Choiseul, and the Duchess de Grammont were there also ; but upon the favorite taking her seat at table they expressed themselves very freely to Louis XV. respecting the insult they conceived offered to the young Dauphiness, left the royal party, and never appeared again at Court till after the King's death. In consequence of this scene, Maria Antoinette, at the instigation of the Abbé Vermond, wrote to her mother, the Empress, complaining of the slight put upon her rank, birth, and dignity, and requesting the Empress would signify her displeasure to the Court of France as she had done to that of Spain on a similar occasion in favor of her sister, the Queen of Naples.

"This letter, which was intercepted, got to the knowledge of the Court and excited some clamor. To say the worst, it could only be looked upon as an ebullition of the folly of youth. But insignificant as such matters were in fact, malignity converted them into the locust, which destroyed the fruit she was sent to cultivate.

"Maria Theresa, like the old fox, too true to her system to retract the policy, which formerly laid her open to the criticism of all the civilized Courts of Europe for opening the correspondence with Pompadour, to whose influence she owed her daughter's footing in France — a correspondence whereby she degraded the dignity of her sex and the honor of her crown — and at the same time suspecting that it was not her daughter, but Vermond, from private motives, who complained, wrote the following laconic reply to the remonstrance :

"'Where the sovereign himself presides, no guest can be exceptionable.'

"Such sentiments are very much in contradiction with the character of Maria Theresa. She was always solicitous to impress the world with her high notion of moral rectitude. Certainly, such advice, however politic, ought not to have proceeded from a mother so religious as Maria Theresa wished herself to be thought; especially to a young Princess who, though enthusiastically fond of admiration, at least had discretion to see and feel the impropriety of her being degraded to the level of a female like Du Barry, and, withal, courage to avow it. This, of itself, was quite enough to shake the virtue of Maria Antoinette; or, at least, Maria Theresa's letter was of a cast to make her callous to the observance of all its scruples. And in that vitiated, depraved Court, she too soon, unfortunately, took the hint of her maternal counselor in not only tolerating, but imitating, the object she despised. Being one day told that Du Barry was the person who most contributed to amuse Louis XV.—'Then,' said she, innocently, 'I declare myself her rival; for I will try who can best amuse my grandpapa for the future. I will exert all my powers to please and divert him, and then we shall see who can best succeed.'

"Du Barry was by when this was said, and she never forgave it. To this, and to the letter, her rancor may principally be ascribed. To all those of the Court party who owed their places and preferments to her exclusive influence and who held them subject to her caprice, she, of course, communicated the venom.

"Meanwhile, the Dauphin saw Maria Antoinette mimicking the monkey tricks with which this low Sultana amused her dotard, without being aware of the cause. He was not pleased; and this circumstance, coupled with his natural coolness and indifference for an union he had been taught to deem impolitic and dangerous to the interests of France, created in his virtuous mind that sort of disgust which remained so long an enigma to the Court and all the kingdom, excepting his royal aunts, who did the best they could to confirm it into so decided an aversion as might induce him to impel his grandfather to annul the marriage and send the Dauphiness back to Vienna."

The execution of this diabolical scheme, with many others of a similar nature, was only prevented by the death of Louis XV. They are not treated by the Princess here, but will be found explained by her in their proper place. She seems to feel as if she had already outrun her story, and therefore returns a little upon her steps. The manuscript continues thus:

"After the Dauphin's marriage, the Count d'Artois and his brother Monsieur * returned from their travels to Versailles. The former was delighted with the young Dauphiness, and, seeing her so decidedly neglected by her husband, endeavored to console her by a marked attention, but for which she would have been totally isolated, for, excepting the old King, who became more and more enraptured with the grace, beauty, and vivacity of his young granddaughter, not another individual in the Royal Family was really interested in her favor. The kindness of a personage so important was of too much weight not to awaken calumny. It was, of course, endeavored to be turned against her. Possibilities, and even probabilities, conspired to give a pretext for the scandal which already began to be whispered about the Dauphiness and d'Artois. It would have been no wonder had a reciprocal attachment arisen between a virgin wife, so long neglected by her husband, and one whose congeniality of character pointed him out as a more desirable partner than the Dauphin. But there is abundant evidence of the perfect innocence of their intercourse. Du Barry was most earnest in endeavoring, from first to last, to establish its impurity, because the Dauphiness induced the gay young Prince to join in all her girlish schemes to tease and circumvent the favorite. But when this young Prince and his brother were married to the two Princesses of Piedmont, the intimacy between their brides and the Dauphiness proved there could have been no doubt that Du Barry had invented a calumny, and that no feeling existed but one altogether sisterly. The three stranger Princesses were indeed inseparable; and

* Afterward Louis XVIII., and the former the present Charles X.

these marriages, with that of the French Princess, Clotilda, to the Prince of Piedmont, created considerable changes in the coteries of Court.

"The machinations against Maria Antoinette could not be concealed from the Empress-mother. An extraordinary ambassador was consequently sent from Vienna to complain of them to the Court of Versailles, with directions that the remonstrance should be supported and backed by the Count de Mercy, then Austrian ambassador at the Court of France. Louis XV. was the only person to whom the communication was news. This old *dilettanti* of the sex was so much engaged between his seraglio of the *Parc aux cerfs* and Du Barry, that he knew less of what was passing in his palace than those at Constantinople. On being informed by the Austrian ambassador, he sent an ambassador of his own to Vienna to assure the Empress that he was perfectly satisfied of the innocent conduct of his newly acquired granddaughter.

"Among the intrigues within intrigues of the time I mention, there was one which shows that perhaps Du Barry's distrust of the constancy of her paramour, and apprehension from the effect on him of the charms of the Dauphiness, in whom he became daily more interested, were not utterly without foundation. In this instance even her friend the Duke de Richelieu, that notorious seducer, by lending himself to the secret purposes of the King, became a traitor to the cause of the King's favorite, to which he had sworn allegiance, and which he had supported by defaming her whom he now became anxious to make his Queen.

"It has already been said, that the famous Duchess de Grammont was one of the confidential friends of Louis XV. before he took Du Barry under his especial protection. Of course, there can be no difficulty in conceiving how likely a person she would be, to aid any purpose of the King, which should displace the favorite, by whom she herself had been obliged to retire, by ties of a higher order, to which she might prove instrumental.

" Louis XV. actually flattered himself with the hope of obtaining advantages from the Dauphin's coolness toward the Dauphiness. He encouraged it, and even threw many obstacles in the way of the consummation of the marriage. The apartments of the young couple were placed at opposite ends of the palace, so that the Dauphin could not approach that of his Dauphiness without a publicity, which his bashfulness could not brook.

"Louis XV. now began to act upon his secret passion to supplant his grandson, and make the Dauphiness his own Queen, by endeavoring to secure her affections to himself. His attentions were backed by gifts of diamonds, pearls, and other valuables, and it was at this period that Bœhmer, the jeweler, first received the order for that famous necklace, which subsequently produced such dreadful consequences, and which was originally meant as a kingly present to the intended Queen; though afterward destined for Du Barry, had not the King died before the completion of the bargain for it.

" The Queen herself one day told me, 'Heaven knows if ever I should have had the blessing of being a mother, had I not one evening surprised the Dauphin, when the subject was adverted to, in the expression of a sort of regret at our being placed so far asunder from each other. Indeed he never honored me with any proof of his affection so explicit as that you have just witnessed'— for the King had that moment kissed her, as he left the apartment —'from the time of our marriage till the consummation. The most I ever received from him was a squeeze of the hand in secret. His extreme modesty, and perhaps his utter ignorance of the intercourse with woman, dreaded the exposure of crossing the palace to my bedchamber; and no doubt the accomplishment would have occurred sooner, could it have been effectuated in privacy. The hint he gave emboldened me with courage, when he next left me, as usual, at the door of my apartment, to mention it to the Duchess of Grammont, then the confidential friend of Louis XV., who laughed me almost out of countenance; saying, in her

gay manner of expressing herself, "IF I were as young
and as beautiful a wife as you are, I should certainly not
trouble myself to remove the obstacle by going to him
while there were others of superior rank ready to supply
his place." Before she quitted me, however, she said:
"Well, child, make yourself easy: you shall no longer be
separated from the object of your wishes: I will mention
it to the King, your grandpapa, and he will soon order
your husband's apartment to be changed for one nearer
your own."' And the change shortly afterward took
place.*

"'Here,' continued the Queen, 'I accuse myself of a
want of that courage which every virtuous wife ought to
exercise in not having complained of the visible neglect
shown me long, long before I did; for this, perhaps,
would have spared both of us the many bitter pangs orig-
inating in the seeming coldness, whence have arisen all
the scandalous stories against my character — which have
often interrupted the full enjoyment I should have felt,
had they not made me tremble for the security of that
attachment, of which I had so many proofs, and which
formed my only consolation amid all the malice, that for
years has been endeavoring to deprive me of it! So far
as regards my husband's estimation, thank fate, I have
defied their wickedness! Would to Heaven I could have
been equally secure in the estimation of my people — the
object nearest to my heart, after the King and my dear
children!'

"The present period appears to have been one of the
happiest of the life of Maria Antoinette. Her intimate
society consisted of the King's brothers, and their Prin-

* The Dauphiness could not understand the first allusion of the Duchess; but it is evident that the vile intriguer took this opportunity of
sounding her upon what she was commissioned to carry on in favor of
Louis XV., and it is equally apparent that when she heard Maria Antoinette express herself decidedly in favor of her young husband, and
distinctly saw how utterly groundless were the hopes of his secret rival,
she was led thereby to abandon her wicked project; and perhaps the
change of apartments was the best mask that could have been devised
to hide the villainy.

cesses, with the King's saint-like sister Elizabeth; and
they lived entirely together, excepting when the Dauphiness dined in public. These ties seemed to be drawn
daily closer for some time, till the subsequent intimacy
with the Polignacs. Even when the Countess d'Artois
lay-in, the Dauphiness, then become Queen, transferred
her parties to the apartments of that Princess, rather
than lose the gratification of her society.

"During all this time, however, Du Barry, the Duke d'-
Aiguillon, and the aunts-Princesses, took special care to
keep themselves between her and any tenderness on the
part of the husband Dauphin, and, from different motives
uniting in one end, tried every means to get the object
of their hatred sent back to Vienna."

CHAPTER III.

"THE Empress-mother was thoroughly aware of all that was going on. Her anxiety, not only about her daughter, but her State policy, which it may be apprehended was in her mind the stronger motive of the two, encouraged the machinations of an individual who must now appear upon the stage of action, and to whose arts may be ascribed the worst of the sufferings of Maria Antoinette.

"I allude to the Cardinal Prince de Rohan.

"At this time he was Ambassador at the Court of Vienna. The reliance the Empress placed on him* favored his criminal machinations against her daughter's reputation. He was the cause of her sending spies to watch the conduct of the Dauphiness, besides a list of persons proper for her to cultivate, as well as of those it was deemed desirable for her to exclude from her confidence.

"As the Empress knew all those who, though high in office in Versailles, secretly received pensions from Vienna, she could, of course, tell without much expense of sagac-

* Madame Campan (vol. i., page 42) is very much in the dark on this subject and totally misinformed. The Cardinal de Rohan did not become obnoxious to Maria Theresa till it was discovered that he had abused her confidence and betrayed that of her ministers.—*Ed.*

ity, who were in the Austrian interest. The Dauphiness was warned that she was surrounded by persons who were not her friends.

"The conduct of Maria Theresa toward her daughter, the Queen of Naples, will sufficiently explain how much the Empress must have been chagrined at the absolute indifference of Maria Antoinette to the State policy, which was intended to have been served in sending her to France. A less fitting instrument for the purpose could not have been selected by the mother. Maria Antoinette had much less of the politician about her than either of her surviving sisters; and so much was she addicted to amusement, that she never even thought of entering into State affairs till forced by the King's neglect of his most essential prerogatives and called upon by the ministers themselves to screen them from responsibility. Indeed, the latter cause prevailed upon her to take her seat in the cabinet council (though she took it with great reluctance) long before she was impelled thither by events and her consciousness of its necessity. She would often exclaim to me : 'How happy I was during the lifetime of Louis XV.! No cares to disturb my peaceful slumbers ! No responsibility to agitate my mind ! No fears of erring, of partiality, of injustice to break in upon my enjoyments ! All, all happiness, my dear Princess, vanishes from the bosom of a female if she once deviate from the prescribed domestic character of her sex! Nothing was ever framed more wise than the Salique Laws, which in France and many parts of Germany exclude females from reigning, for few of us have that masculine capacity so necessary to conduct with impartiality and justice the affairs of State !'

"To this feeling of the impropriety of feminine interference in masculine duties, coupled with her attachment to France, both from principle and feeling, may be ascribed the neglect of her German connections, which led to the many mortifying reproaches, and the still more galling espionage to which she was subjected in her own palace by her mother. These are, however, so many proofs of the falsehood of the allegations by which she suffered so deeply afterward, of having sacrificed the interests of her husband's kingdom to her predilection for her mother's empire.

"The subtile Rohan designed to turn the anxiety of Maria Theresa about the Dauphiness to account, and he was also aware that the ambition of the Empress was paramount in Maria Theresa's bosom to the love for her child. He was about to play a deep and more than double game. By increasing the mother's jealousy of the daughter, and at the same time enhancing the importance of the advantages afforded by her situation, to forward the interests of the mother, he, no doubt, hoped to get both within his power: for who can tell what wild expectation might not have animated such a mind as Rohan's, at the prospect of governing not only the Court of France but that of Austria?—the Court of France, through a secret influence of his own dictation thrown around the Dauphiness by the mother's alarm; and that of Austria, through a way he pointed out, in which the object, that was most longed for by the mother's ambition, seemed most likely to be achieved! While he endeavored to make Maria Theresa beset her daughter with the spies I have mentioned, and which were generally of his own selection, he at the same time endeavored to strengthen her impression of how important it was to her schemes to insure the daughter's co-operation. Conscious of the eagerness of Maria Theresa for the recovery of the rich province which Frederick the Great of Prussia had wrested from her ancient dominions, he pressed upon her credulity the assurance, that the influence, of which the Dauphiness was capable, over Louis XV. by the youthful beauty's charms acting upon the dotard's admiration, would readily induce that monarch to give such aid to Austria as must insure the restoration of what it lost. Silesia, it has been before observed, was always a topic by means of which the weak side of Maria Theresa could be attacked with success. There is generally some peculiar frailty in the ambitious, through which the artful can throw them off their guard. The weak and tyrannical Philip II. whenever the recovery of Holland and the Low Countries was proposed to him was always ready to rush headlong into any scheme for its accomplishment; the bloody Queen Mary, his wife, declared that at her death the loss of Calais would be found engraven on her heart; and to Maria Theresa, Silesia was the Holland and the Calais for which her wounded pride was thirsting.*

"But Maria Theresa was wary, even in the midst of the credulity of her ambition. The Baron de Neni was sent by her privately to Versailles to examine, personally, whether there was anything in Maria Antoinette's conduct requiring the extreme vigilance which had been represented as indispensable. The report of the Baron de Neni to his royal mistress was such as to convince

---

* No doubt if ever Ferdinand of Spain can be made to believe he has lost Spanish America, he may exclaim with equal truth, "I feel it in my head, in every fiber of my racked frame — it gnaws my unrelenting heart!" However ridiculous, it is certainly true, that whenever sovereigns, from their folly, ignorance, oppression, or misrule, lose a part of their States, their reason generally follows, at least upon that one theme. Such is the principle which at this moment actuates the Turks for the recovery of Greece! If the Greeks are not Spaniards, and English valor do not degenerate to French poltroonry, the fatalism by which they are guided will soon convince the Turks that they are playing a losing game. The woeful experience of some of the greatest of the European politicians might afford them a useful lesson. How impolitic is the neutrality of my own country upon this interesting subject! Why is it thus reluctant to assist in tearing off the yoke of an intelligent people's barbarous oppressors, who are as uncivilized at this moment as they were centuries ago, when they first took possession of Byzantium? Ought we not to rejoice in the triumph of those whom God himself commands to propagate human emancipation? For liberty, like religion, must have its martyrs. Its blood is the stamina of its existence. Its opposers may exile, imprison, burn in effigy, and, in fact, hang and shoot; but all these violences only strengthen the creed of the survivors, and must end in the ruin of the unholy cause they would fain strengthen. Nations must be free to be prosperous, and Princes liberal to be happy. Liberty is the phœnix that revives from its ashes! — *Ed.*

her she had been misled and her daughter misrepresented by Rohan. The Empress instantly forbade him her presence.

"The Cardinal upon this, unknown to the Court of Vienna, and indeed, to everyone, except his factotum, principal agent, and secretary, the Abbé Georgel, left the Austrian capital, and came to Versailles, covering his disgrace by pretended leave of absence. On seeing Maria Antoinette he fell enthusiastically in love with her. To gain her confidence he disclosed the conduct which had been observed toward her by the Empress, and, in confirmation of the correctness of his disclosure, admitted that he had himself chosen the spies, which had been set on her. Indignant at such meanness in her mother, and despising the prelate, who could be base enough to commit a deed equally corrupt and uncalled for, and even thus wantonly betrayed when committed, the Dauphiness suddenly withdrew from his presence, and gave orders that he should never be admitted to any of her parties.

"But his imagination was too much heated by a guilty passion of the blackest hue to recede; and his nature too presumptuous and fertile in expedients to be disconcerted. He soon found means to conciliate both mother and daughter; and both by pretending to manage with the one the self-same plot, which, with the other, he was recommending himself by pretending to overthrow. To elude detection he interrupted the regular correspondence between the Empress and the Dauphiness, and created a coolness by preventing the communications which would have unmasked him, that gave additional security to the success of his deception.

"By the most diabolical arts he obtained an interview with the Dauphiness, in which he regained her confidence. He made her believe that he had been commissioned by her mother, as she had shown so little interest for the house of Austria, to settle a marriage for her sister, the Archduchess Elizabeth, with Louis XV. The Dauphiness was deeply affected at the statement. She could not conceal her agitation. She involuntarily confessed how much she should deplore such an alliance. The Cardinal instantly perceived his advantage and was too subtle to let it pass. He declared that as it was to him the negotiation had been confided, if the Dauphiness would keep her own counsel, never communicate their conversation to the Empress, but leave the whole matter to his management and only assure him that he was forgiven, he would pledge himself to arrange things to her satisfaction. The Dauphiness, not wishing to see another raised to the throne over her head and to her scorn, under the assurance that no one knew of the intention or could prevent it but the Cardinal, promised him her faith and favor; and thus rashly fell into the springe of this wily intriguer.

"Exulting to find Maria Antoinette in his power, the Cardinal left Versailles as privately as he arrived there, for Vienna. His next object was to insnare the Empress, as he had done her daughter; and by a singular caprice fortune, during his absence, had been preparing for him the means.

"The Abbé Georgel, his secretary, by underhand maneuvers, to which he was accustomed, had obtained access to all the secret State correspondence, in which the Empress had expressed herself fully to the Count de Mercy relative to the views of Russia and Prussia upon Poland, whereby her own plans were much thwarted. The acquirement of copies of these documents naturally gave the Cardinal free access to the Court and a ready introduction once more to the Empress. She was too much committed by his possession of such weapons, not to be most happy to make her peace with him; and he was too sagacious not to make the best use of his opportunity. To regain her confidence, he betrayed some of the subaltern agents, through whose treachery he had procured his evidences, and, in further confirmation of his resources, showed the Empress several dispatches from her own ministers to the Courts of Russia and Prussia. He had long, he said, been in possession of similar views of aggrandisement, upon which these Courts were about

to act; and had, for a while, even incurred Her Imperial Majesty's displeasure, merely because he was not in
a situation fully to explain; but that he had now thought
of the means to crush their schemes before they could
be put in practice. He apprised her of his being aware
that her Imperial Majesty's ministers were actively carrying on a correspondence with Russia, with a view of
joining Her in checking the French co-operation with the
Grand Signior; and warned her that if this design were
SECRETLY pursued, it would defeat the very views she had
in sharing in the spoliation of Poland; and if OPENLY, it
would be deemed an avowal of hostilities against the
Court of France, whose political system would certainly
impel it to resist any attack upon the divan of Constantinople, that the balance of power in Europe might be maintained against the formidable ambition of Catherine,
whose gigantic hopes had been already too much realized.

"Maria Theresa was no less astonished at these disclosures of the Cardinal than the Dauphiness had been at
his communication concerning her. She plainly saw that
all her plans were known, and might be defeated from
their detection.

"The Cardinal, having succeeded in alarming the Empress, took from his pocket a fabulous correspondence,
hatched by his secretary, the Abbé Georgel. 'There,
madam,' said he, 'this will convince your majesty that
the warm interest I have taken in your Imperial house
has carried me further than I was justified in having
gone; but seeing the sterility of the Dauphiness, or, as
it is reported by some of the Court, the total disgust the
Dauphin has to consummate the marriage, the coldness
of your daughter toward the interest of your Court, and
the prospect of a race from the Countess d'Artois, for the
consequences of which there is no answering, I have, unknown to your Imperial Majesty, taken upon myself to
propose to Louis XV. a marriage with the Archduchess
Elizabeth, who, on becoming Queen of France, will immediately have it in her power to forward the Austrian
interest; for Louis XV., as the first proof of his affection

to his young bride, will at once secure to your Empire the aid you stand so much in need of against the ambition of these two rising states. The recovery of your Imperial Majesty's ancient dominions may then be looked upon as accomplished from the influence of the French cabinet.'

"The bait was swallowed. Maria Theresa was so overjoyed at this scheme that she totally forgot all former animosity against the Cardinal. She was encouraged to ascribe the silence of Maria Antoinette (whose letters had been intercepted by the Cardinal himself) to her resentment of this project concerning her sister; and the deluded Empress, availing herself of the pretended zeal of the Cardinal for the interest of her family, gave him full powers to return to France and secretly negotiate the alliance for her daughter Elizabeth, which was by no means to be disclosed to the Dauphiness till the King's proxy should be appointed to perform the ceremony at Vienna. This was all the Cardinal wished for.

"Meanwhile, in order to obtain a still greater ascendancy over the Court of France, he had expended immense sums to bribe secretaries and ministers; and couriers were even stopped to have copies taken of all the correspondence to and from Austria. At the same crisis the Empress was informed by Prince Kaunitz that the Cardinal and his suite at the palace of the French ambassador carried on such an immense and barefaced traffic of French manufactures of every description that Maria Theresa thought proper, in order to prevent future abuse, to abolish the privilege which gave to ministers and ambassadors an opportunity of defrauding the revenue. Though this law was leveled exclusively at the Cardinal, it was thought convenient under the circumstances to avoid irritating him, and it was consequently made general. But, the Count de Mercy, now obtaining some clue to his duplicity, an intimation was given to the Court at Versailles, to which the King replied, 'If the Empress be dissatisfied with the French ambassador, he shall be recalled.' But though completely unmasked, none dared publicly to accuse him, each party fearing a discovery of its own intrigue. His official recall did not in consequence take place for some time; and the Cardinal, not thinking it prudent to go back till Louis XV. should be no more, lest some unforeseen discovery of his project for supplying her royal paramour with a queen should rouse Du Barry to get his Cardinalship sent to the Bastille for life, remained fixed in his post, waiting for events.

"At length Louis XV. expired, and the Cardinal returned to Versailles. He contrived to obtain a private audience of the young Queen. He presumed upon her former facility in listening to him, and was about to betray the last confidence of Maria Theresa; but the Queen, shocked at the knowledge which she had obtained of his having been equally treacherous to her with her mother, in disgust and alarm left the room without receiving a letter he had brought her from Maria Theresa, and without deigning to address a single word to him. In the heat of her passion and resentment, she was nearly exposing all she knew of his infamies to the King, when the cool-headed Princess Elizabeth opposed her, from the seeming imprudence of such an abrupt discovery; alleging that it might cause an open rupture between the two Courts, as it had already been the source of a reserve and coolness, which had not yet been explained. The Queen was determined never more to commit herself by seeing the Cardinal. She accordingly sent for her mother's letter, which he himself delivered into the hands of her confidential messenger, who advised the Queen not to betray the Cardinal to the King, lest, in so doing, she should never be able to guard herself against the domestic spies. by whom, perhaps, she was even yet surrounded! The Cardinal, conceiving, from the impunity of his conduct, that he still held the Queen in check, through the influence of her fears of his disclosing her weakness upon the subject of the obstruction she threw in the way of her sister's marriage, did not resign the hope of converting that ascendancy to his future profit.

"The fatal silence to which Her Majesty was thus unfortunately advised I regret from the bottom of my soul!

All the successive vile plots of the Cardinal against the peace and reputation of the Queen may be attributed to this ill-judged prudence! Though it resulted from an honest desire of screening Her Majesty from the resentment or revenge to which she might have subjected herself from this villain, who had already injured her in her own estimation for having been credulous enough to have listened to him, yet from this circumstance it is that the Prince de Rohan built the foundation of all the after frauds and machinations with which he blackened the character and destroyed the comfort of his illustrious victim. It is obvious that a mere exclusion from Court was too mild a punishment for such offenses, and it was but too natural that such a mind as his, driven from the royal presence, and, of course, from all the noble societies to which it led (the anti-Court party excepted), should brood over the means of inveigling the Queen into a consent for his reappearance before her and the gay world, which was his only element, and if her favor should prove unattainable to revenge himself by her ruin.

"On the Cardinal's return to France,* all his numerous and powerful friends beset the King and Queen to allow of his restoration to his embassy; but though on his arrival at Versailles, finding the Court had removed to Compeigne, he had a short audience there of the King, all efforts in his favor were thrown away. Equally unsuccessful was every intercession with the Empress-mother. She had become thoroughly awakened to his worthlessness, and she declared she would never more even receive him in her dominions as a visitor. The Cardinal being apprised of this by some of his intimates, was at last persuaded to give up the idea of further importunity; and, pocketing his disgrace, retired with his *hey* dukes and his secretary, the Abbé Georgel, to whom may be attributed all the artful intrigues of his disgraceful diplomacy.†

* This circumstance is mentioned also by Madame Campan.

† The Abbé Georgel, in his memoirs, justifies the conduct of his superior with great ability; and it was very politic in him to do so,

"It is evident that Rohan had no idea, during all his schemes to supplant the Dauphiness by marrying her sister to the King, that the secret hope of Louis XV. had been to divorce the Dauphin and marry the slighted bride himself. Perhaps it is fortunate that Rohan did not know this. A brain so fertile in mischief as his might have converted such a circumstance to baneful uses. But the death of Louis XV. put an end to all the then existing schemes for a change in her position. It was to her a real, though but a momentary triumph. From the hour of her arrival she had a powerful party to cope with; and the fact of her being an Austrian, independent of the jealousy created by her charms, was, in itself, a spell to conjure up armies, against which she stood alone, isolated in the face of embattled myriads! But she now reared her head, and her foes trembled in her presence. Yet she could not guard against the moles busy in the earth secretly to undermine her. Nay, had not Louis XV. died at the moment he did, there is scarcely a doubt, from the number and the quality of the hostile influences working on the credulity of the young Dauphin, that Maria Antoinette would have been very harshly dealt with; even the more so from the partiality of the dotard who believed himself to be reigning. But she has been preserved from her enemies to become their sovereign; and if her crowned brow has erewhile been stung by thorns in its coronal, let me not despair of their being hereafter smothered in yet unblown roses.*

because he thereby exonerates himself from the imputation he would naturally incur from having been a known party, if not a principal, in all which has dishonored the Cardinal.

*The vain wish of friendship, that has been cruelly disappointed! Fortunate would it have been for Maria Antoinette had she been sent back to Vienna! What an ocean of blood, what writhings of human misery, it might have prevented! Had she been sent back, spotless as the first fallen snow, her life might have passed in that domestic bliss which was her sole ambition, and she would have gone down to the peaceful tombs of her august ancestors, leaving, perhaps, the page of history unstained by some of the greatest of its crimes!

CHAPTER IV.

"THE accession of Louis XVI. and Maria Antoinette to
the crown of France took place (May 10, 1774)
under the most propitious auspices !

"After the long, corrupt reign of an old debauched
Prince whose vices were degrading to himself and to a nation groaning under the lash of prostitution and caprice,
the most cheering changes were expected from the known
exemplariness of his successor and the amiableness of his
consort. Both were looked up to as models of goodness.
The virtues of Louis XVI. were so generally known that
all France hastened to acknowledge them, while the Queen's
fascinations acted like a charm on all who had not been
invincibly prejudiced against the many excellent qualities
which entitled her to love and admiration. Indeed, I
never heard an insinuation against either the King or
Queen but from those depraved minds which never possessed virtue enough to imitate theirs, or were jealous of
the wonderful powers of pleasing that so eminently distinguished Maria Antoinette from the rest of her sex.

"On the death of Louis XV. the entire Court removed
from Versailles to the palace of *La Muette*, situate in the
Bois de Boulogne, very near Paris. The confluence of
Parisians, who came in crowds joyfully to hail the death
of the old vitiated Sovereign, and the accession of his
adored successors, became quite annoying to the whole

Royal Family. The enthusiasm with which the Parisians hailed their young King, and in particular his amiable young partner, lasted for many days. These spontaneous evidences of attachment were regarded as prognostics of a long reign of happiness. If any inference can be drawn from public opinion, could there be a stronger assurance than this one of uninterrupted future tranquillity to its objects ?

"To the Queen herself it was a double triumph. The conspirators, whose depravity had been laboring to make her their victim, departed from the scene of power. The husband, who for four years had been callous to her attractions, became awakened to them. A complete change in the domestic system of the palace was wrought suddenly. The young King, during the interval which elapsed between the death and the interment of his grandfather, from Court etiquette was confined to his apartments. The youthful couple therefore saw each other with less restraint. The marriage was consummated. Maria Antoinette from this moment may date that influence over the heart (would I might add over the head and policy !) of the King, which never slackened during the remainder of their lives.

"Madame Du Barry was much better dealt with by the young King, whom she had always treated with the greatest levity, than she, or her numerous courtiers, expected. She was allowed her pension, and the entire enjoyment of all her ill-gotten and accumulated wealth: but, of course, excluded from ever appearing at Court, and politically exiled from Paris to the *Château aux Dames*.

"This implacable foe and her infamous coadjutors being removed from further interference in matters of state by the expulsion of all their own ministers, their rivals, the Duke de Choiseul and his party, by whom Maria Antoinette had been brought to France, were now in high expectation of finding the direction of the Government, by the Queen's influence, restored to that nobleman. But the King's choice was already made. He had been ruled by his aunts, and appointed the ministers suggested by them and his late grandfather's friends, who feared the preponderance of the Austrian influence. The three ladies, Madame la Maréchale de Beauveau, the Duchess de Choiseul, and the Duchess de Grammont, who were all well known to Louis XVI. and stood high in his opinion for many excellent qualities, and especially for their independent assertion of their own and the Dauphiness's dignity by retiring from Court in consequence of the supper at which Du Barry was introduced, these ladies, though received on their return thither with peculiar welcome, in vain united their efforts with those of the Queen and the Abbé Vermond, to overcome the prejudice which opposed Choiseul's reinstatement. It was all in vain. The royal aunts, Adelaide especially, hated Choiseul for the sake of Austria, and his agency in bringing Maria Antoinette to France; and so did the King's tutor and governor, the Duke de Vauguyon, who had ever been hostile to any sort of friendship with Vienna; and these formed a host impenetrable even to the influence of the Queen, which was opposed by all the leaders of the prevailing party, who, though they were beginning externally to court, admire, and idolize her, secretly surrounded her by their noxious and viperous intrigues, and, while they lived in her bosom, fattened on the destruction of her fame!

"One of the earliest of the paltry insinuations against Maria Antoinette emanated from her not counterfeiting deep affliction at the decease of the old King. A few days after that event, the Court received the regular visits of condolence and congratulation of the nobility, whose duty prescribes their attendance upon such occasions; and some of them, among whom were the daughters of Louis XV., not finding a young Queen of nineteen hypocritically bathed in tears, on returning to their abodes declared her the most indecorous of Princesses, and diffused a strong impression of her want of feeling. At the head of these detractors were Mesdames de Guéménée and Marsan, rival pretenders to the favors of the Cardinal de Rohan, who, having by the death of Louis XV. lost

their influence and their unlimited power to appoint and
dismiss ministers, themselves became ministers to their
own evil geniuses, in calumniating her whose legitimate
elevation annihilated their monstrous pretensions!

"The Abbé Vermond, seeing the defeat of the
party of the Duke de Choiseul, by whom he had
been sent to the Court of Vienna on the recommendation of Brienne, began to tremble for his own security.
As soon as the Court had arrived at Choisy and he was
assured of the marriage having been consummated, he
obtained, with the Queen's consent, an audience of the
King, for the purpose of soliciting his sanction to his
continuing in his situation. On submitting his suit to
the King, His Majesty merely gave a shrug of the
shoulders and turned to converse with the Duke d'Aiguillon, who at that moment entered the room. The Abbé
stood stupefied, and the Queen, seeing the crestfallen
humor of her tutor, laughed and cheered him by remarking, 'There is more meaning in the shrug of a
king than in the embrace of a minister. The one always promises, but is seldom sincere; the other is generally sincere, but never promises.' The Abbé, not knowing
how to interpret the dumb answer, finding the King's
back turned and his conversation with d'Aiguillon continuing, was retiring with a shrug of his own shoulders
to the Queen, when she exclaimed good-humoredly to
Louis, laughing and pointing to the Abbé, 'Look! look!
see how readily a Church dignitary can imitate the good
Christian King, who is at the head of the Church.' The
King, seeing the Abbé still waiting, said dryly, 'Sir,
you are confirmed in your situation,' and then resumed
his conversation with the Duke.

"This anecdote is a sufficient proof that Louis XVI.
had no prepossession in favor of the Abbé Vermond, and
that it was merely not to wound the feelings of the
Queen that he was tolerated. The Queen herself was
conscious of this, and used frequently to say to me how
much she was indebted to the King, for such deference
to her private choice, in allowing Vermond to be her

secretary, as she did not remember the King's ever having held any communication with the Abbé during the whole time he was attached to the service, though the Abbé always expressed himself with the greatest respect toward the King.

"The decorum of Maria Antoinette would not allow her to endure those public exhibitions of the ceremony of dressing herself which had been customary at Court. This reserve was highly approved by His Majesty; and one of the first reforms she introduced, after the accession, was in the internal discipline of her own apartment.

"It was during one of the visits, apart from Court etiquette, to the toilet of the Queen, that the Duchess de Chartres, afterward Duchess of Orleans, introduced the famous Mademoiselle Bertin, who afterward became so celebrated as the Queen's milliner; the first that was ever allowed to approach a royal palace; and it was months before Maria Antoinette had courage to receive her milliner in any other than the private apartment, which, by the alteration Her Majesty had made in the arrangements of the household, she set apart for the purposes of dressing in comfort by herself and free from all intruders.

"Till then the Queen was not only very plain in her attire, but very economical; a circumstance which, I have often heard her say, gave great umbrage to the other princesses of the Court of Versailles, who never showed themselves, from the moment they rose till they returned to bed, except in full dress; while she herself made all her morning visits in a simple white cambric gown and straw hat. This simplicity, unfortunately, like many other trifles, whose consequences no foresight would have predicted, tended much to injure Maria Antoinette, not only with the Court dandies, but the nation; by whom, though she was always censured, she was as suddenly imitated in all she wore, or did.

"From the private closet, which Maria Antoinette reserved to herself, and had now opened to her milliner, she would return, after the great points of habiliment were accomplished, to those who were waiting with memorials at her public toilet, where the hairdresser would finish putting the ornaments in Her Majesty's hair.*

"The King made Maria Antoinette a present of *Le Petit Trianon.* Much has been said of the extravagant expense lavished by her upon this spot. I can only declare that the greater part of the articles of furniture which had not been worn out by time or were not worm or moth-eaten, and her own bed among them, were taken from the apartments of former queens, and some of them had actually belonged to Anne of Austria, who, like Maria Antoinette, had purchased them out of her private savings. Hence it is clear that neither of the two Queens were chargeable to the State even for those little indulgences, which every private lady of property is permitted from her husband, without coming under the lash of censure.

*The Count de Fersen relates a curious anecdote of an occurrence which caused a great deal of mirth among the visitors of Her Majesty's toilet rendezvous. Mademoiselle Bertin had invented a new head ornament of gauze, ribbons, flowers, beads, and feathers, for the Queen; but the tire-woman, finding it deficient in the dimensions Her Majesty had ordered, by some folds, directed the gauze architect, Mademoiselle Bertin, to alter it so as to conform thoroughly to the model. The was executed; and Maria Antoinette went to her morning visitors. The royal hairdresser, according to custom, was in attendance there, with an embellishment, of which she did not perceive the use. "What are these steps for?" exclaimed she to the tire-woman. The knight of the comb advanced, and, making a most profound reverence, humbly represented to Her Majesty that, Mademoiselle Bertin having so enormously increased the height of the head ornaments, it would be impossible for him to establish them upon a firm foundation, unless he could have a complete command of the head they were to be fixed on; and, being but of the middle size and Her Majesty very tall, he could not achieve the duty of his office without mounting three or four steps, which he did, to the great amusement of the Queen and the whole party, and thus placed the *ne plus ultra* of Mademoiselle Bertin's invention, to the best of his own judgment, on the pinnacle of the royal head! As Hamlet says of Yorick—" Alas! where be your flashes of merriment now?"—Who would have dared, at that toilet, and among those smiles, to have prognosticated the cruel fate of the head which then attracted such general admiration!

"Her allowance as Queen of France was no more than 300,000 francs (£12,250). It is well known that she was generous, liberal, and very charitable; that she paid all her expenses regularly, respecting her household, Trianon, her dresses, diamonds, millinery, and everything else; her Court establishment excepted, and some few articles, which were paid by the civil list. She was one of the first Queens in Europe, had the first establishment in Europe, and was obliged to keep up the most refined and luxurious Court in Europe; and all upon means no greater than had been assigned to many of the former bigoted queens, who led a cloistered life, retired from the world without circulating their wealth among the nation which supplied them with so large a revenue; and yet who lived and died uncensured for hoarding from the nation what ought at least to have been in part expended for its advantage.*

"And yet of all the extra expenditure which the dignity and circumstances of Maria Antoinette exacted, not a franc came from the public treasury; but everything out of her majesty's private purse and savings from the above three hundred thousand francs, which was an infinitely less sum than Louis XIV. had lavished yearly on the Duchess de Montespan, and less than half what Louis XV. had expended on the two last favorites, Pompadour

---

*The Queens of England, who never had occasion to keep a Court like that of France, besides the revenue allowed them, it is said, and with some authority, have sinecures, resulting merely from the insertion of their names in the liturgy of eighty thousand pounds a year; and it is further added, that Madame Schwallemberg was of no little service to herself and others, in exercising the brokership of these ecclesiastical benefices.

Now, then, for all this outcry against the extravagance of the Court of France, leveled in particular against Maria Antoinette, for having lavished the national wealth, upon which pretext her life was made a scene of suffering, and her death a martyrdom! Let me take a momentary retrospect of the modest expenses of her murderers, the scrupulous *sans culottes*, who succeeded the Court of Louis XVI. and committed all their horrors in the name of national economy; for here is the record

and Du Barry. These two women, as clearly appeared
from the private registers, found among the papers of
Louis XV. after his death, by Louis XVI. (but which,
out of respect for the memory of his grandfather, he
destroyed), these two women had amassed more property
in diamonds and other valuables than all the Queens of
France from the days of Catherine de Medicis up to
those of Maria Antoinette.*

"Such was the goodness of heart of the excellent Queen
of Louis XVI., such the benevolence of her character,
that not only did she pay all the pensions of the invalids
left by her predecessors, but she distributed in public
and private charities greater sums than any of the for-

---

taken from the public register of the 500 tyrants, mountebank ragamuffins,
overthrowers of thrones, king killers, and sworn enemies of royalty, slaves
to the five buffoons of leaders, whose only virtue was that of wearing a
filthy shirt a month, and then turning it for the comfort and enjoyment
of clean linen next their polluted bodies!

MINISTERIAL PUBLIC EXPENSES.

30 millions of francs au ministre de la justice.

900	"	"	à celui de l'interieur.
200	"	"	à celui des finances.
1200	"	"	à celui de la guerre.
50	"	"	à celui des relations extérieures.
600	"	"	à celui de la marine.

Nearly three thousand millions, or three milliards, besides two millions
of secret service money in that particular year, which sometimes, according to the quantity and quality of their spies, exceeded this sum, but
which never was less during this anarchial government of miscreants. I
have appended this trifling account, merely to give the reader an idea of
what naturally became the further expenses with which the nation was
afterward overburdened to support these regicide *sans culottes*, when,
in the short time which elapsed between the plundering bloody government of Robespierre and the return to a taste for *culottes*, no less a sum
than 20 louis was expended on the mere embroidery of the flaps of one
pair for the PUBLIC SERVICE!

* The pensions and private landed property which Du Barry was
allowed to enjoy unmolested till the fatal period of the Revolution,
besides that of her predecessor; being divided at her death among
different branches of her nearest relations, has continued ever since
their legitimate inheritance.

mer Queens, thus increasing her expenses without any proportionate augmentation of her resources." *

* Indeed, could Louis XVI. have foreseen — when, in order not to expose the character of his predecessor and to honor the dignity of the throne and monarchy of France, he destroyed the papers of his grandfather — what an arm of strength he would have possessed in preserving them, against the accusers of his unfortunate Queen and himself, he never could have thrown away such means of establishing a most honorable contrast between his own and former reigns. His career exhibits no superfluous expenditure. Its economy was most rigid. No sovereign was ever more scrupulous with the public money. He never had any public or private predilection; no dilapidated minister for a favorite; no courtezan intrigue. For gaming he had no fondness; and, if his abilities were not splendid, he certainly had no predominating vices.

NOTE.

I MUST once more quit the Journal of the Princess. Her highness here ceases to record particulars of the early part of the reign of Louis XVI. and everything essential upon those times is too well known to render it desirable to detain the reader by an attempt to supply the deficiency. It is enough to state that the secret unhappiness of the Queen at not yet having the assurance of an heir was by no means weakened by the impatience of the people, nor by the accouchement of the Countess d'Artois of the Duke d' Angoulême. While the Queen continued the intimacy, and even held her parties at the apartments of the Duchess that she might watch over her friend, even in this triumph over herself the *poissardes* grossly insulted her in her misfortune, and coarsely called on her to GIVE HEIRS TO THE THRONE!

A consolation, however, for the unkind feeling of the populace was about to arise in the delights of one of her strongest friendships. I am come to the epoch when Her Majesty first formed an acquaintance with the Princess Lamballe.

After a few words of my own on the family of her highness, I shall leave her to pursue her beautiful and artless narrative of her parentage, early sorrows, and introduction to Her Majesty, unbroken.

The Journal of the history of Maria Antoinette. after this slight interruption for the private history of her friend, will become blended with the Journal of the Princess Lamballe, and both thenceforward proceed in their course together, like their destinies, which from that moment never became disunited.

CHAPTER V.

MARIA THERESA LOUISA CARIGNAN, Princess of Savoy,
was born at Turin on the 8th of September, 1749.
She had three sisters: two of them were married
at Rome, one to the Prince Doria Pamfili, the other to
the Prince Colonna; and the third, at Vienna, to the
Prince Lobkowitz, whose son was the great patron of the
immortal Haydn, * the celebrated composer. She had a

---

* The celebrated Haydn was, even at the age of 74, when I last saw
him at Vienna, still the most good-humored *bon vivant* of his age. He
delighted in telling the origin of his good fortune, which he said he entirely owed to a bad wife!

When he was first married, he said, finding no remedy against domestic squabbles, he used to quit his bad half and go and enjoy himself
with his good friends, who were Hungarians and Germans, for weeks
together. Once, having returned home after a considerable absence, his
wife, while he was in bed next morning, followed her husband's example: she did even more, for she took all his clothes, even to his shoes,
stockings, and small clothes, nay, everything he had, along with her!
Thus situated, he was under the necessity of doing something to cover
his nakedness; and this, he himself acknowledged, was the first cause of
his seriously applying himself to the profession which has since made his
name immortal.

He used to laugh, saying: "I was from that time so habituated to
study that my wife, often fearing it would injure me, would threaten
me with the same operation if I did not go out and amuse myself; but
then," added he, "I was grown old, and she was sick and no longer

brother also, the Prince Carignan, who, marrying against
the consent of his family, was no longer received by
them; but the unremitting and affectionate attention which
the Princess Lamballe paid to him and his new connections was an ample compensation for the loss he sustained
in the severity of his other sisters.*

'With regard to the early life of the Princess Lamballe,
the arranger of these pages must now leave her to pursue her own beautiful and artless narrative unbroken,
up to the epoch of her appointment to the household of
the Queen. It will be recollected that the papers of
which the reception has been already described in the
introduction, formed the private journal of this most amiable princess; and those passages relating to her own
early life being the most connected part of them, it has
been thought that to disturb them would be a kind of
sacrilege. After the appointment of her highness to the
superintendence of the Queen's household, her manu-
scripts again become confused, and fall into scraps and
fragments, which will require to be once more rendered
clear by the recollections of events and conversations
by which the preceding chapters have been assisted.

"I was the favorite child of a numerous family, and intended, almost at my birth — as is generally the case
among princes who are nearly allied to crowned heads —
to be united to one of the Princes, my near relation, of
the royal house of Sardinia.

"A few years after this, the Duke and Duchess de Penthièvre arrived at Turin, on their way to Italy, for the

jealous." He spoke remarkably good Italian, though he had never been
in Italy, and on my going to Vienna to hear his "Creation," he promised
to accompany me back to Italy; but he unfortunately died before I returned to Vienna from Carlsbad.

* If I mistake not, the present Prince Carignan, famous in the late
history of Piedmont, is a son of that marriage, the same who is now
distinguished by the title of "Prince of the Epaulets of a French soldier
of the Trocadero."

The Prince Carignan I speak of has been united to the daughter of
the late Grand Duke of Tuscany, and is now the only male heir to the
crown of Sardinia, Piedmont, Savoy, etc.

purpose of visiting the different Courts, to make suitable marriage contracts for both their infant children.

"These two children were Mademoiselle de Penthièvre, afterward the unhappy Duchess of Orleans, and their idolized son, the Prince Lamballe.*

"Happy would it have been both for the Prince who was destined to the former and the Princess who was given to the latter, had these unfortunate alliances never taken place.

"The Duke and Duchess de Penthièvre became so singularly attached to my beloved parents, and, in particular, to myself, that the very day they first dined at the Court of Turin, they mentioned the wish they had formed, of uniting me to their young son, the Prince Lamballe.

"The King of Sardinia, as the head of the house of Savoy and Carignan, said there had been some conversation as to my becoming a member of his Royal Family; but, as I was so very young at the time, many political reasons might arise to create motives for a change in the projected alliance. 'If, therefore, the Prince Carignan,' said the King, 'be anxious to settle his daughter's marriage, by any immediate matrimonial alliance, I certainly shall not avail myself of any prior engagement, nor oppose any obstacle in the way of its solemnization.'

"The consent of the King being thus unexpectedly obtained by the Prince, so desirable did the arrangement seem to the Duke and Duchess that the next day the contract was concluded with my parents for my becoming the wife of their only son, the Prince Lamballe.

---

* The father of Louis Alexander Joseph Stanislaus de Bourbon Penthièvre, Prince Lamballe, was the son of the Count de Toulouse, himself a natural son of Louis XIV. and Madame de Montespan, who was considered as the most wealthy of all the natural children, in consequence of Madame de Montespan, having artfully entrapped the famous Mademoiselle de Montpensier to make over her immense fortune to him as her heir after her death, as the price of liberating her husband from imprisonment in the Bastille, and herself from a ruinous prosecution, for having contracted this marriage contrary to the express commands of her royal cousin, Louis XIV.—*Vide Histoire de Louis* XIV. *par Voltaire.*

"I was too young to be consulted. Perhaps, had I been older the result would have been the same, for it generally happens in these great family alliances that the parties most interested, and whose happiness is most concerned, are the least thought of. The Prince was, I believe, at Paris, under the tuition of his governess, and I was in the nursery, heedless, and totally ignorant of my future good or evil destination!

"So truly happy and domestic a life as that led by the Duke and Duchess de Penthièvre seemed to my family to offer an example too propitious not to secure to me a degree of felicity with a private prince, very rarely the result of royal unions! of course, their consent was given with alacrity. When I was called upon to do homage to my future parents, I had so little idea, from my extreme youthfulness, of what was going on that I set them all laughing, when, on being asked if I should like to become the CONSORT of the Prince Lamballe, I said, 'Yes, I am very fond of music!' 'No my dear,' resumed the good and tender-hearted Duke de Penthièvre, 'I mean, would you have any objection to become his wife?' 'No, nor any other person's!' was the innocent reply, which increased the mirth of all the guests at my expense.

"Happy, happy days of youthful, thoughtless innocence, luxuriously felt and appreciated under the thatched roof of the cottage, but unknown and unattainable beneath the massive pile of a royal palace and a gemmed crown! Scarcely had I entered my teens when my adopted parents strewed flowers of the sweetest fragrance to lead me to the sacred altar, that promised the bliss of blisses, but which, too soon, from the foul machinations of envy, jealously, avarice, and a still more criminal passion, proved to me the altar of my sacrifice!

"My misery and my uninterrupted grief may be dated from the day my beloved sister-in-law, Mademoiselle de Penthièvre, sullied her hand by its union with the Duke de Chartres.* From that moment all comfort, all pros-

*Afterward Duke of Orleans, and the celebrated revolutionary *Philip Égalité.*

pect of connubial happiness, left my young and affectionate heart, plucked thence by the very roots, never more
again to bloom there. Religion and philosophy were the
only remedies remaining.

"I was a bride when an infant, a wife before I was a
woman, a widow before I was a mother, or had
the prospect of becoming one! Our union was, perhaps, an exception to the general rule. We became
insensibly the more attached to each other the more
we were acquainted, which rendered the more severe the
separation, when we were torn asunder never to meet
again in this world!

"After I left Turin, though everything for my reception at the palaces of Toulouse and Rambouillet had been
prepared in the most sumptuous style of magnificence,
yet such was my agitation that I remained convulsively
speechless for many hours, and all the affectionate attention of the family of the Duke de Penthièvre could
not calm my feelings.

"Among those who came about me was the bridegroom
himself, whom I had never yet seen. So anxious was he
to have his first acquaintance *incognito* that he set off
from Paris the moment he was apprised of my arrival
in France and presented himself as the Prince's page.
As he had outgrown the figure of his portrait I received
him as such; but the Prince, being better pleased with
me than he had apprehended he should be, could scarcely
avoid discovering himself. During our journey to Paris
I myself disclosed the interest with which the supposed
page had inspired me. 'I hope,' exclaimed I, 'my
prince will allow his page to attend me, for I like him
much.'

"What was my surprise when the Duke de Penthièvre
presented me to the Prince and I found in him the page
for whom I had already felt such an interest! We both
laughed and wanted words to express our mutual sentiments. This was really love at first sight.*

* The young Prince was enraptured at finding his lovely bride so superior in personal charms to the description which had been given of

"The Duke de Chartres, then possessing a very handsome person and most insinuating address, soon gained the affections of the amiable Mademoiselle Penthièvre. Becoming thus a member of the same family, he paid me the most assiduous attention. From my being his sister-in-law, and knowing he was aware of my great attachment to his young wife, I could have no idea that his views were criminally leveled at my honor, my happiness, and my future peace of mind. How, therefore, was I astonished and shocked when he discovered to me his desire to supplant the legitimate object of my affections, whose love for me equaled mine for him! I did not expose this baseness of the Duke de Chartres out of filial affection for my adopted father, the Duke de Penthièvre; out of the love I bore his amiable daughter, she being pregnant; and above all in consequence of the fear I was under of compromising the life of the Prince, my husband, who I apprehended might be lost to me if I did not suffer in silence. But still, through my silence he was lost —and oh, how dreadfully! The Prince was totally in the dark as to the real character of his brother-in-law. He blindly became every day more and more attached to the man, who was then endeavoring by the foulest means to blast the fairest prospects of his future happiness in life!

her, and even to the portrait sent to him from Turin. Indeed she must have been a most beautiful creature, for when I left her in the year 1792, though then five-and-forty years of age, from the freshness of her complexion, the elegance of her figure, and the dignity of her deportment, she certainly did not appear to be more than thirty. She had a fine head of hair, and she took great pleasure in showing it unornamented. I remember one day, on her coming hastily from the bath, as she was putting on her dress, her cap falling off, her hair completely covered her!

The circumstances of her death always make me shudder at the recollection of this incident! I have been assured by Mesdames Mackau, de Soucle, the Countess de Noailles (not Duchess, as Mademoiselle Bertin has created her in her Memoirs of that name), and others, that the Princess Lamballe was considered the most beautiful and accomplished Princess at the Court of Louis XV., adorned with all the grace, virtue, and elegance of manner which so eminently distinguished her through life.

But my guardian angel protected me from becoming a
a victim to seduction, defeating every attack by that prudence which has hitherto been my invincible shield.

"Guilt unpunished in its first crime, rushes onward, and
hurrying from one misdeed to another, like the flood tide,
drives all before it! My silence and his being defeated
without reproach, armed him with courage for fresh daring, and he too well succeeded in embittering the future
days of my life, as well as those of his own affectionate
wife, and his illustrious father-in-law, the virtuous Duke
de Penthièvre, who was to all a father.

"To revenge himself upon me for the repulse he met
with, this man inveigled my young, inexperienced husband from his bridal bed to those infected with the nauseous poison of every vice! Poor youth! he soon became
the prey of every refinement upon dissipation and studied
debauchery, till at length his sufferings made his life a
burden, and he died in the most excruciating agonies both
of mind and body, in the arms of a disconsolate wife and
a distracted father — and thus, in a few short months, at
the age of eighteen, was I left a widow to lament my
having become a wife!

"I was in this situation, retired from the world and ab-
sorbed in grief, with the ever beloved and revered illustrious father of my murdered lord, endeavoring to soothe
his pangs for the loss of those comforts in a child with
which my cruel disappointment forbade my ever being
blest — though, in the endeavor to soothe, I often only
aggravated both his and my own misery at our irretrievable loss — when a ray of unexpected light burst upon
my dreariness. It was amid this gloom of human agony,
these heart-rending scenes of real mourning, that the brilliant star shone to disperse the clouds, which hovered
over our drooping heads, — to dry the hot briny tears
which were parching up our miserable vegetating existence — it was in this crisis that Maria Antoinette came, like
a messenger sent down from Heaven, graciously to offer
the balm of comfort in the sweetest language of human
compassion. The pure emotions of her generous soul

made her unceasing, unremitting, in her visits to two
mortals who must else have perished under the weight
of their misfortunes. But for the consolation of her warm
friendship we must have sunk into utter despair!

"From that moment I became seriously attached to
the Queen of France. She dedicated a great portion of
her time to calm the anguish of my poor heart, though I
had not yet accepted the honor of becoming a member
of Her Majesty's household. Indeed, it was a considerable time before I could think of undertaking a
charge I felt myself so completely incapable of fulfill-
ing.* I endeavored to check the tears that were pouring down my cheeks, to conceal in the Queen's presence
the real feelings of my heart, but the effort only served
to increase my anguish when she had departed. Her attachment to me, and the cordiality with which she distinguished herself toward the Duke de Penthièvre, gave
her a place in that heart, which had been chilled by the
fatal vacuum left by its first inhabitant; and Maria Antoinette was the only rival through life that usurped his
pretentions, though she could never wean me completely
from his memory.

"My health, from the melancholy life I led, had so
much declined that my affectionate father, the Duke de
Penthièvre, with whom I continued to reside, was anx-

---

* I am under the necessity of correcting an error of Madame Campan's in vol. i., page 129. The Queen had been long attached to the
Princess Lamballe before the sledge parties took place, though
it was only during that amusement that the superintendence
of the household of the Queen was revived in her favor. It
is not at all likely, from the unlimited authority and power
which the situation gave a superintendent over Her Majesty,
that the Queen, who was so scrupulously particular with respect to the
meanest of the persons who held any charge in her household, should
have placed herself under the immediate control of one whose office
might itself be a check upon her own movements without first being
thoroughly assured of the principles, morals, character, and general
conduct of the individual destined to a post of such importance.
Nothing can be more absurd than to believe that the Queen could have
been so heedless as to have nominated the Princess Lamballe her superintendent *ex abrupta* merely because she was the Princess Lamballe.

fous that I should emerge from my retirement for the benefit of my health. Sensible of his affection, and having always honored his counsels, I took his advice in this instance. It being in the hard winter, when so many persons were out of bread, the Queen, the Duchess of Orleans, the Duke de Penthièvre, and myself introduced the German sledges, in which we were followed by most of the nobility and the rich citizens. This afforded considerable employment to different artificers. The first use I made of my own vehicle was to visit, in company of the Duke de Penthièvre, the necessitious poor families and our pensioners. In the course of our rounds we met the Queen.

"'I suppose,' exclaimed Her Majesty, 'you also are laying a good foundation for my work! Heavens! what must the poor feel! I am wrapped up like a diamond in a box, covered with furs, and yet I am chilled with cold!'

"'That feeling sentiment,' said the Duke, 'will soon warm many a cold family's heart with gratitude to bless your Majesty!'

"'Why, yes,' replied Her Majesty, showing a long piece of paper containing the names of those to whom she intended to afford relief — 'I have only collected two hundred yet on my list, but the *curé* will do the rest and help me to draw the strings of my privy purse! But I have not half done my rounds. I dare say before I return to Versailles I shall have as many more, and, since we are engaged in the same business, pray come into my sledge and do not take my work out of my hands! Let me have for once the merit of doing something good!'

"On the coming up of a number of other vehicles belonging to the sledge party, the Queen added, 'Do not say anything about what I have been telling you!' for Her Majesty never wished what she did in the way of charity or donations should be publicly known, the old pensioners excepted, who, being on the list, could not be concealed; especially as she continued to pay all those she found of the late Queen of Louis XV. She was

remarkably delicate and timid with respect to hurting the
feelings of anyone; and, fearing the Duke de Penthièvre
might not be pleased at her pressing me to leave him in
order to join her, she said, 'Well, I will let you off,
Princess, on your both promising to dine with me at
Trianon; for the King is hunting, not deer, but wood for
the poor, and he will see his game off to Paris before he
comes back.'

"The Duke begged to be excused, but wished me to
accept the invitation, which I did, and we parted, each
to pursue our different sledge excursions.

"At the hour appointed, I made my appearance at
Trianon, and had the honor to dine *tête-à-tête* with Her Majesty, which was much more congenial to my feelings than
if there had been a party, as I was still very low-spirited
and unhappy.

"After dinner, 'My dear Princess,' said the Queen to
me, 'at your time of life you must not give yourself up
entirely to the dead. You wrong the living. We have
not been sent into the world for ourselves. I have felt
much for your situation, and still do so, and therefore
hope, as long as the weather permits, that you will favor
me with your company to enlarge our sledge excursions.
The King and my dear sister Elizabeth are also much
interested about your coming on a visit to Versailles.
What think you of our plan?'

"I thanked Her Majesty, the King, and the Princess,
for their kindness, but I observed that my state of health
and mind could so little correspond in any way with the
gratitude I should owe them for their royal favors, that
I trusted a refusal would be attributed to the fact of my
consciousness how much rather my society must prove
an annoyance and a burden than a source of pleasure.

"My tears flowing down my cheeks rapidly while I
was speaking, the Queen, with that kindness for which
she was so eminently distinguished, took me by the
hand, and with her handkerchief dried my face.

"'I am,' said the Queen, 'about to renew a situation,
which has for some time past lain dormant; and I hope,

my dear Princess, therewith to establish my own private views, in forming the happiness of a worthy individual.'

"I replied that such a plan must insure Her Majesty the desired object she had in view, as no individual could be otherwise than happy under the immediate auspices of so benevolent and generous a Sovereign.

"The Queen, with great affability, as if pleased with my observation, only said, 'If you really think as you speak, my views are accomplished.'

"My carriage was announced, and I then left Her Majesty, highly pleased at her gracious condescension, which evidently emanated from the kind wish to raise my drooping spirits from their melancholy.

"Gratitude would not permit me to continue long without demonstrating to Her Majesty the sentiments her kindness had awakened in my heart.

"I returned next day with my sister-in-law, the Duchess of Orleans, who was much esteemed by the Queen, and we joined the sledge parties with Her Majesty.

"On the third or fourth day of these excursions I again had the honor to dine with Her Majesty, when, in the presence of the Princess Elizabeth, she asked me if I were still of the same opinion with respect to the person it was her intention to add to her household?

"I myself had totally forgotten the topic and entreated Her Majesty's pardon for my want of memory, and begged she would signify to what subject she alluded.

"The Princess Elizabeth laughed. 'I thought,' cried she, 'that you had known it long ago! The Queen, with His Majesty's consent, has nominated you, my dear Princess (embracing me), superintendent of her household.'

"The Queen, also embracing me, said, 'Yes; it is very true. You said the individual destined to such a situation could not be otherwise than happy; and I am myself thoroughly happy in being able thus to contribute toward rendering you so.'

"I was perfectly at a loss for a moment or two, but, recovering myself from the effect of this unexpected and unlooked-for preferment, I thanked Her Majesty with the best grace I was able for such an unmerited mark of distinction.

"The Queen, perceiving my embarrassment, observed, 'I knew I should surprise you; but I thought your being established at Versailles much more desirable for one of your rank and youth than to be, as you were, with the Duke de Penthièvre; who, much as I esteem his amiable character and numerous great virtues, is by no means the most cheering companion for my charming Princess. From this moment let our friendships be united in the common interest of each other's happiness.'

"The Queen took me by the hand. The Princess Elizabeth, joining hers, exclaimed to the Queen, 'Oh, my dear sister! let me make the trio in this happy union of friends!'

"In the society of her adored Majesty and of her saint-like sister Elizabeth I have found my only balm of consolation! Their graciously condescending to sympathize in the grief with which I was overwhelmed from the cruel disappointment of my first love, filled up in some degree the vacuum left by his loss, who was so prematurely ravished from me in the flower of youth, leaving me a widow at eighteen; and though that loss is one I never can replace or forget, the poignancy of its effect has been in a great degree softened by the kindnesses of my excellent father-in-law, the Duke de Penthièvre, and the relations resulting from my situation with, and the never-ceasing attachment of my beloved royal mistress."

CHAPTER VI.

THE connection of the Princess Lamballe with the Queen, of which she has herself described the origin in the preceding chapter, proved so important in its influence upon the reputation and fate of both these illustrious victims, that I must once more withdraw the attention of the reader, to explain, from personal observation and confidential disclosures, the leading causes of the violent dislike which was kindled in the public against an intimacy, that it would have been most fortunate had Her Majesty preferred through life to every other.

The selection of a friend by the Queen, and the sudden elevation of that friend to the highest station in the royal household could not fail to alarm the selfishness of courtiers, who always feel themselves injured by the favor shown to others. An obsolete office was revived in favor of the Princess Lamballe. In the time of Maria Leckzinska, wife of Louis XV., the office of superintendent, then held by Mademoiselle de Clermont, was suppressed when its holder died. The office gave a control over the inclinations of queens by which Maria Leckzinska was sometimes inconvenienced; and it had lain dormant ever since. Its restoration by a queen who it was believed could be guided by no motive but the desire to seek pretexts for showing undue favor, was of course eyed askance, and ere long openly calumniated.

The Countess de Noailles, who never could forget the title the Queen gave her of MADAME ETIQUETTE, nor forgive the frequent jokes which Her Majesty passed upon her antiquated formality, availed herself of the opportunity offered by her husband's being raised to the dignity of Marshal of France, to resign her situation on the appointment of the Princess Lamballe as superintendent. The Countess retired with feelings embittered against her royal mistress, and her annoyance in the sequel ripened into enmity. The Countess was attached to a very powerful party, not only at Court but scattered throughout the kingdom. Her discontent arose from the circumstance of no longer having to take her orders from the Queen direct, but from her superintendent. Ridiculous as this may seem to an impartial observer, it created one of the most powerful hostilities against which Her Majesty had afterward to contend.

Though the Queen esteemed the Countess de Noailles for her many good qualities, yet she was so much put out of her way by the rigor with which the Countess enforced forms, which to Her Majesty appeared puerile and absurd, that she felt relieved, and secretly gratified, by her retirement. It will be shown hereafter to what an excess the Countess was eventually carried by her malice.

One of the popular objections to the revival of the office of superintendent in favor of the Princess Lamballe arose from its reputed extravagance. This was as groundless as the other charges against the Queen. The etiquettes of dress, and the requisite increase of every other expense, from the augmentation of every article of the necessaries as well as the luxuries of life, made a treble difference between the expenditure of the circumscribed Court of Maria Leckzinska and that of Louis XVI.; yet the Princess Lamballe received no more salary* than had

* And even that salary she never appropriated to any private use of her own, being amply supplied through the generous bounty of her

been allotted to Mademoiselle de Clermont in the self-same situation half a century before.

So far from possessing the slightest propensity either to extravagance in herself or to the encouragement of extravagance in others, the Princess Lamballe was a model of prudence, and upon those subjects, as indeed upon all others, the Queen could not have had a more discreet counselor. She eminently contributed to the charities of the Queen, who was the mother of the fatherless, the support of the widow, and the general protectress and refuge of suffering humanity. Previous to the purchase of any article of luxury, the Princess would call for the list of the pensioners: if anything were due on that account, it was instantly paid, and the luxury dispensed with.

She never made her appearance in the Queen's apartments except at established hours. This was scrupulously observed till the Revolution. Circumstances then obliged her to break through forms. The Queen would only receive communications, either written or verbal, upon the subjects growing out of that wretched crisis, in the presence of the Princess; and hence her apartments were open to all who had occasion to see Her Majesty. This made their intercourse more constant and unceremonious. But before this, the Princess only went to the royal presence at fixed hours, unless she had memorials to present to the King, Queen, or ministers, in favor of such as asked for justice or mercy. Hence, whenever the Princess entered before the stated times, the Queen would run and embrace her, and exclaim: "Well, my dear Princess Lamballe! what widow, what orphan, what suffering, or oppressed petitioner am I to thank for this visit? for I know you never come to me empty-handed when you come unexpectedly!" The Princess, on these occasions, often had the petitioners waiting in an adjoining apartment, that they might instantly avail them-

father-in-law, the Duke de Penthièvre; and latterly, to my knowledge, so far from receiving any pay, she often paid the Queen's and Princess Elizabeth's bills out of her own purse.

selves of any inclination the Queen might show to see them.

Once the Princess was deceived by a female painter of doubtful character, who supplicated her to present a work she had executed to the Queen. I myself afterward returned that work to its owner. Thenceforward, the Princess became very rigid in her inquiries, previous to taking the least interest in any application, or consenting to present anyone personally to the King or Queen. She required thoroughly to be informed of the nature of the request, and of the merit and character of the applicant, before she would attend to either. Owing to this caution Her Highness scarcely ever after met with a negative. In cases of great importance, though the Queen's compassionate and good heart needed no stimulus to impel her to forward the means of justice, the Princess would call the influence of the Princess Elizabeth to her aid; and Elizabeth never sued in vain.

Maria Antoinette paid the greatest attention to all memorials. They were regularly collected every week by Her Majesty's private secretary, the Abbé Vermond. I have myself seen many of them, when returned from the Princess Lamballe, with the Queen's marginal notes in her own handwriting and the answers dictated by Her Majesty to the different officers of the departments relative to the nature of the respective demands. She always recommended the greatest attention to all public documents, and annexed notes to such as passed through her hands to prevent their being thrown aside or lost.

One of those who were least satisfied with the appointment of the Princess Lamballe to the office of superintendent was her brother-in-law, the Duke of Orleans, who, having attempted her virtue on various occasions and been repulsed, became mortified and alarmed at her situation as a check to his future enterprise.

At one time the Duke and Duchess of Orleans were most constant and assiduous in their attendance on Maria Antoinette. They were at all her parties. The Queen was very fond of the Duchess. It is supposed that the interest Her Majesty took in that lady and the steps to which some time afterward that interest led, planted the first seeds of the unrelenting and misguided hostility which, in the deadliest times of the Revolution, animated the Orleanists against the throne.

The Duke of Orleans, then Duke de Chartres, was never a favorite of the Queen. He was only tolerated at Court on account of his wife and of the great intimacy which subsisted between him and Count d'Artois. Louis XVI. had often expressed his disapprobation of the Duke's character, which his conduct daily justified.

The Princess Lamballe could have no cause to think of her brother-in-law but with horror. He had insulted her, and in revenge at his defeat, had, it was said, deprived her by the most awful means, of her husband. The Princess was tenderly attached to her sister-in-law, the Duchess. Her attachment could not but make her look very unfavorably upon the circumstance of the Duke's subjecting his wife to the humiliation of residing in the palace with Madame de Genlis, and being forced to receive a person of morals so incorrect as the guardian of her children. The Duchess had complained to her father, the Duke de Penthièvre, in the presence of the Princess Lamballe, of the very great ascendancy Madame de Genlis exercised over her husband; and had even requested the Queen to use her influence in detaching the Duke from this connection.* But she had too much gentleness of nature not presently to forget her resentment. Being much devoted to her husband, rather than irritate him to further neglect by personal remonstrance, she determined to make the best of a bad business, and tolerated Madame de Genlis, although she made no secret among her friends and relations of the reason why she did so. Nay, so far did her wish not to disoblige her husband prevail over her own feelings as to induce her to yield at last to his importunities by frequently proposing to present

* It was generally understood that the Duke had a daughter by Madame de Genlis. This daughter, when grown up, was married to the late Irish Lord Robert Fitzgerald.

Madame de Genlis to the Queen. But Madame de Genlis never could obtain either a public or a private audience. Though the Queen was a great admirer of merit and was fond of encouraging talents, of which Madame de Genlis was by no means deficient, yet even the account the Duchess herself had given, had Her Majesty possessed no other means of knowledge, would have sealed that lady's exclusion from the opportunities of display at Court, which she sought so earnestly.

There was another source of exasperation against the Duke of Orleans; and the great cause of a new and, though less obtrusive, yet perhaps an equally dangerous foe under all the circumstances, in Madame de Genlis. The anonymous slander of the one was circulated through all France by the other; and spleen and disappointment feathered the venomed arrows shot at the heart of power by malice and ambition! Be the charge true or false, these anonymous libels were generally considered as the offspring of this lady: they were industriously scattered by the Duke of Orleans; and their frequent refutation by the Queen's friends only increased the malignant industry of their inventor.

An event which proved the most serious of all that ever happened to the Queen, and the consequences of which were distinctly foreseen by the Princess Lamballe and others of her true friends, was now growing to maturity.

The deposed Court oracle, the Countess de Noailles, had been succeeded as literary leader by the Countess Diana Polignac. She was a favorite of the Count d'Artois, and was the first lady in attendance upon the Countess, his wife.* The Queen's conduct had always

* The Countess Diana Polignac had a much better education, and considerably more natural capacity, than her sister-in-law, the Duchess, and the Queen merely disliked her from her prudish affectation. The Countess d'Artois grew jealous of the Count's intimacy with the Countess Diana. While she considered herself as the only one of the Royal Family likely to be mother of a future sovereign, she was silent. or, perhaps, too much engrossed by her castles in the air to think of anything but diadems; but when she saw the Queen producing heirs, she grew out of humor at her lost popularity, and began to turn her atten-

been very cool to her. She deemed her a self-sufficient coquette. However, the Countess Diana was a constant attendant at the gay parties, which were then the fashion of the Court, though not greatly admired.

The reader will scarcely need to be informed that the event to which I have just alluded is the introduction by the Countess Diana of her sister-in-law, the Countess Julie Polignac, to the Queen; and having brought the record up to this point, I here once more dismiss my own pen for that of the Princess Lamballe.

It will be obvious to everyone that I must have been indebted to the conversations of my beloved patroness for most of the sentiments and nearly all the facts I have just been stating; and had the period on which she has written so little as to drive me to the necessity of writing for her been less pregnant with circumstances almost entirely personal to herself, no doubt I should have found more upon that period in her manuscript. But the year of which Her Highness says so little was the year of happiness and exclusive favor; and the Princess was above the vanity of boasting, even privately in the self-confessional of her diary. She resumes her records with her apprehensions; and thus proceeds, describing the introduction of the Countess Julie de Polignac, regretting her ascendancy over the Queen and foreseeing its fatal effects.

———

"I had only been a twelvemonth in Her Majesty's service, which I believe was the happiest period of both

tion to her husband's ENDYMIONSHIP to this new Diana! When she had made up her mind to get her rival out of her house, she consulted one of the family; but being told that the best means for a wife to keep her husband out of harm's way was to provide him with a domestic occupation for his leisure hours at home, than which nothing could be better than a HAND-MAID under the same roof, she made a merit of necessity and submitted ever after to retain the Countess Diana, as she had been prudently advised. The Countess Diana, in consequence, remained in the family even up to the 17th of October, 1789, when she left Versailles in company with the Polignacs and the d'Artois, who all emigrated together from France to Italy and lived at Stria on the Brenta, near Venice, for some time, till the Countess d'Artois went to Turin.

our lives, when, at one of the Court assemblies, the Countess Julie Polignac was first introduced by her sister-in-law, the Countess Diana Polignac, to the Queen.

"She had lived in the country, quite a retired life, and appeared to be more the motherly woman, and the domestic wife, than the ambitious Court lady, or royal sycophant. She was easy of access, and elegantly plain in her dress and deportment.

" Her appearance at Court was as fatal to the Queen as it was propitious to herself!

"She seemed formed by nature to become a royal favorite; unassuming, remarkably complaisant, possessing a refined taste, with a good-natured disposition, not handsome, but well formed, and untainted by haughtiness or pomposity.

"It would appear, from the effect her introduction had on the Queen, that her domestic virtues were written in her countenance, for she became a royal favorite before she had time to become a candidate for royal favor.

"The Queen's sudden attachment to the Countess Julie produced no alteration in my conduct, while I saw nothing extraordinary to alarm me for the consequences of any particular marked partiality, by which the character and popularity of Her Majesty might be endangered.*

" But, seeing the progress this lady made in the feelings of the Queen's enemies, it became my duty, from the situation I held, to caution Her Majesty against the risks she ran in making her favorites friends; for it was very soon apparent how highly the Court disapproved of this intimacy and partiality: and the same feeling soon found its way to the many-headed monster, the people, who only saw the favorite without considering the charge she held. Scarely had she felt the warm rays of royal favor, than the chilling blasts of envy and malice began to nip it in the bud of all its promised bliss. Even long before she

---

* The Princess Lamballe was too virtuous, too handsome, and much too noble in character and sentiment, meanly to nourish jealousy or envy. She was as much above it as her personal and mental qualifications were superior to those of her rival.

touched the pinnacle of her grandeur as governess of the royal children, the blackest calumny began to show itself in prints, caricatures, songs, and pamphlets of every description.

"A reciprocity of friendship between a queen and a subject, by those who never felt the existence of such a feeling as friendship, could only be considered in a criminal point of view. But by what perversion could suspicion frown upon the ties between two married women, both living in the greatest harmony with their respective husbands, especially when both became mothers and so devoted to their offspring? This boundless friendship DID glow between this calumniated pair — calumniated because the sacredness and peculiarity of the sentiment which united them was too pure to be understood by the groveling minds who made themselves their sentencers. The friend is the friend's shadow. The real sentiment of friendship, of which DISINTERESTED sympathy is the sign, cannot exist unless between two of the same sex, because a physical difference involuntarily modifies the complexion of the intimacy where the sexes are opposite, even though there be no physical relations. The Queen of France had love n her eyes and Heaven in her soul. The Duchess of Polignac, whose person beamed with every charm, could never have been condemned, like the Friars of La Trappe, to the mere *memento mori.*

"When I made the representations to Her Majesty which duty exacted from me on perceiving her ungovernable partiality for her new favorite, that I might not importune her by the awkwardness naturally arising from my constant exposure to the necessity of witnessing an intimacy she knew I did not sanction, I obtained permission from my royal mistress to visit my father-in-law, the Duke de Penthièvre, at Rambouillet, his country seat.

"Soon after I arrived there, I was taken suddenly ill after dinner with the most excruciating pains in my stomach. I thought myself dying. Indeed, I should have been so but for the fortunate and timely discovery that I was poisoned: — certainly, not intentionally, by anyone belonging to my dear father's household; but by some execrable hand which had an interest in my death.

"The affair was hushed up with a vague report that some of the made dishes had been prepared in a stew pan long out of use, which the clerk of the Duke's kitchen had forgotten to get properly tinned.

"This was a doubtful story for many reasons. Indeed, I firmly believe that the poison given me had been' prepared in the salt, for everyone at table had eaten of the same dish without suffering the smallest inconvenience.*

"The news of this accident had scarcely arrived at Versailles, when the Queen, astounded, and in excessive anxiety, instantly sent off her physician, and her private secretary, the Abbé Vermond, to bring me back to my apartments at Versailles, with strict orders not to leave me a moment at the Duke's, for fear of a second attempt of the same nature. Her Majesty had imputed the first to the earnestness I had always shown in support of her interests, and she seemed now more ardent in her kindness toward me from the idea of my being exposed through her means to the treachery of assassins in the dark. The Queen awaited our coming impatiently, and, not seeing the carriages return so quickly as she fancied they ought to arrive, she herself set off for Rambouillet, and did not leave me till she had prevailed on me to quit my father-in-law's, and we both returned together the same night to Versailles, where the Queen in person dedicated all her attention to the restoration of my health.

"As yet, however, nothing in particular had discovered that splendor for which the Polignacs were afterward so conspicuous.

* Had not this unfortunate circumstance occurred, it is probable the Duke de Penthièvre would have prevailed on the Princess to have renounced her situation at Court. What heart-rending grief would it not have spared the gray hairs of her doting father-in-law, and what a sea of crime might have been obviated, had it pleased Heaven to have ordained her death under the paternal roof of her second father!

"Indeed, so little were their circumstances calculated for a Court life, that when the friends of Madame Polignac perceived the growing attachment of the young Queen to the palladium of their hopes, in order to impel Her Majesty's friendship to repair the deficiencies of fortune, they advised the magnet to quit the Court abruptly, assigning the want of means as the motive of her retreat. The story got wind, and proved propitious.

"The Queen, to secure the society of her friend, soon supplied the resources she required and took away the necessity for her retirement. But the die was cast. In gaining one friend she sacrificed a host. By this act of imprudent preference she lost forever the affections of the old nobility. This was the gale which drove her back among the breakers.

"I saw the coming storm, and endeavored to make my sovereign feel its danger. Presuming that my example would be followed, I withdrew from the Polignac society, and vainly flattered myself that prudence would impel others not to encourage Her Majesty's amiable infatuation till the consequences should be irretrievable. But sovereigns are always surrounded by those who make it a point to reconcile them to their follies, however flagrant; and keep them on good terms with themselves, however severely they may be censured by the world.

"If I had read the book of fate I could not have seen more distinctly the fatal results which actually took place from this unfortunate connection. The Duchess and myself always lived in the greatest harmony, and equally shared the confidence of the Queen; but it was my duty not to sanction Her Majesty's marked favoritism by my presence. The Queen often expressed her discontent to me upon the subject. She used to tell me how much it grieved her to be denied success in her darling desire of uniting her friends with each other, as they were already united in her own heart. Finding my resolution unalterable, she was mortified, but gave up her pursuit. When she became assured that all importunity was useless, she ever after avoided wounding my feelings by remonstrance, and allowed me to pursue the system I had adopted, rather than deprive herself of my society, which would have been the consequence had I not been left at liberty to follow the dictates of my own sense of propriety in a course from which I was resolved that even Her Majesty's displeasure should not make me swerve.

"Once in particular, at an entertainment given to the Emperor Joseph at Trianon, I remember the Queen took the opportunity to repeat how much she felt herself mortified at the course in which I persisted of never making my appearance at the Duchess of Polignac's parties.

"I replied, 'I believe, madam, we are both of us disappointed; but your Majesty has your remedy, by replacing me by a lady less scrupulous.'

"'I was too sanguine,' said the Queen, 'in having flattered myself that I had chosen two friends who would form, from their sympathizing and uniting their sentiments with each other, a society which would embellish my private life as much as they adorn their public stations.'

"I said it was by my unalterable friendship and my loyal and dutiful attachment to the sacred person of Her Majesty that I had been prompted to a line of conduct in which the motives whence it arose would impel me to persist while I had the honor to hold a situation under Her Majesty's roof.

"The Queen, embracing me, exclaimed, 'That will be for life, for death alone can separate us!'*

"This is the last conversation I recollect to have had with the Queen upon this distressing subject.

"The Abbé Vermond, who had been Her Majesty's tutor, but who was now her private secretary, began to dread that his influence over her from having been her confidential adviser from her youth upward would suffer from the rising authority of the all-predominant new favorite. Consequently, he thought proper to remonstrate, not with Her Majesty, but with those about her royal

---

* Good Heaven! What must have been the feelings of these true, these sacred friends, the shadow of each other, on that fatal Tenth of August, which separated them only to meet in a better world!

person. The Queen took no notice of these side-wind complaints, not wishing to enter into any explanation of her conduct. On this the Abbé withdrew from Court. But he only retired for a short time, and that to make better terms for the future. Here was a new spring for those who were supplying the army of calumniators with poison. Happy had it been, perhaps, for France and the Queen if Vermond had never returned. But the Abbé was something like a distant country cousin of an English minister, a man of no talents, but who hoped for employment through the power of his kinsman. 'There is nothing on hand now,' answered the minister, 'but a bishop's miter or a field marshal's staff.' 'Oh, very well,' replied the countryman; 'either will do for me till something better turns up.' The Abbé, in his retirement finding leisure to reflect that there was no probability of anything 'better turning up' than his post of private secretary, tutor, confidant, and counceler (and that not always the most correct) of a young and amiable Queen of France, soon made his reappearance and kept his jealousy of the Polignacs ever after to himself.*

"The Abbé Vermond enjoyed much influence with regard to ecclesiastical preferments. He was too fond of his situation ever to contradict or thwart Her Majesty in any of her plans; too much of a courtier to assail her ears with the language of truth; and by far too much a clergyman to interest himself but for Mother Church.

"In short, he was more culpable in not doing his duty than in the mischief he occasioned, for he certainly oftener misled the Queen by his silence than by his advice."

* He remained in the same situation till the horrors of the Revolution drove him from it.

CHAPTER VII.

Journal Continued — Slanders against the Empress Maria Theresa, on Account of Metastasio, Give the Queen a Distaste for Patronizing Literature — Private Plays and Acting — Censoriousness of Those Who Were Excluded from Them — The Queen's Love of Music — Gluck Invited from Germany — Anecdotes of Gluck and His "Armida" — Garat — Viotti — Madame St. Huberti — Vestris.

I HAVE already mentioned that Maria Antoinette had no decided taste for literature. Her mind rather sought its amusements in the ballroom, the promenade, the theater, especially when she herself was a performer, and the concert room, than in her library and among her books. Her coldness toward literary men may in some degree be accounted for by the disgust which she took at the calumnies and caricatures resulting from her mother's partiality for her own revered teacher, the great Metastasio. The resemblance of most of Maria Theresa's children to that poet was coupled with the great patronage he received from the Empress; and much less than these circumstances would have been quite enough to furnish a tale for the slanderer, injurious to the reputation of any exalted personage.

"The taste of Maria Antoinette for private theatricals was kept up till the clouds of the Revolution darkened over all her enjoyments.

"These innocent amusements were made subjects of censure against her by the many courtiers who were denied access to them; while some, who were permitted to be present, were too well pleased with the opportunity of sneering at her mediocrity in the art, which those, who could not see her, were ready to criticise with the utmost severity. It is believed that Madame de Genlis found this too favorable an opportunity to be slighted. Anonymous satires upon the Queen's performances, which were attributed to the malice of that authoress, were frequently shown to Her Majesty by good-natured friends. The Duke de Fronsac also, from some situation he held at Court, though not included in the private household of Her Majesty at Trianon, conceiving himself highly injured by not being suffered to interfere, was much exasperated, and took no pains to prevent others from receiving the infection of his resentment.

"Of all the arts, music was the only one which Her Majesty ever warmly patronized. For music she was an enthusiast. Had her talents in this art been cultivated, it is certain from her judgment in it that she would have made very considerable progress. She sang little French airs with great taste and feeling. She improved much under the tuition of the great composer, her master, the celebrated Sacchini. After his death, Sapio* was named his successor; but, between the death of one master and the appointment of another, the revolutionary horrors so increased that her mind was no longer in a state to listen to anything but the howlings of the tempest.

"In her happier days of power, the great Gluck was brought at her request from Germany to Paris. He cost nothing to the public treasury, for Her Majesty paid all his expenses out of her own purse, leaving him the profits of his operas, which attracted immense sums to the theater.†

"Maria Antoinette paid for the musical education of the French singer, Garat, and pensioned him for her private concerts.

"Her Majesty was the great patroness of the celebrated Viotti, who was also attached to her private musical

---

* The father of Sapio, the tenor singer, who on coming to England was much patronized by the Duchess of York and the late old Duke of Queensbury.

† To this very day the music of Gluck in France, like the works of our immortal Shakespeare in England, stands the test of time even amid that versatile nation. To outlive French caprice, his compositions must possess, like those of the immortal Sacchini, something strikingly extraordinary. If they are less frequently performed than inferior productions, it is for want of artists equal to their merit.

parties. Before Viotti began to perform his concertos, Her Majesty, with the most amiable condescension, would go round the music saloon, and say: 'Ladies and gentlemen, I request you will be silent, and very attentive, and not enter into conversation, while Mr. Viotti is playing, for it interrupts him in the execution of his fine performance.'

"Gluck composed his 'Armida' in compliment to the personal charms of Maria Antoinette. I never saw Her Majesty more interested about anything than she was for its success. She became a perfect slave to it. She had the gracious condescension to hear all the pieces through, at Gluck's request, before they were submitted to the stage for rehearsal. Gluck said he always improved his music after he saw the effect it had upon Her Majesty.

"He was coming out of the Queen's apartment one day, after he had been performing one of these pieces for Her Majesty's approbation, when I followed and congratulated him on the increased success he had met with from the whole band of the opera at every rehearsal. 'O my dear Princess!' cried he, 'it wants nothing to make it be applauded up to the seven skies but two such delightful heads as Her Majesty's and your own.' 'Oh, if that be all,' answered I, 'we'll have them painted for you, Mr. Gluck!' 'No, no, no! you do not understand me,' replied Gluck, 'I mean real, real heads.* My actresses are very ugly, and Armida and her confidential lady ought to be very handsome.'

"However great the success of the opera of 'Armida,' and certainly it was one of the best productions ever exhibited on the French stage, no one had a better opinion of its composition than Gluck himself. He was quite mad about it. He told the Queen that the air of France had invigorated his musical genius, and that, after having had the honor of seeing Her Majesty, his ideas were so much inspired that his compositions resembled her, and became alike angelic and sublime!

* How little did Gluck think, when he was paying this compliment, or the Princess, when she recorded it, that these two heads were really to be so cruelly severed from their bodies.

"The first artist who undertook the part of Armida was Madame Saint Huberti. The Queen was very partial to her. She was principal female singer at the French opera, was a German by birth, and strongly recommended by Gluck for her good natural voice. At Her Majesty's request, Gluck himself taught Madame Saint Huberti the part of Armida. Sacchini, also, at the command of Maria Antoinette, instructed her in the style and sublimity of the Italian school, and Mdlle. Bertin, the Queen's dressmaker and milliner, was ordered to furnish the complete dress for the character.

"The Queen, perhaps, was more liberal to this lady than to any actress upon the stage. She had frequently paid her debts, which were very considerable, for she dressed like a queen whenever she represented one.

"Gluck's consciousness of the merit of his own works, and of their dignity, excited no small jealousy, during the getting up of 'Armida,' in his rival with the public, the great Vestris, to whom he scarcely left space to exhibit the graces of his art; and many severe disputes took place between the two rival sharers of the Parisian enthusiasm. Indeed, it was at one time feared that the success of 'Armida' would be endangered, unless an equal share of the performance were conceded to the dancers. But Gluck, whose German obstinacy would not give up a note, told Vestris he might compose a *ballet* in which he would leave him his own way entirely; but that an artist whose profession only taught him to reason with his heels should not kick about works like 'Armida' at his pleasure. 'My subject,' added Gluck, 'is taken from the immortal Tasso. My music has been logically composed, and with the ideas of my head; and, of course, there is very little room left for capering. If Tasso had thought proper to make Rinaldo a dancer he never would have designated him a warrior.'

"Rinaldo was the part Vestris wished to be allotted to his son. However, through the interference of the Queen, Vestris prudently took the part as it had been originally finished by Gluck.

"The Queen was a great admirer and patroness of Augustus Vestris, the god of dance, as he was styled. Augustus Vestris never lost Her Majesty's favor, though he very often lost his sense of the respect he owed to the public, and showed airs and refused to dance. Once he did so when Her Majesty was at the opera. Upon some frivolous pretext he refused to appear. He was, in consequence, immediately arrested. His father, alarmed at his son's temerity, flew to me and with the most earnest supplications implored I would condescend to endeavor to obtain the pardon of Her Majesty. 'My son,' cried he, 'did not know that Her Majesty had honored the theater with her presence. Had he been aware of it, could he have refused to dance for his most bounteous benefactress? I, too, am grieved beyond the power of language to describe, by this *mal àpropos contretemps* between the two houses of Vestris and Bourbon, as we have always lived in the greatest harmony ever since we came from Florence to Paris. My son is very sorry and will dance most bewitchingly if Her Majesty will graciously condescend to order his release!'

"I repeated the conversation *verbatim* to Her Majesty, who enjoyed the arrogance of the Florentine, and sent her page to order young Vestris to be set immediately at liberty.

"Having exerted all the wonderful powers of his art, the Queen applauded him very much. When Her Majesty was about leaving her box, old Vestris appeared at the entrance, leading his son to thank the Queen.

"'Ah, Monsieur Vestris,' said the Queen to the father, 'you never danced as your son has done this evening!'

"'That's very natural, Madame,' answered old Vestris, 'I never had a Vestris, please your Majesty, for a master.'

"'Then you have the greater merit,' replied the Queen, turning round to old Vestris — 'Ah, I shall never forget you and Mademoiselle Guimard dancing the *menuet de la cour*.'

" On this old Vestris held up his head with that peculiar grace for which he was so much distinguished. The old man, though ridiculously vain, was very much of a gentleman in his manners. The father of Vestris was a painter of some celebrity at Florence, and originally from Tuscany.

CHAPTER VIII.

"THE visit of the favorite brother of Maria Antoinette, the Emperor Joseph the Second, to France, had been long and anxiously expected, and was welcomed by her with delight. The pleasure Her Majesty discovered at having him with her is scarcely credible; and the affectionate tenderness with which the Emperor frequently expressed himself on seeing his favorite sister evinced that their joys were mutual.

"Like everything else, however, which gratified and obliged the Queen, her evil star converted even this into a misfortune. It was said that the French treasury, which was not overflowing, was still more reduced by the Queen's partiality for her brother. She was accused of having given him immense sums of money; which was utterly false.

"The finances of Joseph were at that time in a situation too superior to those of France to admit of such extravagance, or even to render it desirable. The circumstance which gave a color to the charge was this:

"The Emperor, in order to facilitate the trade of his Brabant subjects, had it in contemplation to open the navigation of the Scheldt. This measure would have been ruinous to many of the skippers, as well as to the internal commerce of France. It was considered equally dangerous to the trade and navigation of the North Hollanders. To prevent it, negotiations were carried on by the French

(94)

minister, though professedly for the mutual interest of both countries, yet entirely at the instigation and on account of the Dutch. The weighty argument of the Dutch to prevent the Emperor from accomplishing a purpose they so much dreaded was a sum of many millions, which passed by means of some monied speculation in the Exchange through France to its destination at Vienna. It was to see this affair settled that the Emperor declared in Vienna his intention of taking France in his way from Italy, before he should go back to Austria.

"The certainty of a transmission of money from France to Austria was quite enough to awaken the malevolent, who would have taken care even had they inquired into the source whence the money came, never to have made it public. The opportunity was too favorable not to be made the pretext to raise a clamor against the Queen for robbing France to favor and enrich Austria.

"The Emperor, who had never seen me, though he had often heard me spoken of at the Court of Turin, expressed a wish, soon after his arrival, that I should be presented to him. The immediate cause of this let me explain.

"I was very much attached to the Princess Clotilda, whom I had caused to be united to Prince Charles Emanuel of Piedmont. Our family had, indeed, been principally instrumental in the alliances of the two brothers of the King of France with the two Piedmontese Princesses, as I had been in the marriage of the Piedmontese Prince with the Princess of France. When the Emperor Joseph visited the Court of Turin he was requested when he saw me in Paris to signify the King of Sardinia's satisfaction at my good offices. Consequently, the Emperor lost no time in delivering his message.

"When I was just entering the Queen's apartment to be presented, 'Here,' said Her Majesty, leading me to the Emperor, 'is the Princess,' and, then turning to me, exclaimed, 'Mercy, how cold you are!' The Emperor answered Her Majesty in German, 'What heat can you expect from the hand of one whose heart resides with the dead?' and subjoined, in the same language, 'What a pity that so charming a head should be fixed on a dead body!'

"I affected to understand the Emperor literally, and set him and the Queen laughing by thanking His Imperial Majesty for the compliment.

"The Emperor was exceedingly affable and full of anecdote. Maria Antoinette resembled him in her general manners. The similitude in their easy openness of address toward persons of merit was very striking. Both always endeavored to encourage persons of every class to speak their minds freely, with this difference, that Her Majesty in so doing never forgot her dignity nor her rank at Court. Sometimes, however, I have seen her, though so perfect in her deportment with inferiors, much intimidated and sometimes embarrassed in the presence of the Princes and Princesses, her equals, who for the first time visited Versailles: indeed, so much so as to give them a very incorrect idea of her capacity. It was by no means an easy matter to cause Her Majesty to unfold her real sentiments or character on a first acquaintance.

"I remember the Emperor one evening at supper when he was exceedingly good-humored, talkative, and amusing. He had visited all his Italian relations, and had a word for each,—man, woman, or child,—not a soul was spared. The King scarcely once opened his mouth, except to laugh at some of the Emperor's jokes upon his Italian relations.

"He began by asking the Queen if she punished her husband by making him keep as many Lents in the same year as her sister did the King of Naples. The Queen not knowing what the Emperor meant, he explained himself, and said, 'When the King of Naples offends his Queen, she keeps him on short commons and *soupe maigre* till he has expiated the offense by the penance of humbling himself; and then, and not till then, permits him to return and share the nuptial rights of her bed.'

"'This sister of mine,' said the Emperor, 'is a pro-ficient Queen in the art of man training. My other sister, the Duchess of Parma, is equally scientific in breaking-in horses; for she is constantly in the stables with her grooms, by which she GROOMS a pretty sum yearly in buying, selling, and breaking-in; while the simpleton, her husband, is ringing the bells with the Friars of Colorno to call his good subjects to mass.'

"'My brother Leopold, Grand Duke of Tuscany, feeds his subjects with plans of economy, a dish that costs nothing, and not only saves him a multitude of troubles in public buildings and public institutions, but keeps the public money in his private coffers; which is one of the greatest and most classical discoveries a sovereign can possibly accomplish, and I give Leopold much credit for his ingenuity.'

"'My dear brother Ferdinand, Archduke of Milan, considering he is only Governor of Lombardy, is not without industry; and I am told when out of the glimpse of his dragon the holy Beatrix, his Archduchess, sells his corn in the time of war to my enemies, as he does to my friends in the time of peace. So he loses nothing by his speculations!'

"The Queen checked the Emperor repeatedly, though she could not help smiling at his caricatures.

"'As to you, my dear Maria Antoinette,' continued the Emperor, not heeding her, 'I see you have made great progress in the art of painting. You have lavished more color on one cheek than Rubens would have required for all the figures in his cartoons.' Observing one of the ladies of honor still more highly rouged than the Queen, he said, 'I suppose I look like a death's head upon a tombstone, among all these high-colored furies.'

"The Queen again tried to interrupt the Emperor, but he was not to be put out of countenance.

"He said he had no doubt, when he arrived at Brussels, that he should hear of the progress of his sister, the Archduchess Maria Christina, in her money negotiations with the banker Valkeers, who made a good stock for her husband's jobs.

"'If Maria Christina's gardens and palace at Lakin could speak,' observed he, 'what a spectacle of events would they not produce! What a number of fine sights my own family would afford!'

"'When I get to Cologne,' pursued the Emperor, 'there I shall see my great fat brother Maximilian, in his little electorate, spending his yearly revenue upon an ec- clesiastical procession; for priests, like opposition, never bark but to get into the manger; never walk empty- handed; rosaries and good cheer always wind up their holy work; and my good Maximilian, as head of his Church, has scarcely feet to waddle into it. Feasting and fasting produce the same effect. In wind and food he is quite an adept — puffing, from one cause or the other, like a smith's bellows!'

"Indeed, the Elector of Cologne was really grown so very fat, that, like his Imperial mother, he could scarcely walk. He would so over-eat himself at these ecclesiastical dinners, to make his guests welcome, that, from indiges- tion, he would be puffing and blowing, an hour afterward, for breath!

"'As I have begun the family visits,' continued the Emperor, 'I must not pass by the Archduchess Mariana and the lady abbess at Clagenfurt; or, the Lord knows, I shall never hear the end of their *klagens*.* The first, I am told, is grown so ugly, and, of course, so neglected by mankind, that she is become an utter stranger to any at- tachment, excepting the fleshy embraces of the disgusting wen that encircles her neck and bosom, and makes her head appear like a black spot upon a large sheet of white paper! Therefore *klagen* is all I can expect from that quarter of female flesh, and I dare say it will be leveled against the whole race of mankind for their want of taste in not admiring her exuberance of human craw!

"'As to the lady abbess, she is one of my best recruit-

* A German word, which signifies COMPLAINING.

ing sergeants. She is so fond of training cadets for the benefit of the army that they learn more from her system in one month than at the military academy at Neustadt in a whole year. She is her mother's own daughter. She understands military tactics thoroughly. She and I never quarrel, except when I garrison her citadel with invalids. She and the canoness, Mariana, would rather see a few young ensigns than all the staffs of the oldest field marshals!'

"The Queen often made signs to the Emperor to desist from thus exposing every member of his family, and seemed to feel mortified; but the more Her Majesty endeavored to check his freedom, and make him silent, the more he enlarged upon the subject. He did not even omit Maria Theresa, who, he said, in consequence of some papers found on persons arrested as spies from the Prussian camp, during the Seven Years' War, was reported to have been greatly surprised to have discovered that her husband, the Emperor Francis I., supplied the enemy's army with all kinds of provision from her stores.

"The King scarcely ever answered excepting when the Emperor told the Queen that her staircase and antechamber at Versailles resembled more the Turkish bazars of Constantinople* than a royal palace. 'But,' added he, laughing, 'I suppose you would not allow the nuisance of hawkers and peddlers almost under your nose, if the sweet perfumes of a handsome present did not compensate for the disagreeable effluvia exhaling from their filthy traffic.'

"On this, Louis XVI., in a tone of voice somewhat varying from his usual mildness, assured the Emperor that neither himself nor the Queen derived any advantage from the custom, beyond the convenience of purchasing articles inside the palace at the moment they were wanted, without being forced to send for them elsewhere.

---

* It was an old custom, in the passages and staircase of all the royal palaces, for tradespeople to sell their merchandise for the accommodation of the Court.

"'That is the very reason, my dear brother,' replied Joseph, 'why I should not allow these shops to be where they are. The temptation to lavish money to little purpose is too strong; and women have not philosophy enough to resist having things they like, when they can be obtained easily, though they may not be wanted.'

"'Custom, answered the King——

"'True, exclaimed the Queen, interrupting him; 'custom, my dear brother, obliges us to tolerate in France many things which you, in Austria, have long since abolished; but the French are not to be treated like the Germans. A Frenchman is a slave to habit. His very caprice in the change of fashion, proceeds more from habit than genius or invention. His very restlessness of character is systematic; and old customs and national habits in a nation virtually *spirituelle* must not be trifled with. The tree torn up by the roots dies for want of nourishment; but, on the contrary, when lopped carefully only of its branches the pruning makes it more valuable to the cultivator. and more pleasing to the beholder. So it is with national prejudices, which are often but the excrescences of national virtues. Root them out and you root out virtue and all. They must only be pruned and turned to profit. A Frenchman is more easily killed than subdued. Even his follies generally spring from a high sense of national dignity and honor, which foreigners cannot but respect.'*

"The Emperor Joseph while in France mixed in all sorts of society to gain information with respect to the popular feeling toward his sister, and instruction as to the manners and modes of life and thinking of the French. To this end he would often associate with the lowest of the common people, and generally gave them a *louis* for their loss of time in attending to him.

"One day, when he was walking with the young

*Little did she think then that the nation she was eulogizing and so proud of governing would one day cause her to repent her partiality by barbarously dragging her to an ignominious trial and cruel death.

Princess Elizabeth and myself in the public gardens at Versailles and in deep conversation with us, two or three of these LOUIS ladies came up to my side and, not knowing who I was, whispered, 'There's no use in paying such attention to the stranger: After all, when he has got what he wants, he'll only give you a *louis* apiece and then send you about your business.'"

NOTE.

Thus far extend the anecdotes which the Princess Lamballe has recorded of the Emperor Joseph; but I cannot dismiss this part of the subject without noticing some mistakes which Madame Campan has admitted into her account of His Imperial Majesty and his visit.

Maria Antoinette, and not the Queen of Naples, was the Emperor's favorite. The Queen of Naples was the favorite of Leopold, Grand Duke of Tuscany, who succeeded the Emperor Joseph in a brief reign. This assertion is substantiated by the Queen of Naples herself, who could never persuade Joseph II. to allow the two marriages to take place between her two daughters and the present Emperor and his brother Ferdinand, the late Duke of Tuscany. On the contrary, he married the present Emperor, then King of the Romans, when very young, to his first wife, the Princess of Wirtemberg, sister to the Empress Dowager of Russia, to stop the continued importunities of his sister, the Queen of Naples, on that subject; but this Princess dying at Vienna only a few days previous to the death of the Emperor Joseph II., and Leopold succeeding, the marriages between Francis and Ferdinand and the daughters of the Queen of Naples took place soon after Leopold assumed the imperial diadem, when Carolina and Ferdinand, her husband, the late King of Naples, accompanied both their daughters to their respective husbands.

Though Joseph II. freely acknowledged his sister Carolina's capacity for governing Naples, he was very much displeased at her instigating Pope Pius VI. to come to Vienna to remonstrate with him on the suppression of some of his religious houses. He avoided coming to any explanation with the holy father on this or any other subject by never seeing him but in public; and though the Pope resided for some months at Vienna, and traveled to that city from the ancient Christian capital of the world for no other purpose, yet His Holiness was unable to get a sight of the Emperor except at public levee days, and was obliged to return to Rome with the mortification of having humiliated himself by an utterly fruitless journey.

When Joseph II. had been informed that the Queen of Naples had expressed herself hostile to his innovations, he told her Ambassador, "*Tutti son padroni a casa sua.*"

From these circumstances I think it seems pretty evident that Madame Campan has been led into an error when she says that Joseph II. and the Queen of Naples idolized each other. The very reverse is the fact; but it was their mutual interest to keep up political appearances from the two extreme situations they held in Italy.

It was Joseph II., on his leaving Italy and coming to Paris, who interested himself with his favorite sister, the Queen of France, to cause the King, her husband, to settle the differences then subsisting between the Court of Naples and that of Spain; and it was his opinion which some time afterward influenced the Queen of France to refuse the offer of the Queen of Naples to affiance her daughter, the present Duchess d' Angoulême, to the Crown Prince, son of the Queen of Naples, and to propose as more eligible a marriage which, since the Revolution, HAS taken place between the house of Orleans and that of Naples.

I know not whether the individuals since united are the same who were then proposed, but the union of the houses was certainly suggested by Maria Antoinette, with the consent of the Duke and Duchess of Orleans, with whom, or rather with the last of whom, the Queen of France was then upon terms of intimacy.

CHAPTER IX.

"I REMEMBER an old lady who could not bear to be told of deaths. 'Pshaw! Pshaw!' she would exclaim. 'Bring me no tales of funerals! Talk of births and of those who are likely to be blest with them! These are the joys which gladden old hearts and fill youthful ones with ecstasy! It is our own reproduction in children which makes us quit the world happy and contented; because then we only retire to make room for another race, bringing with them all those faculties which are in us decayed; and capable, which we ourselves have ceased to be, of taking our parts and figuring on the stage of life so long as it may please the Supreme Manager to busy them in earthly scenes! Then talk no more to me of weeds and mourning, but show me christenings and all those who give employ to the baptismal font!'

"Such also was the exulting feeling of Maria Antoinette when she no longer doubted of her wished-for pregnancy. The idea of becoming a mother filled her soul with an exuberant delight, which made the very pavement on which she trod vibrate with the words 'I shall be a mother! I shall be a mother!' She was so overjoyed that she not only made it public throughout France but dispatches were sent off to all her royal relatives. And was not her rapture natural? so long as she had waited for the result of every youthful union, and so coarsely as she had been reproached with her misfortune! Now came her triumph. She could now prove to the world, like all the descendants of the house of Austria, that there was no defect with her. The satirists and the malevolent were silenced. Louis XVI., from the cold, insensible bridegroom, became the infatuated admirer of his long-neglected wife. The enthusiasm with which the event was hailed by all France atoned for the partial insults she had received before it. The splendid *fêtes*, balls, and entertainments, indiscriminately lavished by all ranks throughout the kingdom on this occasion, augmented those of the Queen and the Court to a pitch of magnificence surpassing the most luxurious and voluptuous times of the great and brilliant Louis XIV. Entertainments were given even to the domestics of every description belonging to the royal establishments. Indeed, so general was the joy that, among those who could do no more, there could scarcely be found a father or mother in France who, before they took their wine, did not first offer up a prayer for the prosperous pregnancy of their beloved Queen.

"And yet, though the situation of Maria Antoinette was now become the theme of a whole nation's exultation, she herself, the owner of the precious burden, selected by Heaven as its special depositary, was the only one censured for expressing all her happiness!

"Those models of decorum, the VIRTUOUS Princesses, her aunts, deemed it highly indelicate in Her Majesty to have given public marks of her satisfaction to those deputed to compliment her on her prosperous situation. To avow the joy she felt was in their eyes indecent and unqueenly. Where was the shrinking bashfulness of THAT ONE of these Princesses who had herself been so clamorous to Louis XV. against her husband, the Duke of Modena, for not having consummated her own marriage?

"The party of the dismissed favorite Du Barry were still working underground. Their pestiferous vapors issued from the recesses of the earth, to obscure the brightness of the rising sun, which was now rapidly towering to its climax, to obliterate the little planets which had once endeavored to eclipse its beautiful rays, but were now incapable of competition, and unable to endure its luster. This malignant nest of serpents began to poison the minds of the courtiers, as soon as the pregnancy was obvious, by inuendos on the partiality of the Count d'Artois for the Queen; and at length, infamously, and openly, dared to point him out as the cause!

"Thus, in the heart of the Court itself, originated this most atrocious slander, long before it reached the nation, and so much assisted to destroy Her Majesty's popularity with a people, who now adored her amiableness, her general kind-heartedness, and her unbounded charity.

"I have repeatedly seen the Queen and the Count d'Artois together under circumstances in which there could have been no concealment of her real feelings; and I can firmly and boldly assert the falsehood of this allegation against my royal mistress. The only attentions Maria Antoinette received in the earlier part of her residence in France were from her grandfather and her brothers-in-law. Of these, the Count d'Artois was the only one who, from youth and liveliness of character, thoroughly sympathized with his sister. But, beyond the little freedoms of two young and innocent playmates, nothing can be charged upon their intimacy; no familiarity whatever further than was warranted by their relationship. I can bear witness that Her Majesty's attachment for the Count d'Artois never differed in its nature from what she felt for her brother, the Emperor Joseph.*

---

* When the King thought proper to be reconciled to the Queen after the death of his grandfather, Louis XV., and that she became a mother, she really was very much attached to Louis XVI., as may be proved from her never quitting him, and suffering all the horrid sacrifices she endured, through the whole period of the Revolution, rather than leave her husband, her children, or her sister. Maria Antoinette might have

"It is very likely that the slander of which I speak, derived some color of probability afterward with the million, from the Queen's thoughtlessness, relative to the challenge which passed between the Count d'Artois and the Duke de Bourbon. In right of my station, I was one of Her Majesty's confidential counselors, and it became my duty to put restraint upon her inclinations, whenever I conceived they led her wrong. In this instance, I exercised my prerogative decidedly, and even so much so as to create displeasure ; but I anticipated the consequences, which actually ensued, and preferred to risk my royal mistress's displeasure rather than her reputation. The dispute, which led to the duel, was on some point of etiquette ; and the Baron de Besenval was to attend as second to one of the parties. From the Queen's attachment for her royal brother, she wished the affair to be amicably arranged, without the knowledge either of the King, who was ignorant of what had taken place, or of the parties ; which could only be effected by her seeing the baron in the most private manner. I opposed Her Majesty's allowing any interview with the baron upon any terms, unless sanctioned by the King. This unexpected and peremptory refusal obliged the Queen to transfer her confidence to the librarian, who introduced the baron into one of the private apartments of Her Majesty's women, communicating with that of the Queen, where Her Majesty could see the baron without the exposure of passing any of the other attendants. The baron was quite gray, and upward of sixty years of age ! But the self-conceited dotard soon caused the Queen to repent her misplaced confidence, and from his unwarrantable impudence on that occasion, when he found himself alone with the Queen, Her Majesty, though he was a constant member of the societies of the Polignacs, ever after treated him with sovereign contempt.

"The Queen herself afterward described to me the

saved her life twenty times, had not the King's safety united with her own and that of her family, impelled her to reject every proposition of self-preservation.

baron's presumptuous attack upon her credulity. From this circumstance I thenceforward totally excluded him from my parties, where Her Majesty was always a regular visitor.

"The coolness to which my determination not to allow the interview gave rise between Her Majesty and myself was but momentary. The Queen had too much discernment not to appreciate the basis upon which my denial was grounded, even before she was convinced by the result how correct had been my reflections. She felt her error, and, by the mediation of the Duke of Dorset, we were reunited more closely than ever, and so, I trust, we shall remain till death!

"There was much more attempted to be made of another instance, in which I exercised the duty of my office, than the truth justified — the nightly promenades on the terrace at Versailles, or at Trianon. Though no amusement could have been more harmless or innocent for a private individual, yet I certainly disapproved of it for a queen, and therefore withheld the sanction of my attendance. My sole objection was on the score of dignity. I well knew that Du Barry and her infamous party were constant spies upon the Queen on every occasion of such a nature; and that they would not fail to exaggerate her every movement to her prejudice. Though Du Barry could not form one of the party, which was a great source of heartburning, it was easy for her, under the circumstances, to mingle with the throng. When I suggested these objections to the Queen, Her Majesty, feeling no inward cause of reproach, and being sanctioned in what she did by the King himself, laughed at the idea of these little excursions affording food for scandal. I assured Her Majesty that I had every reason to be convinced that Du Barry was often in disguise not far from the seat where Her Majesty and the Princess Elizabeth could be overheard in their most secret conversations with each other. 'Listeners,' replied the Queen, 'never hear any good of themselves.'

"'My dear Lamballe,' she continued, 'you have taken

such a dislike to this woman that you cannot conceive she can be occupied but in mischief. This is uncharitable. She certainly has no reason to be dissatisfied with either the King or myself. We have both left her in the full enjoyment of all she possessed except the right of appearing at Court or continuing in the society her conduct had too long disgraced.'

"I said it was very true, but that I should be happier to find Her Majesty so scrupulous as never to give an opportunity even for the falsehoods of her enemies.

"Her Majesty turned the matter off, as usual, by saying she had no idea of injuring others, and could not believe that anyone would wantonly injure her, adding, 'The Duchess and the Princess Elizabeth, my two sisters, and all the other ladies, are coming to hear the concert this evening, and you will be delighted.'

"I excused myself under the plea of the night air disagreeing with my health, and returned to Versailles without ever making myself one of the nocturnal members of Her Majesty's society, well knowing she could dispense with my presence, there being more than enough ever ready to hurry her by their own imprudence into the folly of despising criticisms, which I always endeavored to avoid, though I did not fear them. Of these I cannot but consider her secretary as one. The following circumstance connected with the promenades is a proof:

"The Abbé Vermond was present one day when Maria Antoinette observed that she felt rather indisposed. I attributed it to Her Majesty's having lightened her dress and exposed herself too much to the night air. 'Heavens, madame!' cried the Abbé, 'would you always have Her Majesty cased up in steel armor and not take the fresh air without being surrounded by a troop of horse and foot, as a field marshal is when going to storm a fortress? Pray, Princess, now that Her Majesty has freed herself from the annoying shackles of Madame Etiquette (the Countess de Noailles), let her enjoy the pleasure of a simple robe and breathe freely the fresh morning dew, as has been her custom all her life (and as her mother

before her, the Empress Maria Theresa, has done and
continues to do, even to this day), unfettered by antiquated absurdities! Let me be anything rather than a
Queen of France, if I must be doomed to the slavery of
such tyrannical rules!'

"'True; but, sir,' replied I, 'you should reflect that if
you were a Queen of France, France, in making you
mistress of her destinies, and placing you at the head of
her nation, would, in return look for respect from you
to her customs and manners. I am born an Italian, but
I renounced all national peculiarities of thinking and acting the moment I set my foot on French ground.'

"'And so did I,' said Maria Antoinette.

"'I know you did, madame,' I answered; 'but I am
replying to your preceptor; and I only wish he saw things
in the same light I do. WHEN WE ARE AT ROME, WE SHOULD
DO AS ROME DOES. You have never had a regicide Bertrand de Gurdon, a Ravillac, or a Damiens in Germany;
but they have been common in France, and the sovereigns of France cannot be too circumspect in their maintenance of ancient etiquette to command the dignified
respect of a frivolous and versatile people.'

"The Queen, though she did not strictly adhere to my
counsels or the Abbé's advice, had too much good sense
to allow herself to be prejudiced against me by her preceptor; but the Abbé never entered on the propriety or
impropriety of the Queen's conduct before me, and from the
moment I have mentioned studiously avoided, in my
presence, anything which could lead to discussion on the
change of dress and amusements introduced by Her
Majesty.

"Although I disapproved of Her Majesty's deviations
from established forms in this, or, indeed, any respect,
yet I never, before or after, expressed my opinion before a third person.

"Never should I have been so firmly and so long attached to Maria Antoinette, had I not known that her
native thorough goodness of heart had been warped and
misguided, though acting at the same time with the best

intentions, by a false notion of her real innocence being a sufficient shield against the public censure of such innovations upon national prejudices, as she thought proper to introduce; the fatal error of conscious rectitude, encouraged in its regardlessness of appearances by those very persons who well knew that it is only by appearances a nation can judge of its rulers.

"I remember a ludicrous circumstance arising from the Queen's innocent curiosity, in which, if there were anything to blame, I myself am to be censured for lending myself to it so heartily to satisfy Her Majesty.

"When the Chevalier d'Eon was allowed to return to France, Her Majesty expressed a particular inclination to see this extraordinary character. From prudential as well as political motives, she was at first easily persuaded to repress her desire. However, by a most ludicrous occurrence, it was revived, and nothing would do but she must have a sight of the being who had for some time been the talk of every society, and at the period to which I allude was become the mirth of all Paris.

"The Chevalier being one day in a very large party of both sexes, in which, though his appearance had more of the old soldier in it than of the character he was compelled *malgré lui* * to adopt, many of the guests having no idea to what sex this nondescript animal really belonged, the conversation after dinner happened to turn on the manly exercise of fencing. Heated by a subject to him so interesting, the Chevalier, forgetful of the respect due to his assumed garb, started from his seat, and pulling up his petticoats, threw himself on guard. Though dressed in male attire underneath, this sudden freak sent all the ladies and many of the gentlemen out of the room in double quick time. The Chevalier, however, instantly recovering from the first impulse, quietly

* It may be necessary to observe here that the Chevalier, having from some particular motives been banished from France, was afterward permitted to return only on condition of never appearing but in the disguised dress of a female, though he was always habited in the male costume underneath it.

put down his upper garment, and begged pardon in a gentlemanly manner for having for a moment deviated from the forms of his imposed situation. All the gossips of Paris were presently amused with the story, which, of course, reached the Court, with every droll particular of the pulling up and clapping down the cumbrous paraphernalia of a hoop petticoat.

"The King and Queen, from the manner in which they enjoyed the tale when told them (and certainly it lost nothing in the report), would not have been the least amused of the party had they been present. His Majesty shook the room with laughing, and the Queen, the Princess Elizabeth, and the other ladies were convulsed at the description.

"When we were alone, 'How I should like,' said the Queen, 'to see this curious man-woman!' 'Indeed,' replied I, 'I have not less curiosity than yourself, and I think we may contrive to let Your Majesty have a peep at him — her, I mean! — without compromising your dignity, or offending the minister who interdicted the Chevalier from appearing in your presence. I know he has expressed the greatest mortification, and that his wish to see Your Majesty is almost irrepressible.'

"'But how will you be able to contrive this without its being known to the King, or to the Count de Vergennes, who would never forgive me?' exclaimed Her Majesty.

"'Why, on Sunday, when you go to chapel, I will cause him, by some means or other, to make his appearance, *en grande costume*, among the group of ladies who are generally waiting there to be presented to Your Majesty.'

"'Oh, you charming creature!' said the Queen. 'But won't the minister banish or exile him for it?'

"'No, no! He has only been forbidden an audience of Your Majesty at Court,' I replied.

"In good earnest, on the Sunday following the Chevalier was dressed *en costume*, with a large hoop, very long train, sack, five rows of ruffles an immensely high powdered female wig, very beautiful lappets, white gloves, an elegant fan in his hand, his beard closely shaved, his neck and ears adorned with diamond rings and necklaces, and assuming all the airs and graces of a fine lady!

"But, unluckily, his anxiety was so great, the moment the Queen made her appearance, to get a sight of Her Majesty, that, on rushing before the other ladies, his wig and headdress fell off his head; and, before they could be well replaced, he made so ridiculous a figure, by clapping them, in his confusion, hind part before, that the King, the Queen, and the whole suite, could scarcely refrain from laughing aloud in the church.

"Thus ended the long longed-for sight of this famous man-woman!

"As to me, it was a great while before I could recover myself. Even now, I laugh whenever I think of this great lady deprived of her head ornaments, with her bald pate laid bare, to the derision of such a multitude of Parisians, always prompt to divert themselves at the expense of others. However, the affair passed off unheeded, and no one but the Queen and myself ever knew that we ourselves had been innocently the cause of this comical adventure. When we met after mass, we were so overpowered, that neither of us could speak for laughing. The bishop who officiated, said it was lucky he had no sermon to preach that day, for it would have been difficult for him to have recollected himself, or to have maintained his gravity. The ridiculous appearance of the Chevalier, he added, was so continually presenting itself before him during the service that it was as much as he could do to restrain himself from laughing, by keeping his eyes constantly riveted on the book. Indeed, the oddity of the affair was greatly heightened when, in the middle of the mass, some charitable hand having adjusted the wig of the Chevalier, he re-entered the chapel as if nothing had happened, and, placing himself exactly opposite the altar, with his train upon his arm, stood fanning himself *à la coquette*, with an inflexible self-possession which only

8

rendered it the more difficult for those around him to maintain their composure.

"Thus ended the Queen's curiosity. The result only made the Chevalier's company in greater request, for everyone became more anxious than ever to know the masculine lady who had lost her wig!"

CHAPTER X.

FROM the time that the Princess Lamballe saw the ties between the Queen and her favorite Polignac drawing closer she became less assiduous in her attendance at Court, being reluctant to importune the friends by her presence at an intimacy which she did not approve. She could not, however, withhold her accustomed attentions, as the period of Her Majesty's *accouchement* approached; and she has thus noted the circumstance of the birth of the Duchess d'Angoulême, on the 19th of December, 1778.

"The moment for the accomplishment of the Queen's darling hope was now at hand: she was about to become a mother.

"It had been agreed between Her Majesty and myself, that I was to place myself so near the *accoucheur*, Vermond,* as to be the first to distinguish the sex of the

---

* Brother to the Abbé, whose pride was so great at this honor conferred on his relative, that he never spoke of him without denominating him *Monsieur mon frère, l'accoucher de sa Majesté, Vermond.*

new-born infant, and if she should be delivered of a Dauphin to say, in Italian, *Il figlio è nato*.

"Her Majesty was, however, foiled even in this the most blissful of her desires. She was delivered of a daughter instead of a Dauphin.

"From the immense crowd that burst into the apartment the instant Vermond said, THE QUEEN IS HAPPILY DELIVERED, Her Majesty was nearly suffocated. I had hold of her hand, and as I said *La regina è andato*, mistaking *andato* for *nato*, between the joy of giving birth to a son and the pressure of the crowd, Her Majesty fainted. Overcome by the dangerous situation in which I saw my royal mistress I myself was carried out of the room in a lifeless state. The situation of Her Majesty was for some time very doubtful till the people were dragged with violence from about her, that she might have air. On her recovering, the King was the first person who told her that she was the mother of a very fine Princess.

"'Well, then,' said the Queen, 'I am like my mother, for at my birth she also wished for a son instead of a daughter; and you have lost your wager': for the King had betted with Maria Theresa that it would be a son.

"The King answered her by repeating the lines Metastasio had written on that occasion:

> "*Io perdei: l'augusta figlia*
> *A pagar, m'a condemnato;*
> *Ma s'è ver che a voi somiglia*
> *Tutto il mondo ha guadagnato.*"

The Princess Lamballe again ceased to be constantly about the Queen. Her danger was over, she was a mother, and the attentions of disinterested friendship were no longer indispensable. She herself about this time met with a deep affliction. She lost both of her own parents; and to her sorrows may, in a great degree, be ascribed her silence upon the events which intervened between the birth of Madame and that of the Dauphin. She was as assiduous as ever in her attentions to Her

Majesty on her second lying-in. The circumstances of the death of Maria Theresa, the Queen's mother, in the interval which divided the two *accouchements*, and Her Majesty's anguish, and refusal to see any but Lamballe and Polignac, are too well known to detain us any longer from the notes of the Princess. It is enough for the reader to know that the friendship of Her Majesty for her superintendent seemed to be gradually reviving in all its early enthusiasm, by her unremitting kindness during the confinements of the Queen; till, at length, they became more attached than ever. But, not to anticipate, let me return to the narrative.

"The public feeling had undergone a great change with respect to Her Majesty from the time of her first *accouchement*. Still, she was not the mother of a future king. The people looked upon her as belonging to them more than she had done before, and faction was silenced by the general delight. But she had not yet attained the climax of her felicity. A second pregnancy gave a new excitement to the nation; and, at length, on the 22d of October, 1781, dawned the day of hope.

"In consequence of what happened on the first *accouchement*, measures were taken to prevent similar disasters on the second. The number admitted into the apartment was circumscribed. The silence observed left the Queen in uncertainty of the sex to which she had given birth, till, with tears of joy, the King said to her: 'Madame, the hopes of the nation, and mine, are fulfilled. You are the mother of a Dauphin.'

"The Princess Elizabeth and myself were so overjoyed that we embraced everyone in the room.

"At this time Their Majesties were adored. Maria Antoinette, with all her beauty and amiableness, was a mere cipher in the eyes of France previous to her becoming the mother of an heir to the Crown; but her popularity now arose to a pitch of unequaled enthusiasm.

"I have heard of but one expression to Her Majesty upon this occasion in any way savoring of discontent. This came from the royal aunts. On Maria Antoinette's expressing to them her joy in having brought a Dauphin to the nation, they replied, 'We will only repeat our father's observation on a similar subject. When one of our sisters complained to his late Majesty that, as her Italian husband had copied the Dauphin's whim, she could not, though long a bride, boast of being a wife, or hope to become a mother'—'a prudent Princess,' replied Louis XV., 'never wants heirs!' But the feeling of the royal aunts was an exception to the general sentiment, which really seemed like madness.

"I remember a proof of this which happened at the time. Chancing to cross the King's path as he was going to Marly and I coming from Rambouillet, my two postilions jumped from their horses, threw themselves on the high road upon their knees, though it was very dirty, and remained there, offering up their benedictions, till he was out of sight.*

"The felicity of the Queen was too great not to be soon overcast. The unbounded influence of the Polignacs was now at its zenith. It could not fail of being attacked. Every engine of malice, envy, and detraction was let loose; and in the vilest calumnies against the character of the Duchess, her royal mistress was included.

"It was, in truth, a most singular fatality in the life of Maria Antoinette that she could do nothing, however beneficial or disinterested, for which she was not either criticised or censured. She had a tenacity of character which made her cling more closely to attachments from which she saw others desirous of estranging her; and this firmness, however excellent in principle, was, in her case, fatal in its effects. The Abbé Vermond, Her Majesty's confessor and tutor, and, unfortunately, in many respects, her ambitious guide, was really alarmed at the rising favor of the Duchess; and though he knew the very obstacles thrown in her way only strengthened her resolution as to any favorite object, yet he ventured to

---

* These very men, perhaps, but a short time after, were among the regicides who caused him to be butchered on the scaffold! What a lesson for Princes!

head an intrigue to destroy the great influence of the
Polignacs, which, as he might have foreseen, only served
to hasten their aggrandisement.

"At this crisis the dissipation of the Duke de Gué-
menée caused him to become a bankrupt. I know not
whether it can be said in principle, but certainly it may
in property, 'It is an ill wind that blows no one any
good.' The Princess, his wife, having been obliged to
leave her residence at Versailles, in consequence of the
Duke's dismissal from the King's service on account of
the disordered state of his pecuniary circumstances, the
situation of governess to the royal children became necessarily vacant, and was immediately transferred to the
Duchess de Polignac. The Queen, to enable her friend
to support her station with all the *éclat* suitable to its
dignity, took care to supply ample means from her own
private purse. A most magnificent suite of apartments was
ordered to be arranged, under the immediate inspection
of the Queen's *maître d'hôtel*, at Her Majesty's expense.

"Is there anything on earth more natural than the
lively interest which inspires a mother toward those
who have the care of her offspring? What then, must
have been the feelings of a Queen of France who had
been deprived of that blessing for which connubial attachments are formed, and which, *vice versâ*, constitutes
the only real happiness of every young female. What
must have been, I say, the ecstasy of Maria Antoinette
when she not only found herself a mother, but the dear
pledges of all her future bliss in the hands of one whose
friendship allowed her the unrestrained exercise of maternal affection: a climax of felicity combining not only the
pleasures of an ordinary mother, but the greatness, the
dignity, and the flattering popularity of a Queen of
France.

"Though the pension of the Duchess de Polignac was
no more than that usually allotted to all former govern-
esses of the royal children of France, yet circumstances
tempted her to a display not a little injurious to her
popularity as well as to that of her royal mistress. She

gave too many pretexts to imputations of extravagance. Yet she had neither patronage, nor sinecures, nor immunities beyond the few inseparable from the office she held, and which had been the same for centuries under the Monarchy of France. But it must be remembered, as an excuse for the splendor of her establishment, that she entered her office upon a footing very different from that of any of her predecessors. Her mansion was not the quiet, retired, simple household of the governess of the royal children, as formerly: it had become the magnificent resort of the first Queen in Europe; the daily haunt of Her Majesty. The Queen certainly visited the former governess, as she had done the Duchess de Duras and many other frequenters of her Court parties; but she made the Duchess de Polignac's her Court; and all the courtiers of that Court, and I may say, the great personages of all France, as well as the ministers and all foreigners of distinction, held there their usual rendezvous; consequently, there was nothing wanting but the guards in attendance in the Queen's apartments to have made it a royal residence suitable for the reception of the illustrious personages that were in the constant habit of visiting these levees, assemblies, balls, routs, picnics, dinner, supper, and card parties. *

"Much as some of the higher classes of the nobility felt aggrieved at the preference given by the Queen to the Duchess de Polignac, that which raised against Her Majesty the most implacable resentment was her frequenting

---

* I have seen ladies at the Princess Lamballe's come from these card parties with their laps so blackened by the quantities of gold received in them, that they have been obliged to change their dresses to go to supper. Many a *chevalier d'industrie* and young military spendthrift has made his harvest here. Thousands were won and lost, and the ladies were generally the dupes of all those who were the constant speculative attendants. The Princess Lamballe did not like play, but when it was necessary she did play, and won or lost to a limited extent; but the prescribed sum once exhausted or gained she left off. In set parties, such as those of whist, she never played except when one was wanted, often excusing herself on the score of its requiring more attention than it was in her power to give to it and her reluctance to sacrifice her partner; though

the parties of her favorite more than those of any other of the *haut ton*. These assemblies, from the situation held by the Duchess, could not always be the most select. Many of the guests who chanced to get access to them from a mere glimpse of the Queen — whose general good humor, vivacity, and constant wish to please all around her would often make her commit herself unconsciously and unintentionally — would fabricate anecdotes of things they had neither seen nor heard; and which never had existence, except in their own wicked imaginations. The scene of the inventions, circulated against Her Majesty through. France, was, in consequence, generally placed at the Duchess's; but they were usually so distinctly and obviously false that no notice was taken of them, nor was any attempt made to check their promulgation.

"Exemplary as was the friendship between this enthusiastic pair, how much more fortunate for both would it have been had it never happened! I foresaw the results long, long before they took place; but the Queen was not to be thwarted. Fearful she might attribute my anxiety for her general safety to unworthy personal views, I was often silent, even when duty bade me speak. I was, perhaps, too scrupulous about seeming officious or jealous of the predilection shown to the Duchess. Experience had taught me the inutility of representing consequences, and I had no wish to quarrel with the Queen. Indeed, there was a degree of coldness toward me on the part of Her Majesty for having gone so far as I had done. It was not till after the birth of the Duke of Normandy, her third child, in March, 1785, that her friendship resumed its primitive warmth.

I have heard *Beau* Dillon, the Duke of Dorset, Lord Edward Dillon, and many others say that she understood and played the game much better than many who had a higher opinion of their skill in it. Lord Edward Fitzgerald was admitted to the parties at the Duchess de Polignac's on his first coming to Paris; but when his connection with the Duke of Orleans and Madame de Genlis became known he was informed that his society would be dispensed with. The famous, or rather the infamous. Beckford was also excluded.

"As the children grew, Her Majesty's attachment for their governess grew with them. All that has been said of Tasso's 'Armida' was nothing to this luxurious temple of maternal affection. Never was female friendship more strongly cemented, or less disturbed by the nauseous poison of envy, malice, or mean jealousy. The Queen was in the plenitude of every earthly enjoyment, from being able to see and contribute to the education of the children she tenderly loved, unrestrained by the gothic etiquette, with which all former royal mothers had been fettered, but which the kind indulgence of the Duchess de Polignac broke through, as unnatural and unworthy of the enlightened and affectionate. The Duchess was herself an attentive, careful mother. She felt for the Queen, and encouraged her maternal sympathies, so doubly endeared by the long, long disappointment which had preceded their gratification. The sacrifice of all the cold forms of state policy by the new governess, and the free access she gave the royal mother to her children, so unprecedented in the Court of France, rendered Maria Antoinette so grateful that it may justly be said she divided her heart between the governess and the governed. Habit soon made it necessary for her existence that she should dedicate the whole of her time, not taken up in public ceremonies or parties, to the cultivation of the minds of her children. Conscious of her own deficiency in this respect, she determined to redeem this error in her offspring. The love of the frivolous amusements of society, for which the want of higher cultivation left room in her mind, was humored by the gayeties of the Duchess de Polignac's assemblies; while her nobler dispositions were encouraged by the privileges of the favorite's station. Thus, all her inclinations harmonizing with the habits and position of her friend, Maria Antoinette literally passed the greatest part of some years in company with the Duchess de Polignac; either amid the glare and bustle of public recreation, or in the private apartment of the governess and her children, increasing as much as possible the kindness of the one for the benefit and comfort of the others.   The attachment of the Duchess to the royal children was returned by the Queen's affection for the offspring of the Duchess.   So much was Her Majesty interested in favor of the daughter of the Duchess, that, before that young lady was fifteen years of age, she herself contrived and accomplished her marriage with the Duke de Guiche, then *maitre de cérémonie* to Her Majesty, and whose interests were essentially promoted by this alliance. *

"The great cabals, which agitated the Court in consequence of the favor shown to the Polignacs, were not slow in declaring themselves.   The Countess de Noailles was one of the foremost among the discontented.   Her resignation, upon the appointment of a superintendent,

* The Duke de Guiche, since Duke de Grammont, has proved how much he merited the distinctions he received, in consequence of the attachment between the Queen and his mother-in-law, by the devotedness with which he followed the fallen fortunes of the Bourbons till their restoration, since which he has not been forgotten.   The Duchess, his wife, who at her marriage was beaming with all the beauties of her age, and adorned by art and nature with every accomplishment, though she came into notice at a time when the Court had scarcely recovered itself from the debauched morals by which it had been so long degraded by a Pompadour and a Du Barry, has yet preserved her character, by the strictness of her conduct, free from the censorious criticisms of an epoch in which some of the purest could not escape unassailed.   I saw her at Pyrmont in 1803; and even then, though the mother of many children, she looked as young and beautiful as ever.   She was remarkably well educated and accomplished, a profound musician on the harp and pianoforte, graceful in her conversation, and a most charming dancer.   She seemed to bear the vicissitudes of fortune with a philosophical courage and resignation not often to be met with in light-headed French women.   She was amiable in her manners, easy of access, always lively and cheerful, and enthusiastically attached to the country whence she was then excluded. She constantly accompanied the wife of the late Louis XVIII. during her travels in Germany, as her husband the Duke did His Majesty during his residence at Mittau, in Courland, etc.   I have had the honor of seeing the Duke twice since the Revolution; once, on my coming from Russia, at General Binkingdroff's, Governor of Mittau, and since, in Portland Place, at the French Ambassador's, on his coming to England in the name of his sovereign, to congratulate the King of England on his accession to the throne.

was a sufficient evidence of her real feeling; but when she now saw a place filled, to which she conceived her family had a claim, her displeasure could not be silent, and her dislike to the Queen began to express itself without reserve.

"Another source of dissatisfaction against the Queen was her extreme partiality for the English. After the peace of Versailles, in 1783, the English flocked into France, and I believe if a poodle dog had come from England it would have met with a good reception from Her Majesty. This was natural enough. The American war had been carried on entirely against her wish; though, from the influence she was supposed to exercise in the cabinet, it was presumed to have been managed entirely by herself. This odious opinion she wished personally to destroy; and it could only be done by the distinction with which, after the peace, she treated the whole English nation. *

"Several of the English nobility were on a familiar footing at the parties of the Duchess de Polignac. This was quite enough for the slanderers. They were all

---

* The daughter of the Duchess de Polignac (of my meeting with whom I have already spoken in a note), entering with me upon the subject of France and of old times, observed that had the Queen limited her attachment to the person of her mother, she would not have given all the annoyance which she did, to the nobility. It was to these partialities to the English, the Duchess de Guiche Grammont alluded. I do not know the lady's name distinctly, but I am certain I have heard the beautiful Lady Sarah Bunbury mentioned by the Princess Lamballe as having received particular attention from the Queen; for the Princess had heard much about this lady and "a certain great personage" in England; but, on discovering her acquaintance with the Duke of Lauzun, Her Majesty withdrew from the intimacy, though not soon enough to prevent its having given food for scandal. "You must remember," added the Duchess de Guiche Grammont, "how much the Queen was censured for her enthusiasm about Lady Spencer." I replied that I did remember the MUCH-ADO ABOUT NOTHING there was regarding some English lady, to whom the Queen took a liking, whose name I could not exactly recall; but I knew well she studied to please the English in general. Of this Lady Spencer it is that the Princess speaks in one of the following pages of this chapter.

ranked, and that publicly, as lovers of Her Majesty. I recollect when there were no less than five different private commissioners out, to suppress the libels that were in circulation over all France, against the Queen and Lord Edward Dillon, the Duke of Dorset, Lord George Conway, Arthur Dillon, as well as Count Fersen, the Duke de Lauzun, and the Count d'Artois, who were all not only constant frequenters of Polignac's but visitors of Maria Antoinette.

"By the false policy of Her Majesty's advisers, these enemies and libelers, instead of being brought to the condign punishment their infamy deserved, were privately hushed into silence, out of delicacy to the Queen's feelings, by large sums of money and pensions, which encouraged numbers to commit the same enormity in the hope of obtaining the same recompense.

"But these were mercenary wretches, from whom no better could have been expected. A legitimate mode of robbery had been pressed upon their notice by the Government itself, and they thought it only a matter of fair speculation to make the best of it. There were some libelers, however, of a higher order, in comparison with whose motives for slander, those of the mere scandal-jobbers were white as the driven snow. Of these, one of the worst was the Duke de Lauzun.

"The first motive of the Queen's strong dislike to the Duke de Lauzun sprang from Her Majesty's attachment to the Duchess of Orleans, whom she really loved. She was greatly displeased at the injury inflicted upon her valued friend by Lauzun, in estranging the affection of the Duke of Orleans from his wife by introducing him to depraved society. Among the associates to which this connection led the Duke of Orleans were a certain Madame Duthée and Madame Buffon.

"When Lauzun, after having been expelled from the drawing-room of the Queen for his insolent presumption,* meeting with coolness at the King's levee, sought to cover his disgrace by appearing at the assemblies of the

* The allusion here is to the affair of the heron plume.

Duchess de Polignac, her grace was too sincerely the friend of her sovereign and benefactress not to perceive the drift of his conduct. She consequently signified to the self-sufficient coxcomb that her assemblies were not open to the public. Being thus shut out from Their Majesties, and, as a natural result, excluded from the most brilliant societies of Paris, Lauzun, from a most diabolical spirit of revenge, joined the nefarious party which had succeeded in poisoning the mind of the Duke of Orleans, and from the hordes of which, like the burning lava from Etna, issued calumnies which swept the most virtuous and innocent victims that ever breathed, to their destruction!*

"Among the Queen's favorites, and those most in request at the Polignac parties, was the good Lady Spencer, with whom I became most intimately acquainted when I first went to England; and from whom, as well as from her two charming daughters, the Duchess of Devonshire and Lady Duncannon, since Lady Besborough, I received the greatest marks of cordial hospitality. In consequence, when her ladyship came to France, I hastened to present her to the Queen. Her Majesty, taking a great liking to the amiable Englishwoman and wishing to profit by her private conversations and society, gave orders that Lady Spencer should pass to her private closet whenever she came to Versailles, without the formal ceremony of waiting in the antechamber to be announced.

"One day, Her Majesty, Lady Spencer, and myself were observing the difficulty there was in acquiring a correct pronunciation of the English language, when Lady Spencer remarked that it only required a little attention.

* These vicious rivals in killing characters and blackening virtue with imputations of every vice, never lost sight of their victims till fate, cutting the thread of their own execrable existence, terminated a long career of crime too horrible to dwell upon! The whole story of the Princess Czartsorinski, to whom I have the honor of being allied, related by Lauzun, is totally destitute of any shadow of truth. This one instance will show how much credit is due to the rest of his infamous assertions against the honor and character of many others of the illustrious persons whom his venomous tongue has traduced.

" 'I beg your pardon,' said the Queen, 'that's not all, because there are many things you do not call by their proper names, as they are in the dictionary.'

" 'Pray what are they, please Your Majesty?'

" 'Well, I will give you an instance. For example, *les culottes* — what do you call them?'

" 'Small clothes,' replied her ladyship.

" '*Ma foi!* how can they be called small clothes for one large man? Now I do look in the dictionary, and I find, *pour le mot culottes* — breeches.'

" 'Oh, please Your Majesty, we never call them by that name in England.'

" '*Voilà donc, j'ai raison!*'

" 'We say inexpressibles!'

" 'Ah, *c'est mieux!* Dat do please me ver much better. *Il y a du bon sens là dedans. C'est une autre chose!*'

" In the midst of this curious dialogue, in came the Duke of Dorset, Lord Edward Dillon, Count Fersen, and several English gentlemen, who, as they were going to the King's hunt, were all dressed in new buckskin breeches.

" 'I do not like,' exclaimed the Queen to them, 'dem yellow irresistibles!'

" Lady Spencer nearly fainted. 'Vat make you so frightful, my dear lady?' said the Queen to her ladyship, who was covering her face with her hands. 'I am terrified at Your Majesty's mistake.' 'Comment? did you no tell me just now, dat in England de lady call de *culottes* IRRESISTIBLES?' 'O mercy! I never could have made such a mistake, as to have applied to that part of the male dress such a word. I said, please Your Majesty, INEXPRESSIBLES.'

" On this the gentlemen all laughed most heartily.

" 'Vell, vell,' replied the Queen, 'do, my dear lady, discompose yourself. I vill no more call de breeches IRRESISTIBLES, but say small clothes, if even *elles sont* upon a giant!'

" At the repetition of the naughty word BREECHES, poor Lady Spencer's English delicacy quite overcame her.

Forgetting where she was, and also the company she was
in, she ran from the room with her cross stick in her
hand, ready to lay it on the shoulders of anyone who
should attempt to obstruct her passage, flew into her carriage, and drove off full speed, as if fearful of being contaminated: all to the no small amusement of the male
guests.

"Her Majesty and I laughed till the very tears ran
down our cheeks.   The Duke of Dorset, to keep up the
joke, said there really were some counties in England
where they called *culottes* IRRESISTIBLES.

"Now that I am upon the subject of England, and the
peace of 1783, which brought such throngs of English
over to France, there occurs to me a circumstance, relating to the treaty of commerce signed at that time, which
exhibits the Count de Vergennes to some advantage; and
with that let me dismiss the topic.

"The Count de Vergennes was one of the most distinguished ministers of France.   I was intimately acquainted with him.   His general character for uprightness
prompted his sovereign to govern in a manner congenial
to his own goodness of heart, which was certainly most
for the advantage of his subjects.   Vergennes cautioned
Louis against the hypocritical adulations of his privileged courtiers.   The Count had been schooled in state
policy by the great Venetian senator, Francis Foscari,
the subtlest politician of his age, whom he consulted during
his life on every important matter; and he was not very
easily to be deceived.

"When the treaty of commerce took place, at the period I mention, experienced Vergennes foresaw — what
afterward really happened — that France would be inundated with British manufactures; but Calonne obstinately
maintained the contrary, till he was severely re-
minded of the consequence of his misguided policy, in
the insults inflicted on him by enraged mobs of thousands
of French artificers, whenever he appeared in public.   But
though the mania for British goods had literally caused
an entire stagnation of business in the French manufac-

turing towns, and thrown throngs upon the *pavé* for want of employment, yet M. de Calonne either did not see, or pretended not to see, the errors he had committed. Being informed that the Count de Vergennes had justly attributed the public disorders to his fallacious policy, M. de Calonne sent a friend to the Count demanding satisfaction for the charge of having caused the riots. The Count calmly replied that he was too much of a man of honor to take so great an advantage, as to avail himself of the opportunity offered, by killing a man who had only one life to dispose of, when there were so many with a prior claim, who were anxious to destroy him *en société.* 'Bid M. de Calonne,' continued the Count, 'first get out of that scrape, as the English boxers do when their eyes are closed up after a pitched battle. He has been playing at blind man's buff, but the poverty to which he has reduced so many of our tradespeople has torn the English bandage from his eyes!' For three or four days the Count de Vergennes visited publicly, and showed himself everywhere in and about Paris; but M. de Calonne was so well convinced of the truth of the old fox's satire that he pocketed his annoyance, and no more was said about fighting. Indeed, the Count de Vergennes gave hints of being able to show that M. de Calonne had been bribed into the treaty."

———

The Princess Lamballe has alluded in a former page to the happiness which the Queen enjoyed during the visits of the foreign princes to the Court of France. Her papers contain a few passages upon the opinions Her Majesty entertained of the royal travelers; which, although in the order of time they should have been mentioned before the peace with England, yet, not to disturb the chain of the narrative, respecting the connection with the Princess Lamballe, of the prevailing libels, and the partiality shown toward the English, I have reserved them for the conclusion of the present chapter. The timidity of the Queen in the presence of the illustrious strangers, and her agitation when about to receive them, have, I think, been

9

already spoken of.   Upon the subject of the royal travelers
themselves, and other personages, the Princess expresses
herself thus.

———

"The Queen had never been an admirer of Catharine
II.   Notwithstanding her studied policy for the advance-
ment of civilization in her internal empire, the means
which, aided by the Princess Dashkoff, she made use of
to seat herself on the imperial throne of her weak husband, Peter the Third, had made her more understood
than esteemed.   Yet when her son, the Grand Duke
of the North,* and the Grand Duchess, his wife, came to
France, their description of Catharine's real character so
shocked the maternal sensibility of Maria Antoinette that
she could scarcely hear the name of the Empress without
shuddering.   The Grand Duke spoke of Catharine without the least disguise.   He said he traveled merely for
the security of his life from his mother, who had surrounded him with creatures that were his sworn enemies,
her own spies and infamous favorites, to whose caprices
they were utterly subordinate.   He was aware that the
dangerous credulity of the Empress might be every hour
excited by these   wretches to the destruction of himself
and his Duchess, and, therefore, he had in absence sought
the only refuge.   He had no wish, he said, ever to return
to his native country, till Heaven should check his mother's doubts respecting his dutiful filial affection toward
her, or till God should be pleased to take her into his
sacred keeping.

"The King was petrified at the Duke's description of
his situation, and the Queen could not refrain from tears
when the Duchess, his wife, confirmed all her husband
had uttered on the subject.   The Duchess said she had
been warned by the untimely fate of the Princess d'Armstadt, her predecessor, the first wife of the Grand Duke,
to elude similar jealousy and suspicion on the part of her
mother-in-law, by seclusion from the Court, in a country
residence with her husband; indeed, that she had made

* Afterward the unhappy Emperor Paul.

it a point never to visit Petersburg, except on the express invitation of the Empress, as if she had been a foreigner.

"In this system the Grand Duchess persevered, even after her return from her travels. When she became pregnant, and drew near her *accouchement*, the Empress-mother permitted her to come to Petersburg for that purpose; but, as soon as the ceremony required by the etiquette of the Imperial Court on those occasions ended, the Duchess immediately returned to her hermitage.

"This Princess was remarkably well educated; she possessed a great deal of good, sound sense, and had profited by the instructions of some of the best German tutors during her very early years. It was the policy of her father, the Duke of Wirtemberg, who had a large family, to educate his children as QUIETISTS in matters of religion. He foresaw that the natural charms and acquired abilities of his daughters would one day call them to be the ornaments of the most distinguished Courts in Europe, and he thought it prudent not to instill early prejudices in favor of peculiar forms of religion which might afterward present an obstacle to their aggrandisement.*

"The notorious vices of the King of Denmark, and his total neglect both of his young Queen, Carolina Matilda, and of the interest of his distant dominions, while in

---

* The first daughter of the Duke of Wirtemberg was the first wife of the present Emperor of Austria. She embraced the Catholic faith and died very young, two days before the Emperor Joseph the Second, at Vienna. The present Empress Dowager, late wife to Paul, became a proselyte to the Greek religion on her arrival at Petersburg. The son of the Duke of Wirtemberg, who succeeded him in the Dukedom, was a Protestant, it being his interest to profess that religion for the security of his inheritance. Prince Ferdinand, who was in the Austrian service, and a long time Governor of Vienna, was a Catholic, as he could not otherwise have enjoyed that office. He was of a very superior character to the Duke, his brother. Prince Louis, who held a commission under the Prussian Monarch, followed the religion of the country where he served, and the other Princes, who were in the employment of Sweden and other countries, found no difficulty in conforming themselves to the religion of the sovereigns under whom they served. None of them having any established forms of worship, they naturally embraced that which conduced most to their aggrandisement, emolument, or dignity.

Paris, created a feeling in the Queen's mind toward that
house which was not a little heightened by her disgust
at the King of Sweden, when he visited the Court of
Versailles. This King, though much more crafty than
his brother-in-law, the King of Denmark, who reveled
openly in his depravities, was not less vicious. The deception he made use of in usurping part of the rights of
his people, combined with the worthlessness and duplicity
of his private conduct, excited a strong indignation in
the mind of Maria Antoinette, of which she was scarcely
capable of withholding the expression in his presence.

"It was during the visit of the Duke and Duchess of
the North, that the Cardinal de Rohan again appeared
upon the scene. For eight or ten years he had never
been allowed to show himself at Court, and had been
totally shut out of every society where the Queen visited.
On the arrival of the illustrious travelers at Versailles,
the Queen, at her own expense, gave them a grand *fête* at her
private palace, in the gardens of Trianon, similar to the
one given by the Count de Provence * to Her Majesty, in
the gardens of Brunoi.

" On the eve of the *fête*, the Cardinal waited upon me
to know if he would be permitted to appear there in the
character he had the honor to hold at Court. I replied
that I had made it a rule never to interfere in the private or public amusements of the Court, and that his
Eminence must be the best judge how far he could ob-
trude himself upon the Queen's private parties, to which
only a select number had been invited, in consequence
of the confined spot where the *fête* was to be given.

"The Cardinal left me, not much satisfied at his reception. Determined to follow, as usual, his own misguided passion, he immediately went to Trianon, disguised
with a large cloak. He saw the porter, and bribed him.
He only wished, he said, to be placed in a situation
whence he might see the Duke and Duchess of the North
without being seen; but no sooner did he perceive the
porter engaged at some distance than he left his cloak

* Afterward Louis XVIII.

at the lodge, and went forward in his cardinal's dress, as if he had been one of the invited guests, placing himself purposely in the Queen's path to attract her attention as she rode by in the carriage with the Duke and Duchess.

"The Queen was shocked and thunderstruck at seeing him. But, great as was her annoyance, knowing the Cardinal had not been invited and ought not to have been there, she only discharged the porter who had been seduced to let him in; and though the King, on being made acquainted with his treachery, would have banished his Eminence a hundred leagues from the capital, yet the Queen, the royal aunts, the Princess Elizabeth, and myself, not to make the affair public, and thereby disgrace the high order of his ecclesiastical dignity, prevented the King from exercising his authority by commanding instant exile.

"Indeed, the Queen could never get the better of her fears of being some day, or in some way or other, betrayed by the Cardinal, for having made him the confidant of the mortification she would have suffered if the projected marriage of Louis XV. and her sister had been solemnized. On this account she uniformly opposed whatever harshness the King at any time intended against the Cardinal.

"Thus was this wicked prelate left at leisure to premeditate the horrid plot of the famous necklace, the ever memorable fraud, which so fatally verified the presentiments of the Queen."

CHAPTER XI.

THE production of "The Marriage of Figaro," by Beaumarchais, upon the stage at Paris, so replete with
indecorous and slanderous allusions to the Royal
Family, had spread the prejudices against the Queen
through the whole kingdom and every rank of France,
just in time to prepare all minds for the deadly blow
which Her Majesty received from the infamous plot of
the diamond necklace. From this year, 1785, crimes and
misfortunes trod closely on each others' heels in the history of the ill-starred Queen; and one calamity only disappeared to make way for a greater.

The destruction of the papers, which would have thoroughly explained the transaction, has still left all its essential particulars in some degree of mystery; and the
interest of the clergy, who supported one of their own
body, coupled with the arts and bribes of the high houses
connected with the plotting prelate, must, of course, have
discolored greatly even what was well known.

It will be recollected that before the accession of Louis
XVI. the Cardinal de Rohan was disgraced in consequence
of his intrigues — that all his ingenuity was afterward
unremittingly exerted to obtain renewed favor — that he

once obtruded himself upon the notice of the Queen in the gardens of Trianon — and that his conduct in so doing excited the indignation it deserved, but was left unpunished owing to the entreaties of the best friends of the Queen, and her own secret horror of a man who had already caused her so much anguish.

With the histories of the fraud everyone is acquainted. That of Madame Campan, as far as it goes, is sufficiently detailed a. d correct to spare me the necessity of expatiating upon tL.'s theme of villainy. Yet, to assist the reader's memory, before returning to the Journal of the Princess Lamballe, I shall recapitulate the leading particulars.

The Cardinal had become connected with a young, but artful and necessitous, woman, of the name of Lamotte. It was known that the darling ambition of the Cardinal was to regain the favor of the Queen.

The necklace, which has been already spoken of, and which was originally destined by Louis XV. for Maria Antoinette — had her hand, by divorce, been transferred to him, but which, though afterward intended by Louis XV. for his mistress, Du Barry, never came to her in consequence of his death — this fatal necklace was still in existence, and in the possession of the crown jewelers, Bœhmer and Bassange. It was valued at eighteen hundred thousand livres. The jewelers had often pressed it upon the Queen, and even the King himself had enforced its acceptance. But the Queen dreaded the expense, especially at an epoch of pecuniary difficulty in the state, much more than she coveted the jewels, and uniformly and resolutely declined them, although they had been proposed to her on very easy terms of payment, as she really did not like ornaments.

It was made to appear at the parliamentary investigation that the artful Lamotte had impelled the Cardinal to believe that she herself was in communication with the Queen; that she had interested Her Majesty in favor of the long slighted Cardinal; that she had fabricated a correspondence, in which professions of penitence on the part of Rohan were answered by assurances of forgiveness from the Queen. The result of this correspondence was represented to be the engagement of the Cardinal to negotiate the purchase of the necklace secretly, by a contract for periodical payments. To the forgery of papers was added, it was declared, the substitution of the Queen's person, by dressing up a girl of the Palais Royal to represent Her Majesty, whom she in some degree resembled, in a secret and rapid interview with Rohan in a dark grove of the gardens of Versailles, where she was to give the Cardinal a rose, in token of her royal approbation, and then hastily disappear. The importunity of the jewelers, on the failure of the stipulated payment, disclosed the plot. A direct appeal of theirs to the Queen, to save them from ruin, was the immediate source of detection. The Cardinal was arrested, and all the parties tried. But the Cardinal was acquitted, and Lamotte and a subordinate agent alone punished. The quack Cagliostro was also in the plot, but he, too, escaped, like his confederate the Cardinal, who was made to appear as the dupe of Lamotte.

The Queen never got over the effect of this affair. Her friends well knew the danger of severe measures toward one capable of collecting around him strong support against a power already so much weakened by faction and discord. But the indignation of conscious innocence insulted, prevailed, though to its ruin!

But it is time to let the Princess Lamballe give her own impressions upon this fatal subject, and in her own words.

" How could Messieurs Bœhmer and Bassange presume that the Queen would have employed any third person to obtain an article of such value, without enabling them to produce an unequivocal document signed by her own hand and countersigned by mine, as had ever been the rule during my superintendence of the household, whenever anything was ordered from the jewelers by Her Majesty? Why did not Messieurs Bœhmer and Bassange wait on me, when they saw a document unauthorized by

me, and so widely departing from the established forms?
I must still think, as I have often said to the King, that
Bœhmer and Bassange wished to get rid of this dead
weight of diamonds in any way, and the Queen having
unfortunately been led by me to hush up many foul libels against her reputation, as I then thought it prudent
she should do, rather than compromise her character with
wretches capable of doing anything to injure her, these
jewelers, judging from this erroneous policy of the past,
imagined that in this instance, also, rather than hazard
exposure, Her Majesty would pay them for the necklace.
This was a compromise which I myself resisted, though
so decidedly adverse to bringing the affair before the
nation by a public trial. Of such an explosion, I foresaw
the consequences, and I ardently entreated the King and
Queen to take other measures. But, though till now so
hostile to severity with the Cardinal, the Queen felt herself so insulted by the proceeding that she gave up every
other consideration to make manifest her innocence.

"The wary Count de Vergennes did all he could to
prevent the affair from getting before the public. Against
the opinion of the King and the whole council of ministers he opposed judicial proceedings. Not that he conceived the Cardinal altogether guiltless; but he foresaw
the fatal consequences that must result to Her Majesty,
from bringing to trial an ecclesiastic of such rank; for he
well knew that the host of the higher orders of the nobility, to whom the prelate was allied, would naturally
strain every point to blacken the character of the King
and Queen, as the only means of exonerating their kinsman in the eyes of the world from the criminal mystery
attached to that most diabolical intrigue against the fair
fame of Maria Antoinette. The Count could not bear
the idea of the Queen's name being coupled with those
of the vile wretches, Lamotte and the mountebank Cagliostro, and therefore wished the King to chastise the
Cardinal by a partial exile, which might have been removed at pleasure. But the Queen's party too fatally
seconded her feelings, and prevailed.

"I sat by Her Majesty's bedside the whole of the night, after I heard what had been determined against the Cardinal by the council of ministers, to beg her to use all her interest with the King to persuade him to revoke the order of the warrant for the prelate's arrest. To this the Queen replied, 'Then the King, the ministers, and the people, will all deem me guilty.'

"Her Majesty's remark stopped all further argument upon the subject, and I had the inconsolable grief to see my royal mistress rushing upon dangers which I had no power of preventing her from bringing upon herself.

"The slanderers who had imputed such unbounded influence to the Queen over the mind of Louis XVI. should have been consistent enough to consider that with but a twentieth part of the tithe of her imputed power, uncontrolled as she then was by national authority, she might, without any exposure to third persons, have at once sent one of her pages to the *garde-meuble* and other royal depositaries, replete with hidden treasures of precious stones which never saw the light, and thence have supplied herself with more than enough to form ten necklaces, or to have fully satisfied, in any way she liked, the most unbounded passion for diamonds, for the use of which she would never have been called to account.

"But the truth is, the Queen had no love of ornaments. A proof occurred very soon after I had the honor to be nominated Her Majesty's superintendent. On the day of the great *fête* of the *Cordon Bleu*, when it was the etiquette to wear diamonds and pearls, the Queen had omitted putting them on. As there had been a greater affluence of visitors than usual that morning, and Her Majesty's toilet was overthronged by princes and princesses, I fancied in the bustle that the omission proceeded from forgetfulness. Consequently, I sent the tire-woman, in the Queen's hearing, to order the jewels to be brought in. Smilingly, Her Majesty replied, 'No, no! I have not forgotten these gaudy things; but I do not intend that the luster of my eyes should be outshone by the one, or the whiteness of my teeth by the other; however, as you

wish art to eclipse nature, I'll wear them to satisfy you,
ma belle dame!'

"The King was always so thoroughly indulgent to Her
Majesty with regard both to her public and private conduct that she never had any pretext for those reserves
which sometimes tempt queens as well as the wives of
private individuals to commit themselves to third persons
for articles of high value, which their caprice indiscreetly
impels them to procure unknown to their natural guardians. Maria Antoinette had no reproach or censure for
plunging into expenses beyond her means to apprehend
from her royal husband. On the contrary, the King himself had spontaneously offered to purchase the necklace
from the jèwelers, who had urged it on him without
limiting any time for payment. It was the intention of
His Majesty to have liquidated it out of his private purse.
But Maria Antoinette declined the gift. Twice in my
presence was the refusal repeated before Messieurs
Bœhmer and Bassange. Who, then, can for a moment
presume, after all these circumstances, that the Queen of
France, with a nation's wealth at her feet and thousands
of individuals offering her millions, which she never accepted, would have so far degraded herself and the honor
of the nation, of which she was born to be the ornament,
as to place herself gratuitously in the power of a knot of
wretches, headed by a man whose general bad character
for years had excluded him from Court and every respectable
society, and had made the Queen herself mark him as an
object of the utmost aversion.

"If these circumstances be not sufficient adequately to
open the eyes of those whom prejudice has blinded, and
whose ears have been deafened against truth, by the
clamors of sinister conspirators against the monarchy instead of the monarchs; if all these circumstances, I repeat,
do not completely acquit the Queen, argument, or even
ocular demonstration itself, would be thrown away.
Posterity will judge impartially, and with impartial judges
the integrity of Maria Antoinette needs no defender.

"When the natural tendency of the character of Rohan

to romatic and extraordinary intrigue is considered in connection with the associates he had gathered around him, the plot of the necklace ceases to be a source of wonder. At the time the Cardinal was most at a loss for means to meet the necessities of his extravagance, and to obtain some means of access to the Queen, the mountebank quack, Cagliostro, made his appearance in France. His fame had soon flown from Strasburg to Paris, the magnet of vices and the seat of criminals. The Prince-Cardinal, known of old as a seeker after everything of notoriety, soon became the intimate of one who flattered him with the accomplishment of all his dreams in the realization of the philosopher's stone; converting puffs and French paste into brilliants; Roman pearls into Oriental ones; and turning earth to gold. The Cardinal, always in want of means to supply the insatiable exigencies of his ungovernable vices, had been the dupe through life of his own credulity — a drowning man catching at a straw! But instead of making gold of base materials, Cagliostro's brass soon relieved his blind adherent of all his sterling metal. As many needy persons enlisted under the banners of this nostrum speculator, it is not to be wondered at that the infamous name of the Countess de Lamotte, and others of the same stamp, should have thus fallen into an association of the Prince-Cardinal; or that her libelous stories of the Queen of France should have found eager promulgators, where the real diamonds of the famous necklace being taken apart were divided piecemeal among a horde of the most depraved sharpers that ever existed to make human nature blush at its own degradation! *

* Cagliostro, when he came to Rome, for I know not whether there had been any previous intimacy, got acquainted with a certain Marchese Vivaldi, a Roman, whose wife had been for years the *chère amie* of the last Venetian ambassador, Peter Pesaro, a noble patrician, and who has ever since his embassy at Rome been his constant companion and now resides with him in England. No men in Europe are more constant in their attachments than the Venetians. Pesaro is the sole proprietor of one of the most beautiful and magnificent palaces on the Grand Canal at Venice, though he now lives in the outskirts of London, in a small

"Eight or ten years had elapsed from the time Her Majesty had last seen the Cardinal to speak to him, with the exception of the casual glance as she drove by when he furtively ntroduced himself into the garden at the *fête* at Trianon, till he was brought to the King's cabinet when arrested, and interrogated, and confronted with her face to face. The Prince started when he saw her. The comparison of her features with those of the guilty wretch who had dared to personate her in the garden at Versailles completely destroyed his self-possession. Her Majesty's person was become fuller, and her face was much longer than that of the infamous d'Oliva. He could neither speak nor write an intelligible reply to the questions put to him. All he could utter, and that only in broken accents, was, 'I'll pay! I'll pay Messieurs Bassange.'

"Had he not speedily recovered himself, all the mystery in which this affair has been left, so injuriously to the Queen, might have been prevented. His papers would have declared the history of every particular, and dis-

house, not so large as one of the offices of his immense noble palace, where his agent transacts his business. The husband of Pesaro's *chère amie*, the Marchese Vivaldi, when Cagliostro was arrested and sent to the Castello Santo Angelo at Rome, was obliged to fly his country, and went to Venice, where he was kept secreted and maintained by the Marquis Solari, and it was only through his means and those of the Cardinal Consalvi, then known only as the MUSICAL Abbé Consalvi, from his great attachment to the immortal Cimarosa, that Vivaldi was ever allowed to return to his native country; but Consalvi, who was the friend of Vivaldi, feeling with the Marquis Solari much interested for his situation, they together contrived to convince Pius VI. that he was more to be pitied than blamed, and thus obtained his recall. I have merely given this note as a further warning to be drawn from the connections of the Cardinal de Rohan, to deter hunters after novelty from forming ties with innovators and impostors. Cagliostro was ultimately condemned, by the Roman laws under Pope Pius VI. for life, to the galleys, where he died.

Proverbs ought to be respected; for it is said that no phrase becomes a proverb until after a century's experience of its truth. In England, it is proverbial to judge of men by the company they keep. To judge of the Cardinal de Rohan from his most intimate friend, the galley slave, Cagliostro, what shall we say of his dignity as a prince, and his purity as a prelate?

tinctly established the extent of his crime and the thorough innocence of Maria Antoinette of any connivance at the fraud, or any knowledge of the necklace. But when the Cardinal was ordered by the King's council to be put under arrest, his self-possession returned. He was given in charge to an officer totally unacquainted with the nature of the accusation. Considering only the character of his prisoner as one of the highest dignitaries of the Church, from ignorance and inexperience, he left the Cardinal an opportunity to write a German note to his factotum, the Abbé Georgel. In this note the trusty secretary was ordered to destroy all the letters of Cagliostro, Madame de Lamotte, and the other wretched associates of the infamous conspiracy; and the traitor was scarcely in custody when every evidence of his treason had disappeared. The note to Georgel saved his master from expiating his offense at the Place de Grêve.

"The consequences of the affair would have been less injurious, however, had it been managed, even as it stood, with better judgment and temper. But it was improperly intrusted to the Baron de Bréteuil and the Abbé Vermond, both sworn enemies of the Cardinal. Their main object was the ruin of him they hated, and they listened only to their resentments. They never weighed the danger of publicly prosecuting an individual whose condemnation would involve the first families in France, for he was allied even to many of the Princes of the blood. They should have considered that exalted personages, naturally feeling as if any crime proved against their kinsman would be a stain upon themselves, would of course resort to every artifice to exonerate the accused. To criminate the Queen was the only and the obvious method. Few are those nearest the Crown who are not most jealous of its wearers! Look at the long civil wars of York and Lancaster, and the short reign of Richard. The downfall of kings meets less resistance than that of their inferiors.

"Still, notwithstanding all the deplorable blunders committed in this business of Rohan, justice was not smothered without great difficulty. His acquittal cost the families of Rohan and Condé more than a million of livres, distributed among all ranks of the clergy; besides immense sums sent to the Court of Rome to make it invalidate the judgment of the civil authority of France upon so high a member of the Church, and to induce it to order the Cardinal's being sent to Rome by way of screening him from the prosecution, under the plausible pretext of more rigid justice.

"Considerable sums in money and jewels were also lavished on all the female relatives of the peers of France, who were destined to sit on the trial. The Abbé Georgel bribed the press, and extravagantly paid all the literary pens in France to produce the most Jesuitical and sophisticated arguments in his patron's justification. Though these writers dared not accuse or in any way criminate the Queen, yet the respectful doubts, with which their defense of her were seasoned, did infinitely more mischief than any direct attack, which could have been directly answered.

"The long cherished, but till now smothered, resentment of the Countess de Noailles, the scrupulous Madame Etiquette, burst forth on this occasion. Openly joining the Cardinal's party against her former mistress and sovereign, she recruited and armed all in favor of her *protégé;* for it was by her intrigues Rohan had been nominated ambassador to Vienna. Mesdames de Guéménée and Marsan, rival pretenders to favors of His Eminence, were equally earnest to support him against the Queen. In short, there was scarcely a family of distinction in France that, from the libels which then inundated the kingdom, did not consider the King as having infringed on their prerogatives and privileges in accusing the Cardinal.

"Shortly after the acquittal of this most artful, and, in the present instance, certainly too fortunate prelate, the Princess Condé came to congratulate me on the Queen's innocence, and her kinsman's liberation from the Bastille.

"Without the slightest observation, I produced to the Princess documents in proof of the immense sums she alone had expended in bribing the judges and other persons, to save her relation, the Cardinal, by criminating Her Majesty.

"The Princess Condé instantly fell into violent hysterics, and was carried home apparently lifeless.

"I have often reproached myself for having given that sudden shock and poignant anguish to her highness, but I could not have supposed that one who came so barefacedly to impress me with the Cardinal's innocence, could have been less firm in refuting her own guilt.

"I never mentioned the circumstance to the Queen. Had I done so, her highness would have been forever excluded from the Court and the royal presence. This was no time to increase the enemies of Her Majesty, and, the affair of the trial being ended, I thought it best to prevent any further breach from a discord between the Court and the house of Condé. However, from a coldness subsisting ever after between the Princess and myself, I doubt not that the Queen had her suspicions that all was not as it should be in that quarter. Indeed, though Her Majesty never confessed it, I think she herself had discovered something at that very time not altogether to the credit of the Princess Condé, for she ceased going, from that period, to any of the *fêtes* given at Chantilly.

"These were but a small portion of the various instruments successfully leveled by parties, even the least suspected, to blacken and destroy the fair fame of Maria Antoinette.

"The document which so justly alarmed the Princess Condé when I showed it to her came into my hands in the following manner:

"Whenever a distressed family, or any particular individual, applied to me for relief, or was otherwise recommended for charitable purposes, I generally sent my little English *protégée*,—on whose veracity, well knowing the goodness of her heart, I could rely,*—to ascertain whether their claims were really well grounded.

"One day, I received an earnest memorial from a family, desiring to make some private communications of peculiar delicacy. I sent my usual ambassadress to inquire into its import. On making her mission known, she found no difficulty in ascertaining the object of the application. It proceeded from conscientious distress of mind. A relation of this family had been the regular confessor of a convent. With the Lady Abbess of this convent and her trusty nuns the Princess Condé had deposited considerable sums of money, to be bestowed in creating influence in favor of the Cardinal de Rohan. The confessor, being a man of some consideration among the clergy, was applied to, to use his influence with the needier members of the Church more immediately about him, as well as those of higher station, to whom he had access, in furthering the purposes of the Princess Condé. The bribes were applied as intended. But, at the near approach of death, the confessor was struck with remorse. He begged his family, without mentioning his name, to send the accounts and vouchers of the sums he had so distributed, to me, as a proof of his contrition, that I might make what use of them I should think proper. The papers were handed to my messenger, who pledged her word of honor that I would certainly adhere to the dying man's last injunctions. She desired they might be sealed up by the family, and by them directed to me.† She then hastened back to our place of rendezvous, where I waited for her, and where she consigned the packet into my own hands.

"That part of the papers which compromised only the Princess Condé was shown by me to the Princess on the

---

* Indeed, I never deceived the Princess on these occasions. She was so generously charitable that I should have conceived it a crime. When I could get no satisfactory information, I said I could not trace anything undeserving her charity, and left her highness to exercise her own discretion.

† To this day, I neither know the name of the convent or the confessor.

occasion I have mentioned. It was natural enough that she should have been shocked at the detection of having suborned the clergy and others with heavy bribes to avert the deserved fate of the Cardinal. I kept this part of the packet secret till the King's two aunts, who had also been warm advocates in favor of the prelate, left Paris for Rome. Then, as Pius VI. had interested himself as head of the Church for the honor of one of its members, I gave them these very papers to deliver to His Holiness for his private perusal. I was desirous of enabling this truly charitable and Christian head of our sacred religion to judge how far his interference was justified by facts. I am thoroughly convinced, that had he been sooner furnished with these evidences, instead of blaming the royal proceeding he would have urged it on, nay, would himself have been the first to advise that the foul conspiracy should be dragged into open day.*

"The Count de Vergennes told me that the King displayed the greatest impartiality throughout the whole investigation for the exculpation of the Queen, and made good his title on this, as he did on every occasion where his own unbiased feelings and opinions were called into action, to great esteem for much higher qualities than the world has usually given him credit for.

"I have been accused of having opened the prison doors of the culprit Lamotte for her escape; but the charge is false. I interested myself, as was my duty, to shield the Queen from public reproach by having Lamotte sent to a place of penitence; but I never interfered, except to lessen her punishment, after the judicial proceedings. The diamonds, in the hands of her vile associates at Paris, procured her ample means to escape. I should have been the Queen's greatest enemy had I been the cause of giving liberty to one who acted, and might

---

* But these proofs came too late to redeem the character of her, whom fate, cruel fate! had written in the book of destinies a victim in this world, for her immortal salvation in the next. Never saint more merited to be ranked in the long list of martyrs than Maria Antoinette.

naturally have been expected to act, as this depraved woman did.

"Through the private correspondence which was carried on between this country and England, after I had left it, I was informed that M. de Calonne, whom the Queen never liked, and who was called to the administration against her will—which he knew, and consequently became one of her secret enemies in the affair of the necklace—was discovered to have been actively employed against Her Majesty in the work published in London by Lamotte.

"Mr. Sheridan was the gentleman who first gave me this information.

"I immediately sent a trusty person by the Queen's orders to London, to buy up the whole work. It was too late. It had been already so widely circulated that its consequences could no longer be prevented. I was lucky enough, however, for a considerable sum to get a copy from a person intimate with the author, the margin of which, in the handwriting of M. de Calonne, actually contained numerous additional circumstances which were to have been published in a second edition! This publication my agent, aided by some English gentlemen, arrived in time to suppress.

"The copy I allude to was brought to Paris and shown to the Queen. She instantly flew with it in her hands to the King's cabinet.

"'Now, sire,' exclaimed she, 'I hope you will be convinced that my enemies are those whom I have long considered as the most pernicious of Your Majesty's councilors—your own cabinet ministers—your M. de Calonne! respecting whom I have often given you my opinion, which, unfortunately, has always been attributed to mere female caprice, or as having been biased by the intrigues of Court favorites! This, I hope, Your Majesty will now be able to contradict!'

"The King all this time was looking over the different pages containing M. de Calonne's additions on their margins. On recognizing the handwriting, His Majesty was so affected by this discovered treachery of his

minister and the agitation of his calumniated Queen that
he could scarcely articulate.

"'Where,' said he, 'did you procure this?'

"'Through the means, sire, of some of the worthy
members of that nation your treacherous ministers made
our enemy — from England! where your unfortunate
Queen, your injured wife, is compassionated!'

"'Who got it for you?'

"'My dearest, my real, and my only sincere friend,
the Princess Lamballe!'

"The King requested I should be sent for. I came.
As may be imagined, I was received with the warmest
sentiments of affection by both Their Majesties. I then
laid before the King the letter of Mr. Sheridan, which
was, in substance, as follows:*

"'MADAM:— A work of mine, which I did not choose should be
printed, was published in Dublin and transmitted to be sold in London.
As soon as I was informed of it, and had procured a spurious copy, I
went to the bookseller to put a stop to its circulation. I there met with
a copy of the work of Madame de Lamotte, which has been corrected
by some one at Paris and sent back to the bookseller for a second edition.
Though not in time to suppress the first edition, owing to its rapid circulation, I have had interest enough, through the means of the bookseller of whom I speak, to remit you the copy which has been sent as the
basis of a new one. The corrections, I am told, are by one of the King's
ministers. If true, I should imagine the writer will be easily traced.

"'I am happy that it has been in my power to make this discovery,
and I hope it will be the means of putting a stop to this most scandalous
publication. I feel myself honored in having contributed thus far to the
wishes of Her Majesty, which I hope I have fulfilled to the entire satisfaction of your highness.

"'Should anything further transpire on this subject, I will give you
the earliest information.

"'I remain, madam, with profound respect, your highness' most devoted,   Very humble servant,

                              "'RICHARD BRINSLEY SHERIDAN.'†

* The letter was, of course, translated in the Journal of the Princess
into Italian; and is thence here restored into English. The original letter probably shared the fate of other papers of her highness in the revolutionary riots.

† Madame Campan mentions in her work that the Queen had informed
her of the treachery of the minister, but did not enter into particulars,

"M. de Calonne immediately received the King's mandate to resign the portfolio. The minister desired that he might be allowed to give his resignation to the King himself. His request was granted. The Queen was present at the interview. The work in question was produced. On beholding it, the minister nearly fainted. The King got up and left the room. The Queen, who remained, told M. de Calonne that His Majesty had no further occasion for his services. He fell on his knees. He was not allowed to speak, but was desired to leave Paris.

"The dismissal and disgrace of M. de Calonne were scarcely known before all Paris vociferated that they were owing to the intrigues of the favorite, Polignac, in consequence of his having refused to administer to her own superfluous extravagance and the Queen's repeated demands on the treasury to satisfy the numerous dependants of the Duchess.

"This, however, was soon officially disproved by the exhibition of a written proposition of Calonne's to the Queen, to supply an additional hundred thousand francs that year to her annual revenue, which Her Majesty refused. As for the Duchess de Polignac, so far from having caused the disgrace, she was not even aware of the circumstance from which it arose; nor did the minister himself ever know how, or by what agency his falsehood was so thoroughly unmasked."

nor explain the mode or source of its detection. Notwithstanding the parties had bound themselves for the sums they received not to reprint the work, a second edition appeared a short time afterward in London. This, which was again bought up by the French ambassador, was the same which was to have been burned by the King's command at the china manufactory at Sêvres.

NOTE.

THE work which is here spoken of the Queen kept, as a proof of the treachery of Calonne toward her and his sovereign, till the storming of the Tuileries on the 10th of August, 1792, when, with the rest of the papers and property plundered on that memorable occasion, it fell into the hands of the ferocious mob.

M. de Calonne soon after left France for Italy. There he lived for some time in the palace of a particular friend of mine and the Marquis, my husband, the Countess Francese Tressino, at Vicenza.

In consequence of our going every season to take the mineral waters and use the baths at Valdagno, we had often occasion to be in company with M. de Calonne, both at Vicenza and Valdagno, where I must do him the justice to say he conducted himself with the greatest circumspection in speaking of the Revolution.

Though he evidently avoided the topic which terminates this chapter, yet one day, being closely pressed upon the subject, he said forgeries were daily committed on ministers, and were most particularly so in France at the period in question; that he had borne the blame of various imprudencies neither authorized nor executed by him; that much had been done and supposed to have been done with his sanction, of which he had not the slightest knowledge. This he observed generally, without specifying any express instance.

He was then asked whether he did not consider himself responsible for the mischief he occasioned by declaring the nation in a state of bankruptcy. He said, "No, not in the least. There was no other way of preventing enormous sums from being daily lavished, as they then were, on herds of worthless beings; that the Queen had sought to cultivate a state of private domestic society, but that, in the attempt, she only warmed in her bosom domestic vipers, who fed on the vital spirit of her generosity." He mentioned no names.

I then took the liberty of asking him his opinion of the Princess Lamballe.

"Oh, madam! had the rest of Her Majesty's numerous attendants possessed the tenth part of that unfortunate victim's virtues, Her Majesty would never have been led into the errors which all France must deplore!

"I shall never forget her," continued he, "the day I went to take leave of her. She was sitting on a sofa when I entered. On seeing me, she rose immediately. Before I could utter a syllable, 'Sir,' said the Princess 'you are accused of being the Queen's enemy. Acquit yourself of the foul deed imputed to you, and I shall be happy to serve you as far as lies in my power. Till then, I must decline holding any communication with an individual thus situated. I am her friend, and cannot receive anyone known to be otherwise.'"

"There was something," added he, "so sublime, so dignified, and altogether so firm, though mild in her manner, that she appeared not to belong to a race of earthly beings!"

Seeing the tears fall from his eyes, while he was thus eulogizing her whose memory I shall ever venerate, I almost forgave him the mischief of his imprudence, which led to her untimely end. I therefore carefully avoided wounding his few gray hairs and latter days, and left him still untold that it was by her, of whom he thought so highly, that his uncontradicted treachery had been discovered.

CHAPTER XII.

"OF THE many instances in which the Queen's exertions to serve those whom she conceived likely to benefit and relieve the nation, turned to the injury, not only of herself, but those whom she patronized and the cause she would strengthen, one of the most unpopular was that of the promotion of Brienne, Archbishop of Sens, to the ministry. Her interest in his favor was entirely created by the Abbé Vermond, himself too superficial to pronounce upon any qualities, and especially such as were requisite for so high a station. By many, the partiality which prompted Vermond to espouse the interests of the Archbishop was ascribed to the amiable sentiment of gratitude for the recommendation of that dignitary, by which Vermond himself first obtained his situation at Court; but there were others, who have been deemed deeper in the secret, who impute *it* to the less honorable source of self-interest, to the mere spirit of ostentation, to the hope of its enabling him to bring about the destruction of the Polignacs. Be this as it may, the Abbé well knew that a minister indebted for his elevation solely to the Queen would be supported by her to the last.

"This, unluckily, proved the case. Maria Antoinette persisted in upholding every act of Brienne, till his ignorance and unpardonable blunders drew down the general indignation of the people against Her Majesty and her *protégé*, with whom she was identified. The King had assented to the appointment with no other view than that of not being utterly isolated and to show a respect for his consort's choice. But the incapable minister was presently compelled to retire, not only from office but from Paris. Never was a minister more detested while in power, or a people more enthusiastically satisfied at his going out. His effigy was burnt in every town of France, and the general illuminations and bonfires in the capital were accompanied by hooting and hissing the deposed statesman to the barriers.

"The Queen, prompted by the Abbé Vermond, even after Brienne's dismission, gave him tokens of her royal munificence. Her Majesty feared that her acting otherwise to a minister, who had been honored by her confidence, would operate as a check to prevent all men of celebrity from exposing their fortunes to so ungracious a return for lending their best services to the state, which now stood in need of the most skillful pilots. Such were the motives assigned by Her Majesty herself to me, when I took the liberty of expostulating with her respecting the dangers which threatened herself and family, from this continued devotedness to a minister against whom the nation had pronounced so strongly. I could not but applaud the delicacy of the feeling upon which her conduct had been grounded; nor could I blame her, in my heart, for the uprightness of her principle, in showing that what she had once undertaken should not be abandoned through female caprice. I told Her

Majesty that the system upon which she acted was praiseworthy; and that its application in the present instance
would have been so had the Archbishop possessed as
much talent as he lacked; but that now it was quite requisite for her to stop the public clamor by renouncing
her protection of a man who had so seriously endangered
the public tranquillity and her own reputation.*

"As a proof how far my caution was well founded,
there was an immense riotous mob raised about this time
against the Queen, in consequence of her having appointed the dismissed minister's niece, Madame de Canisy,
to a place at Court, and having given her picture, set in
diamonds, to the Archbishop himself.

"The Queen, in many cases, was by far too com-
municative to some of her household, who immediately
divulged all they gathered from her unreserve. How
could these circumstances have transpired to the people
but from those nearest the person of Her Majesty, who,
knowing the public feeling better than their royal mistress could be supposed to know it, did their own feeling little credit by the mischievous exposure. The people were exasperated beyond all conception. The Abbé
Vermond placed before Her Majesty the consequences of
her communicativeness, and from this time forward she
never repeated the error. After the lesson she had received, none of her female attendants, not even the
Duchess de Polignac, to whom she would have confided
her very existence, could, had they been ever so much
disposed, have drawn anything upon public matters from
her. With me, as her superintendent and entitled by my
situation to interrogate and give her counsel, she was
not, of course, under the same restriction. To his other
representations of the consequences of the Queen's indis-

---

* The Princess Lamballe had no particularly shining talents; but her
understanding was sound, and she seldom gave her opinion without ma-
ture reflection, and never without being called upon, or when she distinctly foresaw the danger which must accrue from its being withheld.
Would to Heaven the Queen had had more advisers like her, who felt so
little for herself and so much for the welfare of her royal mistress!

creet openness, the Abbé Vermond added that, being obliged to write all the letters, private and public, he often found himself greatly embarrassed by affairs having gone forth to the world beforehand. One misfortune of putting this seal upon the lips of Her Majesty was that it placed her more thoroughly in the Abbé's power. She was, of course, obliged to rely implicitly upon him concerning many points, which, had they undergone the discussion necessarily resulting from free conversation, would have been shown to her under very different aspects. A man with a better heart, less Jesuitical, and not so much interested as Vermond was to keep his place, would have been a safer monitor.

"Though the Archbishop of Sens was so much hated and despised, much may be said in apology for his disasters. His unpopularity, and the Queen's support of him against the people, was certainly a vital blow to the monarchy. There is no doubt of his having been a poor substitute for the great men who had so gloriously beaten the political paths of administration, particularly the Count de Vergennes and Necker. But at that time, when France was threatened by its great convulsion, where is the genius which might not have committed itself? And here is a man coming to rule amid revolutionary feelings, with no knowledge whatever of revolutionary principles; a pilot steering into one harbor by the chart of another. I am by no means a vindicator of the Archbishop's obstinacy in offering himself a candidate for a situation entirely foreign to the occupations, habits, and studies of his whole life; but his intentions may have been good enough, and we must not charge the physician with murder who has only mistaken the disease, and, though wrong in his judgment, has been zealous and conscientious; nor must we blame the comedians for the faults of the comedy. The errors were not so much in the men who did not succeed, as in the manners of the times.

" The part which the Queen was now openly compelled to bear in the management of public affairs, increased the public feeling against her from dislike to hatred.

Her Majesty was unhappy, not only from the necessity which called her out of the sphere to which she thought her sex ought to be confined, but from the divisions which existed in the Royal Family upon points in which their common safety required a common scheme of action. Her favorite brother-in-law, d'Artois, had espoused the side of d'Orleans, and the popular party seemed to prevail against her, even with the King.

"The various parliamentary assemblies, which had swept on their course, under various denominations, in rapid and stormy succession, were now followed by one which, like Aaron's rod, was to swallow up the rest. Its approach was regarded by the Queen with ominous reluctance. At length, however, the moment for the meeting of the States-General at Versailles arrived. Necker was once more in favor, and a sort of forlorn hope of better times dawned upon the perplexed monarch, in his anticipations from this assembly.

"The night before the procession of the installment of the States-General was to take place, it being my duty to attend Her Majesty, I received an anonymous letter, cautioning me not to be seen that day by her side. I immediately went to the King's apartments and showed him the letter. His Majesty humanely enjoined me to abide by its counsels. I told him I hoped he would for once permit me to exercise my own discretion; for if my royal sovereign were in danger, it was then that her attendants should be most eager to rally round her, in order to watch over her safety and encourage her fortitude.

"While we were thus occupied, the Queen and my sister-in-law, the Duchess of Orleans, entered the King's apartment, to settle some part of the etiquette respecting the procession.

"'I wish,' exclaimed the Duchess, 'that this procession were over; or that it were never to take place; or that none of us had to be there; or else, being obliged, that we had all passed, and were comfortably at home again.'

"'Its taking place,' answered the Queen, 'never had my sanction, especially at Versailles. M. Necker appears to be in its favor, and answers for its success. I wish he may not be deceived; but I much fear that he is guided more by the mistaken hope of maintaining his own popularity by this impolitic meeting, than by any conscientious confidence in its advantage to the King's authority.'

"The King, having in his hand the letter which I had just brought him, presented it to the Queen.

"'This, my dear Duchess,' cried the Queen, 'comes from the Palais Royal manufactory, to poison the very first sentiments of delight at the union expected between the King and his subjects, by inuendos of the danger which must result from my being present at it. Look at the insidiousness of the thing! Under a pretext of kindness, cautions against the effect of their attachment are given to my most sincere and affectionate attendants, whose fidelity none dare attack openly. I am, however, rejoiced that Lamballe has been cautioned.'

"'Against what?' replied I.

"'Against appearing in the procession,' answered the Queen.

"'It is only,' I exclaimed, 'by putting me in the grave they can ever withdraw me from Your Majesty. While I have life and Your Majesty's sanction, force only will prevent me from doing my duty. Fifty thousand daggers, Madame, were they all raised against me, would have no power to shake the firmness of my character or the earnestness of my attachment. I pity the wretches who have so little penetration. Victim or no victim, nothing shall ever induce me to quit Your Majesty.'

"The Queen and the Duchess, both in tears, embraced me. After the Duchess had taken her leave, the King and Queen hinted their suspicions that she had been apprised of the letter and had made this visit expressly to observe what effect it had produced, well knowing at the time that some attempt was meditated by the hired mob and purchased deputies already brought over to the Orleans faction. Not that the slightest suspicion of collusion could ever be attached to the good Duchess of

Orleans against the Queen. The intentions of the Duchess were known to be as virtuous and pure as those of her husband's party were criminal and mischievous. But, no doubt, she had intimations of the result intended; and, unable to avert the storm or prevent its cause, had been instigated by her strong attachment to me, as well as the paternal affection her father, the Duke de Penthièvre, bore me, to attempt to lessen the exasperation of the Palais Royal party and the Duke, her husband, against me, by dissuading me from running any risk upon the occasion.

"The next day, May 5th, 1789, at the very moment when all the resources of nature and art seemed exhausted to render the Queen a paragon of loveliness beyond anything I had ever before witnessed, even in her; when every impartial eye was eager to behold and feast on that form whose beauty warmed every heart in her favor; at that moment a horde of miscreants, just as she came within sight of the assembly, thundered in her ears, 'ORLEANS FOREVER!' three or four times,* while she and the King were left to pass unheeded. Even the warning of the letter, from which she had reason to expect some commotions, suggested to her imagination nothing like this, and she was dreadfully shaken. I sprang forward to support her. The King's party, prepared for the attack, shouted '*Vive le roi! vive la reine!*' As I turned, I saw some of the members lividly pale, as if fearing their machinations had been discovered; but, as they passed, they said in the hearing of Her Majesty, 'REMEMBER, YOU ARE THE DAUGHTER OF MARIA THERESA.' 'TRUE,' answered the Queen. The Duke de Biron, Orleans, La Fayette, Mirabeau, and the Mayor of Paris, seeing Her Majesty's emotion, came up, and were going to stop the procession. All, in apparent agitation, cried out 'HALT!' The Queen, sternly looking at them, made a sign with her head to proceed, recovered herself, and moved forward in the

* At that moment her loveliness received its blight. From the instant she heard that cry, her severest sorrows and their effects began. It proved her death cry.

train, with all the dignity and self-possession for which she was so eminently distinguished.

"But this self-command in public proved nearly fatal to Her Majesty on her return to her apartment. There her real feelings broke forth, and their violence was so great as to cause the bracelets on her wrists and the pearls in her necklace to burst from the threads and settings, before her women and the ladies in attendance could have time to take them off. She remained many hours in a most alarming state of strong convulsions. Her clothes were obliged to be cut from her body, to give her ease; but as soon as she was undressed, and tears came to her relief, she flew alternately to the Princess Elizabeth and to myself; but we were both too much overwhelmed to give her the consolation of which she stood so much in need.

"Barnave that very evening came to my private apartment, and tendered his services to the Queen. He told me he wished Her Majesty to be convinced that he was a Frenchman; that he only desired his country might be governed by salutary laws, and not by the caprice of weak sovereigns, or a vitiated, corrupt ministry; that the clergy and nobility ought to contribute to the wants of the state equally with every other class of the King's subjects; that when this was accomplished, and abuses were removed, by such a national representation as would enable the minister, Necker, to accomplish his plans for the liquidation of the national debt, I might assure Her Majesty that both the King and herself would find themselves happier in a constitutional government than they had ever yet been; for such a government would set them free from all dependence on the caprice of ministers, and lessen a responsibility of which they now experienced the misery; that if the King sincerely entered into the spirit of regenerating the French nation, he would find among the present representatives many members of probity, loyal and honorable in their intentions, who would never become the destroyers of a limited legitimate monarchy, or the corrupt regicides of a rump parliament, such as brought the wayward Charles the First, of England, to the fatal block.

"I attempted to relate the conversation to the Queen. She listened with the greatest attention till I came to the part concerning the constitutional King, when Her Majesty lost her patience, and prevented me from proceeding.*

"The expense of the insulting scene, which had so overcome Her Majesty, was five hundred thousand francs! This sum was paid by the agents of the Palais Royal, and its execution intrusted principally to Mirabeau, Bailly, the Mayor of Paris, and another individual, who was afterward brought over to the Court party.

"The history of the assembly itself on the day following, the 6th of May, is too well known. The sudden perturbation of a guilty conscience, which overcame the Duke of Orleans, seemed like an awful warning. He had scarcely commenced his inflammatory address to the assembly, when some one, who felt incommoded by the stifling heat of the hall, exclaimed, 'Throw open the windows!' The conspirator fancied he heard in this his death sentence. He fainted, and was conducted home in the greatest agitation. Madame de Bouffon was at the Palais

---

*This and other conversations which will be found in subsequent pages, will prove that Barnave's sentiments in favor of the Royal Family long preceded the affair at Varennes, the beginning of which Madame Campan assigns to it. Indeed, it must by this time be evident to the reader, that Madame Campan, though very correct in relating all she knew, with respect to the history of Maria Antoinette, was not in possession of matters foreign to her occupation about the person of the Queen, and, in particular, that she could communicate little concerning those important intrigues carried on respecting the different deputies of the first assembly, till, in the latter days of the Revolution, when it became necessary, from the pressure of events, that she should be made a sort of confidante, in order to prevent her from compromising the persons of the Queen and the Princess Lamballe: a trust, of her claim to which her undoubted fidelity was an ample pledge. Still, however, she was often absent from Court at moments of great importance, and was obliged to take her information, upon much which she has recorded, from hearsay, which has led her, as I have before stated, into frequent mistakes.

Royal when the Duke was taken thither. The Duchess of Orleans was at the palace of the Duke de Penthièvre, her father, while the Duke himself was at the Hotel Thoulouse with me, where he was to dine, and where we were waiting for the Duchess to come and join us, by appointment. But Madame de Bouffon was so alarmed by the state in which she saw the Duke of Orleans that she instantly left the Palais Royal, and dispatched his valet express to bring her thither. My sister-in-law sent an excuse to me for not coming to dinner, and an explanation to her father for so abruptly leaving his palace, and hastened home to her husband. It was some days before he recovered; and his father-in-law, his wife, and myself were not without hopes that he would see in this an omen to prevent him from persisting any longer in his opposition to the Royal Family.

"The effects of the recall of the popular minister, Necker, did not satisfy the King. Necker soon became an object of suspicion to the Court party, and especially to His Majesty and the Queen. He was known to have maintained an understanding with Orleans. The miscarriage of many plans and the misfortunes which succeeded were the result of this connection, though it was openly disavowed. The first suspicion of the coalition arose thus:

"When the Duke had his bust carried about Paris, after his unworthy schemes against the King had been discovered, it was thrown into the mire. Necker passing, perhaps by mere accident, stopped his carriage, and expressing himself with some resentment for such treatment to a Prince of the blood and a friend of the people, ordered the bust to be taken to the Palais Royal, where it was washed, crowned with laurel, and thence, with Necker's own bust, carried to Versailles. The King's aunts, coming from Belvue as the procession was upon the road, ordered the guards to send the men away who bore the busts, that the King and Queen might not be insulted with the sight. This circumstance caused another riot, which was attributed to Their Majesties. The dismission of the minister was the obvious result. It is certain, however, that, in obeying the mandate of exile, Necker had no wish to exercise the advantage he possessed from his great popularity. His retirement was sudden and secret; and, although it was mentioned that very evening by the Baroness de Staël to the Count de Chinon, so little bustle was made about his withdrawing from France, that it was even stated at the time to have been utterly unknown, even to his daughter.

"Necker himself ascribed his dismission to the influence of the Polignacs; but he was totally mistaken, for the Duchess de Polignac was the last person to have had any influence in matters of state, whatever might have been the case with those who surrounded her. She was devoid of ambition or capacity to give her weight; and the Queen was not so pliant in points of high import as to allow herself to be governed or overruled, unless her mind was thoroughly convinced. In that respect, she was something like Catharine II., who always distinguished her favorites from her ministers; but in the present case she had no choice, and was under the necessity of yielding to the boisterous voice of a faction.

"From this epoch, I saw all the persons who had any wish to communicate with the Queen on matters relative to the public business, and Her Majesty was generally present when they came, and received them in my apartments. The Duchess de Polignac never, to my knowledge, entered into any of these state questions; yet there was no promotion in the civil, military, or ministerial department, which she has not been charged with having influenced the Queen to make, though there were few of them who were not nominated by the King and his ministers, even unknown to the Queen herself.

"The prevailing dissatisfaction against Her Majesty and the favorite Polignac now began to take so many forms, and produce effects so dreadful, as to wring her own feelings, as well as those of her royal mistress, with the most intense anguish. Let me mention one gross and barbarous instance in proof of what I say.

"After the birth of the Queen's second son, the Duke of Normandy, who was afterward Dauphin, the Duke and Duchess of Harcourt, outrageously jealous of the ascendancy of the governess of the Dauphin, excited the young prince's hatred toward Madame de Polignac to such a pitch that he would take nothing from her hands, but often, young as he was at the time, order her out of the apartment, and treat her remonstrances with the utmost contempt. The Duchess bitterly complained of the Harcourts to the Queen; for she really sacrificed the whole of her time to the care and attention required by this young prince, and she did so from sincere attachment, and that he might not be irritated in his declining state of health. The Queen was deeply hurt at these dissensions between the governor and governess. Her Majesty endeavored to pacify the mind of the young prince, by literally making herself a slave to his childish caprices, which in all probability would have created the confidence so desired, when a most cruel, unnatural, I may say diabolical, report prevailed, to alienate the child's affections even from his mother, in making him believe that, owing to his deformity and growing ugliness, she had transferred all her tenderness to his younger brother, who certainly was very superior in health and beauty to the puny Dauphin. Making a pretext of this calumny, the governor of the heir apparent was malicious enough to prohibit him from eating or drinking anything but what first passed through the hands of his physicians; and so strong was the impression made by this interdict on the mind of the young Dauphin that he never after saw the Queen but with the greatest terror. The feelings of his disconsolate parent may be more readily conceived than described. So may the mortification of his governess, the Duchess de Polignac, herself so tender, so affectionate a mother. Fortunately for himself, and happily for his wretched parents, this royal youth, whose life, though short, had been so full of suffering, died at Versailles on the 4th of June, 1789, and, though only between seven and eight years of age at the time of his decease, he had given proofs of intellectual precocity, which would probably have made continued life, amid the scenes of wretchedness which succeeded, anything to him but a blessing.

"The cabals of the Duke of Harcourt, to which I have just adverted, against the Duchess de Polignac, were the mere result of foul malice and ambition. Harcourt wished to get his wife, who was the sworn enemy of Polignac, created governess to the Dauphin instead of the Queen's favorite. Most of the criminal stories against the Duchess de Polignac, and which did equal injury to the Queen, were fabricated by the Harcourts, for the purpose of excluding their rival from her situation.

"Barnave, meanwhile, continued faithful to his liberal principles, but equally faithful to his desire of bringing Their Majesties over to those principles, and making them republican sovereigns. He lost no opportunity of availing himself of my permission for him to call whenever he chose on public business; and he continued to urge the same points, upon which he had before been so much in earnest, although with no better effect. Both the King and Queen looked with suspicion upon Barnave, and with still more suspicion upon his politics.

"The next time I received him, 'Madam,' exclaimed the deputy to me, 'since our last interview I have pondered well on the situation of the King; and, as an honest Frenchman, attached to my lawful sovereign, and anxious for his future prosperous reign, I am decidedly of opinion that his own safety, as well as the dignity of the crown of France, and the happiness of his subjects, can only be secured by his giving his country a constitution, which will at once place his establishment beyond the caprice and the tyranny of corrupt administrations, and secure hereafter the first monarchy in Europe from the possibility of sinking under weak princes, by whom the royal splendor of France has too often been debased into the mere tool of vicious and mercenary *noblesse*, and sycophantic courtiers. A King, protected by a constitution, can do no wrong. He is unshackled with responsibility.

He is empowered with the comfort of exercising the executive authority for the benefit of the nation, while all the harsher duties, and all the censures they create, devolve on others. It is, therefore, madam, through your means, and the well-known friendship you have ever evinced for the Royal Family and the general welfare of the French nation, that I wish to obtain a private audience of Her Majesty, the Queen, in order to induce her to exert the never-failing ascendancy she has ever possessed over the mind of our good King, in persuading him to the sacrifice of a small proportion of his power, for the sake of preserving the monarchy to his heirs; and posterity will record the virtues of a prince who has been magnanimous enough, of his own free will, to resign the unlawful part of his prerogatives, usurped by his predecessors, for the blessing and pleasure of giving liberty to a beloved people, among whom both the King and Queen will find many Hampdens and Sidneys, but very few Cromwells. Besides, madam, we must make a merit of necessity. The times are pregnant with events, and it is more prudent to support the palladium of the ancient monarchy than risk its total overthrow; and fall it must, if the diseased excrescences, of which the people complain, and which threaten to carry death into the very heart of the tree, be not lopped away in time by the sovereign himself.'

"I heard the deputy with the greatest attention. I promised to fulfill his commission. The better to execute my task, I retired the moment he left me, and wrote down all I could recollect of his discourse, that it might be thoroughly placed before the Queen the first opportunity.

"When I communicated the conversation to Her Majesty, she listened with the most gracious condescension, till I came to the part wherein Barnave so forcibly impressed the necessity of adopting a constitutional monarchy. Here, as she had done once before, when I repeated some former observations of Barnave to her, Maria Antoinette somewhat lost her equanimity. She rose from her seat. and exclaimed:

" 'What! is an absolute prince, and the hereditary sovereign of the ancient monarchy of France, to become the tool of a plebeian faction, who will, their point once gained, dethrone him for his imbecile complaisance? Do they wish to imitate the English Revolution of 1648, and reproduce the sanguinary times of the unfortunate and weak Charles the First? To make France a commonwealth! Well! be it so! But before I advise the King to such a step, or give my consent to it, they shall bury me under the ruins of the monarchy.'

" 'But what answer,' said I, 'does Your Majesty wish me to return to the deputy's request for a private audience?'

" 'What answer?' exclaimed the Queen. 'No answer at all is the best answer to such a presumptuous proposition! I tremble for the consequences of the impression their disloyal maneuvers have made upon the minds of the people, and I have no faith whatever in their proffered services to the King. However, on reflection, it may be expedient to temporize. Continue to see him. Learn, if possible, how far he may be trusted; but do not fix any time, as yet, for the desired audience. I wish to apprise the King, first, of his interview with you, Princess. This conversation does not agree with what he and Mirabeau proposed about the King's recovering his prerogatives. Are these the prerogatives with which he flattered the King? Binding him hand and foot, and excluding him from every privilege, and then casting him a helpless dependant on the caprice of a volatile plebeian faction! The French nation is very different from the English. The first rules of the established ancient order of the government broken through, they will violate twenty others, and the King will be sacrificed, before this frivolous people again organize themselves with any sort of regular government.'

" Agreeably to Her Majesty's commands, I continued to see Barnave. I communicated with him by letter,* at his private lodgings at Passy, and at Vitry; but it

* Of these letters I was generally the bearer.

was long before the Queen could be brought to consent to the audience he solicited.

"Indeed Her Majesty had such an aversion to all who had declared themselves for any innovation upon the existing power of the monarchy, that she was very reluctant to give audience upon the subject to any person, not even excepting the Princes of the blood. The Count d'Artois himself, leaning as he did to the popular side, had ceased to be welcome. Expressions he had made use of, concerning the necessity for some change, had occasioned the coolness, which was already of considerable standing.

"One day the Prince of Conti came to me, to complain of the Queen's refusing to receive him, because he had expressed himself to the same effect as had the Count d'Artois on the subject of the *Tiers États.**

---

* I recollect that day perfectly. I was copying some letters for the Princess Lamballe, when the Prince of Conti came in. The Prince lived not only to see, but to feel the errors of his system. He attained a great age. He outlived the glory of his country. Like many others, the first gleam of political regeneration led him into a system, which drove him out of France, to implore the shelter of a foreign asylum, that he might not fall a victim to his own credulity. I had an opportunity of witnessing in his latter days his sincere repentance; and to this it is fit that I should bear testimony. There were no bounds to the execration with which he expressed himself toward the murderers of those victims, whose death he lamented with a bitterness, in which some remorse was mingled, from the impression that his own early errors in favor of the Revolution had unintentionally accelerated their untimely end. This was a source to him of deep and perpetual self-reproach.

There was an eccentricity in the appearance, dress, and manners of the Prince of Conti, which well deserves recording.

He wore, to the very last — and it was in Barcelona, so late as 1803, that I last had the honor of conversing with him — a white rich stuff dress frock coat, of the cut and fashion of Louis XIV. which, being without any collar, had buttons and buttonholes from the neck to the bottom of the skirt, and was padded and stiffened with buckram. The cuffs were very large, of a different color, and turned up to the elbows. The whole was lined with white satin, which, from its being very much moth-eaten, appeared as if it had been dotted on purpose to show the buckram between the satin lining. His waistcoat was of rich green striped silk, bound with gold lace; the buttons and buttonholes of gold; the flaps very large, and completely covering his small clothes; which happened very

" 'And does your highness,' replied I, 'imagine that the Queen is less displeased with the conduct of the Count d'Artois on that head, than she is with you, Prince? I can assure your highness, that at this moment there subsists a very great degree of coolness between Her Majesty and her royal brother-in-law, whom she loves as if he were her own brother. Though she makes every allowance for his political inexperience, and well knows the goodness of his heart and the rectitude of his intentions, yet policy will not permit her to change her sentiments.'

" 'That may be,' said the Prince, 'but while Her Majesty continues to honor with her royal presence the Duchess de Polignac, whose friends, as well as herself, are all enthusiastically mad in favor of the constitutional system, she shows an undue partiality, by countenancing one branch of the party and not the other; particularly so, as the great and notorious leader of the opposition, which the Queen frowns upon, is the sister-in-law of this very Duchess de Polignac, and the avowed favorite of the Count d'Artois, by whom, and the councils of the Palais Royal, he is supposed to be totally governed in his political career.'

" 'The Queen,' replied I, 'is certainly her own mis-

àpropos, for they scarcely reached his knees, over which he wore large striped silk stockings, that came halfway up his thighs. His shoes had high heels, and reached halfway up his legs; the buckles were small, and set round with paste. A very narrow stiff stock decorated his neck. He carried a hat, with a white feather on the inside, under his arm. His ruffles were of very handsome point lace. His few gray hairs were gathered in a little round bag. The wig alone was wanting to make him a thorough picture of the polished age of the founder of Versailles and Marly.

He had all that princely politeness of manner which so eminently distinguished the old school of French nobility, previous to the Revolution. He was the thorough gentleman, a character by no means so readily to be met with in these days of refinement as one would imagine. He never addressed the softer sex but with ease and elegance, and admiration of their persons.

Could Louis XIV. have believed, had it been told to him when he placed this branch of the Bourbons on the throne of Iberia, that it would one day refuse to give shelter at the Court of Madrid to one of his family, for fear of offending a Corsican usurper!

tress. She sees, I believe, many persons more from habit than any other motive; to which, your highness is aware, many princes often make sacrifices. Your highness cannot suppose I can have the temerity to control Her Majesty in the selection of her friends, or in her sentiments respecting them.'

"'No,' exclaimed the Prince, 'I imagine not. But she might just as well see any of us; for we are no more enemies of the crown than the party she is cherishing by constantly appearing among them; which, according to her avowed maxims concerning the not sanctioning any but supporters of the absolute monarchy, is in direct opposition to her own sentiments.'

"'Who,' continued his highness, 'caused that infernal comedy, "The Marriage of Figaro," to be brought out, but the party of the Duchess de Polignac?* The play is a *critique* on the whole Royal Family, from the drawing up of the curtain to its fall. It burlesques the ways and manners of every individual connected with the Court of Versailles. Not a scene but touches some of their characters. Are not the Queen herself and the Count d'Artois lampooned and caricatured in the garden scenes, and the most slanderous ridicule cast upon their innocent evening walks on the terrace? Does not Beaumarchais plainly show in it, to every impartial eye, the means which the Countess Diana has taken publicly to demonstrate her jealousy of the Queen's ascendancy over the Count d'Artois? Is it not from the same sentiment that she has roused the jealousy of the Countess d'Artois against Her Majesty?'

*Note of the Princess Lamballe. — The Prince of Conti never could speak of Beaumarchais but with the greatest contempt. There was something personal in this exasperation. Beaumarchais had satirized the Prince. "The Spanish Barber" was founded on a circumstance which happened at a country house between Conti and a young lady, during the reign of Louis XV., when intrigues of every kind were practiced and almost sanctioned. The poet has exposed the Prince by making him the Doctor Bartolo of his play. The affair which supplied the story was hushed up at Court, and the Prince was only punished by the loss of his mistress, who became the wife of another.

"'All these circumstances,' observed I, 'the King prudently foresaw when he read the manuscript, and caused it to be read to the Queen, to convince her of the nature of its characters and the dangerous tendency likely to arise from its performance. Of this your highness is aware. It is not for me to apprise you that, to avert the excitement inevitable from its being brought upon the stage, and under a thorough conviction of the mischief it would produce in turning the minds of the people against the Queen, His Majesty solemnly declared that the comedy should not be performed in Paris; and that he would never sanction its being brought before the public on any stage in France.'

"'Bah! bah! madam!' exclaimed Conti. 'The Queen has acted like a child in this affair, as in many others. In defiance of His Majesty's determination, did not the Queen herself, through the fatal influence of her favorite, whose party wearied her out by continued importunities, cause the King to revoke his express mandate? And what has been the consequence of Her Majesty's ungovernable partiality for these Polignacs?'

"'You know, Prince,' said I, 'better than I do.'

"'The proofs of its bad consequences,' pursued his highness, 'are more strongly verified than ever by your own withdrawing from the Queen's parties since her unreserved acknowledgment of her partiality (fatal partiality!) for those who will be her ruin; for they are her worst enemies.'

"'Pardon me, Prince,' answered I, 'I have not withdrawn myself from the Queen, but from the new parties with whose politics I cannot identify myself, besides some exceptions I have taken against those who frequent them.'

"'Bah! bah!' exclaimed Conti, 'your sagacity has got the better of your curiosity. All the wit and humor of that traitor Beaumarchais never seduced you to cultivate his society, as all the rest of the Queen's party have done.'

"'I never knew him to be accused of treason.'

"'Why, what do you call a fellow, who sent arms to the Americans before the war was declared, without his sovereign's consent?'

"'In that affair, I consider the ministers as criminal as himself; for the Queen, to this day, believes that Beaumarchais was sanctioned by them; and, you know, Her Majesty has ever since had an insuperable dislike to both De Manrepas and De Vergennes. But I have nothing to do with these things.'

"'Yes, yes, I understand you, Princess. Let her romp and play with the *compate vous*,* but who will *compatire*† (make allowance for) her folly. Bah! bah! bah! She is inconsistent, Princess. Not that I mean by this to insinuate that the Duchess is not the sincere friend and wellwisher of the Queen. Her immediate existence, her interest, and that of her family, are all dependent on the royal bounty. But can the Duchess answer for the same sincerity toward the Queen, with respect to her innumerable guests? No! Are not the sentiments of the Duchess's sister-in-law, the Countess Diana, in direct opposition to the absolute monarchy? Has she not always been an enthusiastic advocate for all those that have supported the American war? Who was it that crowned, at a public assembly, the democratical straight hairs of Dr. Franklin? Why the same Madame Countess Diana! Who was *capa turpa* in applauding the men who were framing the American constitution at Paris? Madame Countess Diana! Who was it, in like manner, that opposed all the Queen's arguments against the political conduct of France and Spain, relative to the war with England, in favor of the American Independence? The Countess Diana! Not for the love of that rising nation, or for the sacred cause of liberty; but from a taste for notoriety, a spirit of envy and jealousy, an apprehension lest the personal charms of the Queen might rob her of a part of those affections, which she herself exclusively hoped to alienate from that

*A kind of game of forfeits, introduced for the diversion of the royal children and those of the Duchess de Polignac.

† This play upon the words is untranslatable.

abortion, the Countess d'Artois, in whose service she is maid of honor, and handmaid to the Count. My dear Princess, these are facts proved. Beaumarchais has delineated them all. Why, then, refuse to see me? Why withdraw her former confidence from the Count d'Artois, when she lives in the society which promulgates anti-monarchical principles? These are sad evidences of Her Majesty's inconsistency. She might as well see the Duke of Orleans'——

"Here my feelings overwhelmed me. I could contain myself no longer. The tears gushed from my eyes.

"'Oh, Prince!' exclaimed I, in a bitter agony of grief — 'Oh, Prince! touch not that fatal string. For how many years has he not caused these briny tears of mine to flow from my burning eyes! The scalding drops have nearly parched up the spring of life!'"

CHAPTER XIII.

"THE dismissal of M. Necker irritated the people beyond description. They looked upon themselves
as insulted in their favorite. Mob succeeded mob,
each more mischievous and daring than the former. The
Duke of Orleans continued busy in his work of secret destruction. In one of the popular risings, a saber struck
his bust, and its head fell, severed from its body. Many
of the rioters (for the ignorant are always superstitious)
shrunk back at this omen of evil to their idol. His real
friends endeavored to deduce a salutary warning to him
from the circumstance. I was by when the Duke de
Penthièvre told him, in the presence of his daughter,
that he might look upon this accident as prophetic of the
fate of his own head, as well as the ruin of his family,
if he persisted. He made no answer, but left the room.

"On the 14th of July, and two or three days preceding, the commotions took a definite object. The destruction of the Bastille was the point proposed, and it
was achieved. Arms were obtained from the old pensioners at the Hotel des Invalides. Fifty thousand livres

were distributed among the chiefs of those who influenced the Invalides to give up the arms.

"The massacre of the Marquis de Launay, commandant of the place, and of M. de Flesselles, and the fall of the citadel itself, were the consequence.

"Her Majesty was greatly affected when she heard of the murder of these officers and the taking of the Bastille. She frequently told me that the horrid circumstance originated in a diabolical Court intrigue, but never explained the particulars of the intrigue. She declared that both the officers and the citadel might have been saved had not the King's orders for the march of the troops from Versailles and the environs of Paris, been disobeyed. She blamed the precipitation of De Launay in ordering up the drawbridge and directing the few troops on it to fire upon the people. 'There,' she added, 'the Marquis committed himself; as, in case of not succeeding, he could have no retreat, which every commander should take care to secure, before he allows the commencement of a general attack.'*

"The death of the Dauphin; the horrible Revolution of the 14th of July; the troubles about Necker; the insults and threats offered to the Count d'Artois and her-

---

* Certainly, the French Revolution may date its epoch as far back as the taking of the Bastille; from that moment the troubles progressively continued, till the final extirpation of its illustrious victims.

I was just returning from a mission to England when the storms began to threaten not only the most violent effects to France itself, but to all the land which was not divided from it by the watery element. The spirit of liberty, as the vine, which produces the most luxurious fruit, when abused becomes the most pernicious poison, was stalking abroad and reveling in blood and massacre. I myself was a witness to the enthusiastic national ball given on the ruins of the Bastille, while it was still stained and reeking with the hot blood of its late keeper, whose head I saw carried in triumph. Such was the effect on me that the Princess Lamballe asked me if I had known the Marquis de Launay. I answered in the negative; but told her from the knowledge I had of the English Revolution, I was fearful of a result similar to what followed the fall of the heads of Buckingham and Stafford. The Princess mentioning my observation to the Duke de Penthièvre, they both burst into tears.

self; overwhelmed the Queen with the most poignant grief.

"She was most desirous of some understanding being established between the government and the representatives of the people, which she urged upon the King the expendiency of personally attempting.

"The King, therefore, at her reiterated remonstrances and requests, presented himself, on the following day, with his brothers, to the national assembly, to assure them of his firm determination to support the measures of the deputies, in everything conducive to the general good of his subjects. As a proof of his intentions, he said he had commanded the troops to leave Paris and Versailles.

"The King left the assembly, as he had gone thither, on foot, amid the vociferations of '*Vive le roi !*' and it was only through the enthusiasm of the deputies, who thus hailed His Majesty, and followed him in crowds to the palace, that the Count d'Artois escaped the fury of an outrageous mob.

"The people filled every avenue of the palace, which vibrated with cries for the King, the Queen, and the Dauphin to show themselves at the balcony.

"'Send for the Duchess de Polignac to bring the royal children,' cried I to Her Majesty.

"'Not for the world!' exclaimed the Queen. 'She will be assassinated, and my children too, if she make her appearance before this infuriate mob. Let Madame and the Dauphin be brought unaccompanied.'

"The Queen, on this occasion, imitated her imperial mother, Maria Theresa. She took the Dauphin in her arms, and Madame by her side, as that empress had done when she presented herself to the Hungarian magnates; but the reception here was very different. It was not *moriamur pro nostra reginâ*. Not that they were ill received; but the furious party of the Duke of Orleans often interrupted the cries of '*Vive le roi ! Vive la reine !*' etc., with those of '*Vive la nation ! Vive d'Orleans !*' and many severe remarks on the family of the Polignacs, which proved that the Queen's caution on this occasion was exceedingly well judged.

"Not to wound the feelings of the Duchess de Polignac, I kept myself at a distance behind the Queen; but I was loudly called for by the mobility, and, *malgrè moi*, was obliged, at the King and Queen's request, to come forward.

"As I approached the balcony, I perceived one of the well-known agents of the Duke of Orleans, whom I had noticed some time before in the throng, menacing me, the moment I made my appearance, with his upreared hand in fury. I was greatly terrified, but suppressed my agitation, and saluted the populace; but, fearful of exhibiting my weakness in sight of the wretch who had alarmed me, withdrew instantly, and had no sooner re-entered than I sunk motionless in the arms of one of the attendants. Luckily, this did not take place till I left the balcony. Had it been otherwise, the triumph to my declared enemies would have been too great.*

"Recovering, I found myself surrounded by the Royal Family, who were all kindness and concern for my situation; but I could not subdue my tremor and affright. The horrid image of that monster seemed still to threaten me.

"'Come, come!' said the King, 'be not alarmed. I shall order a council of all the ministers and deputies to-morrow, who will soon put an end to these riots!'†

"We were ere long joined by the Prince de Condé, the Duke de Bourbon, and others, who implored the King not to part with the army, but to place himself, with all the Princes of the blood, at its head, as the only means to restore tranquillity to the country, and secure his own safety.

---

*Heavens! who could have been that angel's enemy!

†Poor, deluded Prince! How often do we confound our wishes with the logic of circumstances! The horrid riots that succeeded have been so often described as to render it unnecessary to supply the *hiatus* of this journal by repeating the afflicting scenes which were the consequence.

"The Queen was decidedly of the same opinion; and added, that if the army were to depart the King and his family ought to go with it; but the King, on the contrary, said he would not decide upon any measures whatever till he had heard the opinion of the council.

"The Queen, notwithstanding the King's indecision, was occupied, during the rest of the day and the whole of the night, in preparing for her intended journey, as she hoped to persuade the King to follow the advice of the Princes, and not wait the result of the next day's deliberation. Nay, so desirous was she of this, that she threw herself on her knees to the King, imploring him to leave Versailles and head the army, and offering to accompany him herself, on horseback, in uniform; but it was like speaking to a corpse: he never answered.

"The Duchess de Polignac came to Her Majesty in a state of the greatest agitation, in consequence of M. de Chinon having just apprised her that a most malicious report had been secretly spread among the deputies at Versailles that they were all to be blown up at their next meeting.

"The Queen was as much surprised as the Duchess, and scarcely less agitated. These wretched friends could only, in silence, compare notes of their mutual cruel misfortunes. Both for a time remained speechless at this new calamity. Surely this was not wanting to be added to those by which the Queen was already so bitterly oppressed.

"I was sent for by Her Majesty. Count Fersen accompanied me. He had just communicated to me what the Duchess had already repeated from M. Chinon to the Queen.

"The rumor had been set afloat merely as a new pretext for the continuation of the riots.

"The communication of the report, so likely to produce a disastrous effect, took place while the King was with his ministers deliberating whether he should go to Paris, or save himself and family by joining the army.

"His Majesty was called from the council to the Queen's apartment, and was there made acquainted with the circumstance which had so awakened the terror of the royal party. He calmly replied, 'It is some days since this invention has been spread among the deputies; I was aware of it from the first; but from its being utterly impossible to be listened to for a moment by anyone, I did not wish to afflict you by the mention of an impotent fabrication, which I myself treated with the contempt it justly merited. Nevertheless, I did not forget, yesterday, in the presence of both my brothers, who accompanied me to the national assembly, there to exculpate myself from an imputation at which my nature revolts; and, from the manner in which it was received, I flatter myself that every honest Frenchman was fully satisfied that my religion will ever be an insurmountable barrier against my harboring sentiments allied in the slightest degree to such actions.'

"The King embraced the Queen, begged she would tranquilize herself, calmed the fears of the two ladies, thanked the gentlemen for the interest they took in his favor, and returned to the council, who, in his absence, had determined on his going to the Hotel de Ville at Paris, suggesting at the same time the names of several persons likely to be well received, if His Majesty thought proper to allow of their accompanying him.

"During this interval, the Queen, still flattering herself that she should pursue her wished-for journey, ordered the carriages to be prepared and sent off to Rambouillet, where she said she should sleep; but this Her Majesty only stated for the purpose of distracting the attention of her pages and others about her from her real purpose. As it was well known that M. de St. Priest had pointed out Rambouillet as a fit asylum from the mob, she fancied that an understanding on the part of her suite that they were to halt there, and prepare for her reception, would protect her project of proceeding much further.

"When the council had broken up and the King returned, he said to the Queen, 'It is decided.'

" 'To go, I hope ?' said Her Majesty.

" 'No'—(though in appearance calm, the words remained on the lips of the King, and he stood for some moments incapable of utterance; but, recovering, added) —'To Paris!'

"The Queen, at the word Paris, became frantic. She flung herself wildly into the arms of her friends. '*Nous sommes perdus ! nous sommes perdus !*' cried she, in a passion of tears. But her dread was not for herself. She felt only for the danger to which the King was now going to expose himself; and she flew to him, and hung on his neck.

" 'And what,' exclaimed she, 'is to become of all our faithful friends and attendants!'

" 'I advise them all,' answered His Majesty, 'to make the best of their way out of France; and that as soon as possible.'

"By this time, the apartments of the Queen were filled with the attendants and the royal children, anxiously expecting every moment to receive the Queen's command to proceed on their journey, but they were all ordered to retire to whence they came.

"The scene was that of a real tragedy. Nothing broke the silence but groans of the deepest affliction. Our consternation at the counter order cast all into a state of stupefied insensibility.

"The Queen was the only one whose fortitude bore her up proudly under this weight of misfortunes. Recovering from the frenzy of the first impression, she adjured her friends, by the love and obedience they had ever shown her and the King, to prepare immediately to fulfill his mandate and make themselves ready for the cruel separation!

"The Duchess de Polignac and myself were, for some hours, in a state of agony and delirium.

"When the Queen saw the bodyguards drawn up to accompany the King's departure, she ran to the window, threw apart the sash, and was going to speak to them, to recommend the King to their care; but the Count de Fersen prevented it.

"'For God's sake, madam,' exclaimed he, 'do not commit yourself to the suspicion of having any doubts of the people!'

"When the King entered to take leave of her, and of all his most faithful attendants, he could only articulate, 'Adieu!' But when the Queen saw him accompanied by the Count d'Estaing and others, whom, from their new principles, she knew to be popular favorites, she had command enough of herself not to shed a tear in their presence.

"No sooner, however, had the King left the room than it was as much as the Count de Fersen, Princess Elizabeth, and all of us could do to recover her from the most violent convulsions. At last, coming to herself, she retired with the Princess, the Duchess, and myself to await the King's return; at the same time requesting the Count de Fersen to follow His Majesty to the Hotel de Ville. Again and again she implored the Count, as she went, in case the King should be detained, to interest himself with all the foreign ministers to interpose for his liberation.

"Versailles, when the King was gone, seemed like a city deserted in consequence of the plague. The palace was completely abandoned. All the attendants were dispersed. No one was seen in the streets. Terror prevailed. It was universally believed that the King would be detained in Paris. The high road from Versailles to Paris was crowded with all ranks of people, as if to catch a last look of their sovereign.

"The Count de Fersen set off instantly, pursuant to the Queen's desire. He saw all that passed, and on his return related to me the history of that horrid day.

"He arrived at Paris just in time to see His Majesty take the national cockade from M. Bailly and place it in his hat. He felt the Hotel de Ville shake with the long-continued cries of ' *Vive le roi!* ' in consequence, which so affected the King that, for some moments, he was unable to express himself. 'I myself,' added the Count, 'was so moved at the effect on His Majesty, in being thus warmly received by his Parisian subjects, which portrayed the paternal emotions of his long-lacerated heart, that every other feeling was paralyzed for a moment, in exultation at the apparent unanimity between the sovereign and his people. But it did not,' continued the ambassador, 'paralyze the artful tongue of Bailly, the mayor of Paris. I could have kicked the fellow for his malignant impudence; for, even in the cunning compliment he framed, he studied to humble the afflicted monarch by telling the people it was to them he owed the sovereign authority.'

"'But,' pursued the Count, 'considering the situation of Louis XVI. and that of his family, agonized as they must have been during his absence, from the Queen's impression that the Parisians would never again allow him to see Versailles, how great was our rapture when we saw him safely replaced in his carriage, and returning to those who were still lamenting him as lost!'

"'When I left Her Majesty in the morning, she was nearly in a state of mental aberration. When I saw her again in the evening, the King by her side, surrounded by her family, the Princess Elizabeth, and yourself, madam,' said the kind Count, 'she appeared to me like a person risen from the dead and restored to life. Her excess of joy at the first moment was beyond description.'

"Count de Fersen might well say THE FIRST MOMENT, for the pleasure of the Queen was of short duration. Her heart was doomed to bleed afresh, when the thrill of delight, at what she considered the ESCAPE of her husband, was past, for she had already seen her chosen friend, the Duchess de Polignac, for the last time.*

* The LAST, indeed! Little did the Princess Lamballe, when she wrote, conceive the full and prophetic extent of her phrase. At that time the Duchess was still living; but a little more than three years afterward, the Queen, the Princess Lamballe, and the Duchess herself had all perished by untimely death.

The manner of the death of the Duchess speaks friendship — rare, indeed, except in poets' fancies! She was residing at the palace of the Prince Esterhazy, having been fortunate enough to escape from the torrent of blood then bursting over this horrid country, when informed that

"Her Majesty was but just recovered from the effects of the morning's agitation, when the Duchess, the Duke, his sister, and all his family set off. It was impossible for her to take leave of her friend. The hour was late — about midnight. At the same time departed the Count d'Artois and his family, the Prince of Condé and his, the Prince of Hesse d'Armstadt, and all those who were likely to be suspected by the people.

"Her Majesty desired the Count de Fersen to see the Duchess in her name. When the King heard the request, he exclaimed:

"'What a cruel state for sovereigns, my dear Count! To be compelled to separate ourselves from our most faithful attendants, and not be allowed, for fear of compromising others or our own lives, to take a last farewell!'

"'Ah!' said the Queen, 'I fear so too. I fear it is a last farewell to all our friends!'

"The Count saw the Duchess a few moments before she left Versailles. Pisani, the Venetian ambassador, and Count Fersen, helped her on the coach box, where she rode disguised.

"What must have been most poignantly mortifying to the fallen favorite was, that, in the course of her journey, she met with her greatest enemy, Necker, who was returning, triumphant, to Paris, called by the voice of that very nation by whom she and her family were now forced from its territory: Necker, who himself conceived that she, who now went by him into exile, while he himself returned to the greatest of victories, had thwarted all his former plans of operation, and, from her influence over the Queen, had caused his dismission and temporary banishment.

"For my own part, I cannot but consider this sudden desertion of France by those nearest the throne as ill-

her friend and sovereign had been beheaded. Though so long prepared, by previous events and previous murders of the Royal Family, for this fatal news, so great was the shock to her that she gave but one shriek and expired!

judged. Had all the Royal Family remained, is it likely that the King and Queen would have been watched with such despotic vigilance? Would not confidence have created confidence, and the breach have been less wide between the King and his people?

"When the father and his family will now be thoroughly reconciled, Heaven alone can tell!"

NOTE.

I CANNOT allow this portion of the Journal of the Princess Lamballe to pass from under my hands without offering a few observations upon the intimacy, of which we have now seen the disastrous *dénouement*, between Her Majesty and the Duchess de Polignac. It will not, I trust be deemed impertinent in me to enlarge a little upon a circumstance so important in its effects upon the Queen's character with the nation, and so instrumental in producing the Revolution itself. I must be understood as substantially describing the impressions of her highness upon these subjects, confirmed by my own observation.

To this intimacy of the Queen with the governess of her children may be referred the first direct blows at the royal dignity. It is a fact which cannot be denied, that however Maria Antoinette might have been beset by partial animadversions, the crown had never yet been shorn of its prerogatives, nor had any attempt been made upon them by democratic innovations, until the period of Her Majesty's connection with the family of the Polignacs. The spirit of national independence certainly made rapid strides from the moment of the arrival of the military from America. The enthusiasm with which all ranks hailed the return of La Fayette no doubt promulgated the dangerous overthrow of absolute monarchy; but a constitutional one would have been firmly established, had not the primitive steps toward it met with a total opposition, while the Queen herself encouraged the very system against which she protested, by being herself the first innovator, in abolishing the old customs of the Court, and placing the provincial family of the new raised nobility of the Polignacs in the situations of those who, from their ancient stem, considered themselves the exclusive palladium of absolute monarchy. The most powerful in the kingdom became, from that time, indifferent to the King, who showed so little hesitation in weakening his own authority, by humbling the old aristocracy for a new race with no quarterings beyond their own, but that of favoritism. By remaining neutral, when a strong party was forging its thunderbolts, they left the throne exposed. Their united movement might have interposed a shield, which their disgust influenced them not even to attempt to rear. It is therefore evident how hostile the very heart of the Court must have been to the power of a Queen who valued merit above birth. These selfish and short-sighted censors did not consider that the grave they were digging for their royal mistress would be filled up by themselves, and that every blow leveled at Her Majesty or her favorites shook the throne itself.

It may be said that Maria Antoinette should have steadfastly avoided the dangers that threatened the monarchy; yet when it is considered how much she relied upon the authority of the Abbé Vermond to check, correct, and counsel her inexperience, an authority so often fatal in its silence, her errors will be readily pardoned. They alone, who had the power of preventing them, should bear the whole weight of the censure resulting from the consequences of their unpardonable apathy; and she will then appear in the eyes of an impartial world, less guilty than her sworn enemies have endeavored hitherto to represent her. In justice to the Abbé it must be owned that he attempted to check the evil; but never till it had taken too deep a root. He should have PREVENTED the extreme intimacy; he knew the character of his royal pupil well enough to be aware, that, once formed, she would have conceived herself to be betraying a want of steadiness in her friendship to have retracted any of the purposes to which it gave the impulse.

The Duke of Dorset and Count Fersen were perhaps the only persons who could have taken the liberty of counseling Her Majesty at this crisis, without their motives being exposed to misconstruction. Though they both were of the parties that constantly attended the drawing-room of the Duchess, and esteemed her and her family as private individuals, yet they, as well as many other of the Queen's friends, were fully persuaded that the vindictive spirit of all those who became jealous of her intimacy, and the higher orders of the nobility, who would not condescend to be put on a level with the new raised favorite, besides the other party whom she had been the means of excluding from a distinction which they deemed their due, formed a host of disaffected persons, ready to strike at the heart of those who caused their protracted humiliation.

Crosses and ribbons are necessary in a monarchical government, and most essentially so in that of an absolute despotic one, as, in many cases, they enable the sovereign to pay debts without money; for the cross never crosses the king's treasury, nor is the ribbon taken from his purse strings. No provision of any consequence being added to the baubles, many a dirty crossing is trodden under foot, and many a ribbon tarnished by the rain, before the knight who wears it arrives at the palace gate, to get his shoes blacked by the Court shoeblack. But nothing weakens the sovereign power more than the superfluous aristocracy. Queen Elizabeth was so fully persuaded of this that she was the least lavish in that way of any sovereign that ever reigned. Perhaps to that very wisdom alone she owed the continuation of her unlimited power and masculine strength of government. She knew that energies must be weakened by being scattered.

A sovereign who creates a numerous aristocracy commits two substantial errors. First, he lessens his own dignity. Secondly, he alienates the affections of the bulk of his subjects. Every lord has his followers. This necessarily reduces the direct influence of the crown. What were even absolute sovereigns under the feudal system? — subservient to their barons! so are they since to the aristocracy. The only difference produced by the difference of the ages is that a sovereign now has an army at his own command. But that army forms the smallest part of his subjects. True, they owe their allegiance exclusively to their sovereign. So ought the sovereign to prefer the majority of his people to a circumscribed number, who very often have little more merit than that of their birth, and who constitute the least respectable part of the community. Besides, the aristocracy which has no means of self support is a degradation to the institution, lessens its consequence, and subjects its members to the discretion of its inferiors, who, instead of being respected, often become the ridicule of their own domestics, from the daily shifts resorted to in their economy, to support an empty title; and fall into the power of their own tradesmen, and far below the level of wealthy merchants. The titled gentry, who are obliged to walk on foot for the want of the means of supporting a carriage, are, vulgarly speaking, like a pudding without eggs, and cannot rise above the level.

This vicious condescension, and, I may say, abuse of the royal power, was one of the many causes of the French Revolution. It was, if I may be allowed the expression, principally that supernumerous plebeian aristocracy, who, jealous of the exclusive prerogatives of the higher classes of nobility, and wishing to humble them and share their immunities, shook the fabric to its foundation, were crushed themselves by its fall, and with it buried the monarchy under the ruins of the nation!

It is only necessary, in proof of the sound policy of this principle respecting the influence of an overflow of the hungry aristocracy, to refer to the primitive factions of the Revolution. These will demonstrate how very few of the ancient nobility were implicated in exciting attacks upon the royal authority, in comparison with the second orders. ONE only maintained, for a short time, a degree of purchased popularity for a change; and he wished only for a change of dynasty, which his father before him had vainly sought to establish in his own family; but the vices of the debauched Court of Louis XV.'s minority were by far too deeply implanted and paramount to excite any serious apprehension of a new order of things; because the very vices of the existing government established its authority; everything was in character; corruption was at its zenith in every branch of the administration; but when, in the Court of Louis XVI. virtue was feebly blended and interwoven with the old-established vices, the former not vigorously enough enforced to support itself and the latter weakened by contrast, when the two came in contact, the sovereign power was seen to fall — as the rogue who turns honest loses his character even as a rogue, and never can acquire that of an honest man. Hence it is clear that half measures are the worst of measures, and sure to work their own ruin.

To attempt to reform a Court without radically reforming the courtiers was, therefore, an absurdity; the proof of which has been written, in France, in characters of blood.

CHAPTER XIV.

"BARNAVE often lamented his having been betrayed, by
a love of notoriety, into many schemes, of which
his impetuosity blinded him to the consequences.
With tears in his eyes, he implored me to impress the
Queen's mind with the sad truths he inculcated. He said
his motives had been uniformly the same, however he
might have erred in carrying them into action; but now
he relied on my friendship for my royal mistress to give
efficacy to his earnest desire to atone for those faults, of
which he had become convinced by dear-bought experience. He gave me a list of names * for Her Majesty, in
which were specified all the Jacobins who had emissaries

---

* A few hours after one of her interviews with Barnave, the Princess
Lamballe gave me this list to copy, without assigning any reason. I
made the copy. Her highness then ordered me to take the original to
the *Benedictins Anglais*. She told me I should there find, near the
tomb of the late *Suards*, a friar, who would be making a drawing of
some saint in the church. To this friar the paper was to be delivered.
I went to the spot, found the friar, and gave him the paper.

throughout France, for the purpose of creating on the same day, and at the same hour, an alarm of something like the *Vesparo Siciliano* (a general insurrection to murder all the nobility and burn their palaces, which, in fact, took place in many parts of France), the object of which was to give the assembly, by whom all the regular troops were disbanded, a pretext for arming the people as a national guard, thus creating a perpetual national faction.*

"The hordes of every fauxbourg now paraded in this new democratic livery. Even some of them, who were in the actual service of the Court, made no scruple of decorating themselves thus, in the very face of their sovereign. The King complained, but the answer made to him was that the nation commanded.

"The very first time Their Majesties went to the royal chapel, after the embodying of the troops with the national guards, all the persons belonging to it were accoutred in the national uniform. The Queen was highly incensed, and deeply affected at this insult offered to the King's authority by the persons employed in the sacred occupations of the Church. 'Such persons,' said Her Majesty, 'would, I had hoped, have been the last to interfere with politics.' She was about to order all those who preferred their uniforms to their employments, to be discharged from the King's service; but my advice, coupled with that of Barnave, dissuaded her from executing so dangerous a threat. On being assured that those, perhaps, who might be selected to replace the offenders might refuse the service, if not allowed the same ridiculous prerogatives, and thus expose Their Royal Majesties to double mortification, the Queen

* This horrible operation cost six hundred thousand francs! Mirabeau was the paymaster-general, and Orleans the banker. Thousands of wretches from all parts of France received daily, from five francs to a louis and upward, for the outrage and plunder of all those opposing the popularity of the Duke, who, while stooping to mix with the lowest class of society, had no other view than that of dethroning the King, and ruling in his stead.

seemed satisfied, and no more was said upon the subject, except to an ITALIAN SOPRANO, to whom the King signified his displeasure at his singing a *salva regina* in the dress of a grenadier of the new faction. The singer took the hint and never again intruded his uniform into the chapel.

"Necker, notwithstanding the enthusiasm his return produced upon the people, felt mortified in having lost the confidence of the King. He came to me, exclaiming that unless Their Majesties distinguished him by some mark of their royal favor his influence must be lost with the national assembly. He perceived, he said, that the councils of the King were more governed by the advice of the Queen's favorite, the Abbé Vermond, than by his (Necker's). He begged I would assure Her Majesty that Vermond was quite as obnoxious to the people as the Duchess de Polignac had ever been; for it was generally known that Her Majesty was completely guided by him, and, therefore, for her own safety and the tranquillity of national affairs, he humbly suggested the prudence of sending him from the Court, at least for a time.

"I was petrified at hearing a minister dare presume thus to dictate the line of conduct which the Queen of France, his sovereign, should pursue with respect to her most private servants. Such was my indignation at this cruel wish to dismiss every object of her choice, especially one from whom, owing to long habits of intimacy since her childhood, a separation would be rendered, by her present situation, peculiarly cruel, that nothing but the circumstances in which the Court then stood could have given me patience to listen to him.

"I made no answer. Upon my silence, Necker subjoined, 'You must perceive, Princess, that I am actuated for the general good of the nation.'

"'And I hope, sir, for the prerogatives of the monarchy also,' replied I.

"'Certainly,' said Necker. 'But if Their Majesty continue to be guided by others, and will not follow my advice, I cannot answer for the consequences.'

"I assured the minister that I would be the faithful bearer of his commission, however unpleasant.

"Knowing the character of the Queen, in not much relishing being dictated to with respect to her conduct in relation to the persons of her household, especially the Abbé Vermond, and aware, at the same time, of her dislike to Necker, who thus undertook to be her director, I felt rather awkward in being the medium of the minister's suggestions. But what was my surprise, on finding her prepared, and totally indifferent as to the privation.

"'I foresaw,' replied Her Majesty, 'that Vermond would become odious to the present order of things, merely because he had been a faithful servant, and long attached to my interest; but you may tell M. Necker that the Abbé leaves Versailles this very night, by my express order, for Vienna.'

"If the proposal of Necker astonished me, the Queen's reception of it astonished me still more. What a lesson is this for royal favorites! The man who had been her tutor, and who, almost from her childhood, never left her, the constant confidant for fifteen or sixteen years, was now sent off without a seeming regret.

"I doubt not, however, that the Queen had some very powerful secret motive for the sudden change in her conduct toward the Abbé, for she was ever just in all her concerns, even to her avowed enemies; but I was happy that she seemed to express no particular regret at the minister's suggested policy. I presume, from the result, that I myself had overrated the influence of the Abbé over the mind of his royal pupil; that he had by no means the sway imputed to him; and that Maria Antoinette merely considered him as the necessary instrument of her private correspondence, which he had wholly managed.'*

"But a circumstance presently occurred which aroused Her Majesty from this calmness and indifference. The King came in to inform her that La Fayette, during the

* The truth is, Her Majesty had already taken leave of the Abbé, in the presence of the King, unknown to the Princess, or more properly the Abbé had taken an affectionate leave of them.

night, had caused the guards to desert from the palace of Versailles.

"The effect on her of this intelligence was like the lightning which precedes a loud clap of thunder. Everything that followed was perfectly in character, and shook every nerve of the royal authority.

"'Thus,' exclaimed Maria Antoinette, 'thus, sire, have you humiliated yourself, in condescending to go to Paris, without having accomplished the object. You have not regained the confidence of your subjects. Oh, how bitterly do I deplore the loss of that confidence! It exists no longer. Alas! when will it be restored!'

"The French guards, indeed, had been in open insurrection through the months of June and July, and all that could be done was to preserve one single company of grenadiers, by means of their commander, the Baron de Leval, faithful to their colors. This company had now been influenced by General La Fayette to desert and join their companions, who had enrolled themselves in the Paris national guard.

"Messieurs de Bouillé and Luxemburg being interrogated by the Queen respecting the spirit of the troops under their immediate command, M. de Bouillé answered, 'Madam, I should be very sorry to be compelled to undertake any internal operation with men who have been seduced from their allegiance, and are daily paid by a faction which aims at the overthrow of its legitimate sovereign. I would not answer for a man that has been in the neighborhood of the seditious national troops, or that has read the inflammatory discussions of the national assembly. If Your Majesty and the King wish well to the nation,— I am sorry to say it,— its happiness depends on your quitting immediately the scenes of riot and placing yourselves in a situation to treat with the national assembly on equal terms, whereby the King may be unbiased and unfettered by a compulsive, overbearing mob; and this can only be achieved by your flying to a place of safety. That you may find such a place, I will answer with all my life!'

" 'Yes,' said M. de Luxemburg, 'I think we may both safely answer that, in such a case, you will find a few Frenchmen ready to risk a little to save all!' And both concurred that there was no hope of salvation for the King or country but through the resolution they advised.

" 'This,' said the Queen, 'will be a very difficult task. His Majesty, I fear, will never consent to leave France.'

" 'Then, madam,' replied they, 'we can only regret that we have nothing to offer but our own perseverance in the love and service of our King and his oppressed family, to whom we deplore we can now be useful only with our feeble wishes.'

" 'Well, gentlemen,' answered Her Majesty, 'you must not despair of better prospects. I will take an early opportunity of communicating your loyal sentiments to the King, and will hear his opinion on the subject before I give you a definitive answer. I thank you, in the name of His Majesty, as well as on my own account, for your good intentions toward us.'

"Scarcely had these gentlemen left the palace, when a report prevailed that the King, his family, and ministers, were about to withdraw to some fortified situation. It was also industriously rumored that, as soon as they were in safety, the national assembly would be forcibly dismissed, as the parliament had been by Louis XIV. The reports gained universal belief when it became known that the King had ordered the Flanders regiment to Versailles.

"The national assembly now daily watched the royal power more and more assiduously. New sacrifices of the prerogatives of the nobles were incessantly proposed by them to the King.

"When His Majesty told the Queen that he had been advised by Necker to sanction the abolition of the privileged nobility, and that all distinctions, except the order of the Holy Ghost to himself and the Dauphin, were also annihilated by the assembly, even to the order of Maria Theresa, which she could no longer wear — 'These, sire,' answered she, in extreme anguish, 'are trifles, so far as they regard myself. I do not think I have twice worn the order of Maria Theresa since my arrival in this once happy country. I need it not. The immortal memory of her who gave me being, is engraven on my heart; THAT I shall wear forever, none can wrest it from me. But what grieves me to the soul is your having sanctioned these decrees of the national assembly upon the mere *ipse dixit* of M. Necker.'

"'I have only given my sanction to such as I thought most necessary to tranquilize the minds of those who doubted my sincerity; but I have withheld it from others, which, for the good of my people, require maturer consideration. On these, in a full council, and in your presence, I shall again deliberate.'

"'Oh,' said the Queen, with tears in her eyes, 'could but the people hear you, and know, once for all, how to appreciate the goodness of your heart, as I do now, they would cast themselves at your feet, and supplicate your forgiveness for having shown such ingratitude to your paternal interest for their welfare!'

"But this unfortunate refusal to sanction all the decrees sent by the national assembly, though it preceded from the best motives, produced the worst effects. Dupont, Lameth, and Barnave well knew the troubles such a course must create. Of this they forewarned His Majesty, before any measure was laid before him for approval. They cautioned him not to trifle with the deputies. They assured him that half measures would only rouse suspicion. They enforced the necessity of uniform assentation, in order to lull the Mirabeau party, who were canvassing for a majority to set up Orleans, to whose interest Mirabeau and his myrmidons were then devoted. The scheme of Dupont, Lameth, and Barnave was to thwart and weaken the Mirabeau and Orleans faction, by gradually persuading them, in consequence of the King's compliance with whatever the assembly exacted, that they could do no better than to let him into a share of the executive power: for now nothing was left to His Majesty but responsibility, while the privileges of grace and

justice had become merely nominal, with the one dangerous exception of the VETO, to which he could never have
recourse without imminent peril to his cause and to himself.

"Unfortunately for His Majesty's interest, he was too
scrupulous to act, even through momentary policy, distinctly against his conscience. When he gave way, it
was with reluctance, and often with an avowal, more or
less express, that he only complied with necessity against
conviction. His very sincerity made him appear the reverse. His adherents consequently dwindled, while the
Orleans faction became immeasurably augmented.

"In the midst of these perplexities, an Austrian courier was stopped with dispatches from Prince Kaunitz.
These, though unsought for on the part of Her Majesty,
though they contained a friendly advice to her to submit
to the circumstances of the times, and though, luckily,
they were couched in terms favorable to the constitution,
showed the mob that there WAS a correspondence with
Vienna, carried on by the Queen, and neither Austria
nor the Queen were deemed the friends either of the
people or of the constitution. To have received the letters was enough for the faction.

"Affairs were now ripening gradually into something
like a crisis, when the Flanders regiment arrived. The
note of preparation had been sounded. 'Let us go to
Versailles, and bring the King away from his evil counselors,' was already in the mouths of the Parisians.

"In the meantime, Dumourier, who had been leagued
with the Orleans faction, became disgusted with it. He
knew the deep schemes of treason which were in train
against the Royal Family, and, in disguise, sought the
Queen at Versailles, and had an interview with Her
Majesty in my presence. He assured her that an abominable insurrection was ripe for explosion among the mobs
of the fauxbourgs; gave her the names of the leaders,
who had received money to promote its organization; and
warned her that the massacre of the Royal Family was
the object of the maneuver, for the purpose of declaring

the Duke of Orleans the constitutional King; that he was to be proclaimed by Mirabeau, who had already received a considerable sum in advance, for distribution among the populace, to insure their support; and that Mirabeau, in return for his co-operation, was to be created a duke, with the office of prime minister and secretary of state, and to have the framing of the constitution, which was to be modeled from that of Great Britain. It was further concerted that d'Orleans was to show himself in the midst of the confusion, and the crown to be conferred upon him by public acclamation.

"On his knees Dumourier implored Her Majesty to regard his voluntary discovery of this infamous and diabolical plot as a proof of his sincere repentance. He declared he came disinterestedly to offer himself as a sacrifice to save her, the King, and her family from the horrors then threatening their lives, from the violence of an outrageous mob of regicides; he called God to witness that he was actuated by no other wish than to atone for his error and die in their defense; he looked for no reward beyond the King's forgiveness of his having joined the Orleans faction; he never had any view in joining that faction but that of aiding the Duke, for the good of his country, in the reform of ministerial abuses, and strengthening the royal authority by the salutary laws of the national assembly; but he no sooner discovered that impure schemes of personal aggrandisement gave the real impulse to these pretended reformers than he forsook their unholy course. He supplicated Her Majesty to lose no time, but to allow him to save her from the destruction to which she would inevitably be exposed; that he was ready to throw himself at the King's feet, to implore his forgiveness also, and to assure him of his profound penitence, and his determination to renounce forever the factious Orleans party.

"As Her Majesty would not see any of those who offered themselves, except in my presence, I availed myself, in this instance, of the opportunity it gave me by enforcing the arguments of Dumourier. But all I could say, all the earnest representations to be deduced from this critical crisis could not prevail with her, even so far as to persuade her to temporize with Dumourier, as she had done with many others on similar occasions. She was deaf and inexorable. She treated all he had said as the effusion of an overheated imagination, and told him she had no faith in traitors. Dumourier remained upon his knees while she was replying, as if stupefied; but at the word TRAITOR he started and roused himself; and then, in a state almost of madness, seized the Queen's dress, exclaiming, 'Allow yourself to be persuaded before it is too late! Let not your misguided prejudice against me hurry you to your own and your children's destruction; let it not get the better, madam, of your good sense and reason; the fatal moment is near; it is at hand!' Upon this, turning, he addressed himself to me.

"'Oh, Princess,' he cried, 'be her guardian angel, as you have hitherto been her only friend, and use your never-failing influence. I take God once more to witness, that I am sincere in all I have said; that all I have disclosed is true. This will be the last time I shall have it in my power to be of any essential service to you, madam, and my sovereign. The national assembly will put it out of my power for the future, without becoming a traitor to my country.'

"'Rise, sir,' said the Queen, 'and serve your country better than you have served your King!'

"'Madam, I obey.'——

"When he was about to leave the room, I again, with tears, besought Her Majesty not to let him depart thus, but to give him some hope, that, after reflection, she might perhaps endeavor to soothe the King's anger. But in vain. He withdrew very much affected.* I even ventured, after his departure, to intercede for his recall.

* I saw him as he left the apartment, but had no idea, at the time, who he was. He was a little, thin man. He wore a high, quaker-like, round, slouched hat. He was covered down to the very shoes by a great coat. This, I imagine, was for the sake of disguise. I saw him put a handkerchief to his eyes. I met him some time after

"'He has pledged himself,' said I, 'to save you, madam!'

"'My dear Princess,' replied the Queen, 'the goodness of your own heart will not allow you to have sinister ideas of others. This man is like all of the same stamp. They are all traitors; and will only hurry us the sooner, if we suffer ourselves to be deceived by them, to an ignominious death! I seek no safety for myself.'

"'But he offered to serve the King also, madam.'

"'I am not,' answered Her Majesty, 'Henrietta of France. I will never stoop to ask a pension of the murderers of my husband; nor will I leave the King, my son, or my adopted country, or ever meanly owe my existence to wretches who have destroyed the dignity of the crown and trampled under foot the most ancient monarchy in Europe! Under its ruins they will bury their King and myself. To owe our safety to them would be more hateful than any death they can prepare for us.'

"While the Queen was in this state of agitation, a note was presented to me with a list of the names of the officers of the Flanders regiment, requesting the honor of an audience of the Queen.

"The very idea of seeing the Flanders officers flushed Her Majesty's countenance with an ecstasy of joy.

"She said she would retire to compose herself, and receive them in two hours.

"The Queen saw the officers in her private cabinet, and in my presence. They were presented to her by me. They told Her Majesty that, though they had changed their paymaster, they had not changed their allegiance to their sovereign or herself, but were ready to defend both with their lives. They placed one hand on the hilt of their swords, and, solemnly lifting the other up to Heaven,

---

at Hamburg, and I am confident that all his ntended operations in the royal cause were given up in consequence of the exasperation he felt at the Queen's rejection of his services, though he continued to correspond with the Princess for a considerable time subsequently to the interview.

swore that the weapons should never be wielded but
for the defense of the King and Queen, against all foes,
whether foreign or domestic.

"This unexpected loyalty burst on us like the beau-
teous rainbow after a tempest, by the dawn of which we
are taught to believe the world is saved from a second
deluge.

"The countenance of Her Majesty brightened over the
gloom which had oppressed her, like the heavenly sun
dispersing threatening clouds, and making the heart of
the poor mariner bound with joy. Her eyes spoke her
secret rapture. It was evident she felt even unusual dignity in the presence of these noble-hearted warriors,
when comparing them with him whom she had just
dismissed. She graciously condescended to speak to every
one of them, and one and all were enchanted with her
affability.

"She said she was no longer the Queen who could
compensate loyalty and valor; but the brave soldier found
his reward in the fidelity of his service, which formed the
glory of his immortality. She assured them she had ever
been attached to the army, and would make it her study
to recommend every individual, meriting attention, to the
King.

"Loud bursts of repeated acclamations and shouts of
Vive la reine!' instantly followed her remarks. She
thanked the officers most graciously; and fearing to commit herself, by saying more, took her leave, attended by
me; but immediately sent me back, to thank them again
in her name.

"They departed, shouting as they went, '*Vive la
reine! Vive la Princesse! Vive la roi, le Dauphin, et toute
la famille royale!*'

"When the national assembly saw the officers going
to and coming from the King's palace with such demonstrations of enthusiasm they took alarm, and the regicide
faction hastened on the crisis for which it had been longing. It was by no means unusual for the chiefs of regiments, destined to form part of the garrison of a royal

residence, to be received by the sovereign on their arrival, and certainly only natural that they should be so; but in times of excitement trifling events have powerful effects.

"But if the national assembly began to tremble for their own safety, and had already taken secret measures to secure it, by conspiring to put an instantaneous end to the King's power, against which they had so long been plotting, when the Flanders regiment arrived, it may be readily conceived what must have been their emotions on the fraternization of this regiment with the bodyguard, and on the scene to which the dinner, given to the former troops by the latter, so unpremeditatedly led.

"On the day of this fatal dinner I remarked to the Queen, 'What a beautiful sight it must be to behold, in these troublesome times, the happy union of such a meeting!'

"'It must indeed!' replied the King; 'and the pleasure I feel in knowing it would be redoubled had I the privilege of entertaining the Flanders regiment, as the bodyguards are doing.'

"'Heaven forbid!' cried Her Majesty; 'Heaven forbid that you should think of such a thing! The assembly would never forgive us!'

"After we had dined, the Queen sent to the Marchioness Tourzel for the Dauphin. When he came, the Queen told him about her having seen the brave officers on their arrival; and how gayly those good officers had left the palace, declaring they would die rather than suffer any harm to come to him, or his papa and mamma; and that at that very time they were all dining at the theater.

"'Dining in the theater, mamma?' said the young Prince. 'I never heard of people dining in a theater!'

"'No, my dear child,' replied Her Majesty, 'it is not generally allowed; but they are doing so, because the bodyguards are giving a dinner to this good Flanders regiment; and the Flanders regiment are so brave that the guards chose the finest place they could think of to entertain them in, to show how much they like them;

that is the reason why they are dining in the gay, painted theater.'

"'Oh, mamma!' exclaimed the Dauphin, whom the Queen adored, 'Oh, papa!' cried he, looking at the King, 'how I should like to see them!'

"'Let us go and satisfy the child!' said the King, instantly starting up from his seat.

"The Queen took the Dauphin by the hand, and they proceeded to the theater. It was all done in a moment. There was no premeditation on the part of the King or Queen; no invitation on the part of the officers. Had I been asked, I should certainly have followed the Queen; but just as the King rose, I left the room. The Prince being eager to see the festival, they set off immediately, and when I returned to the apartment they were gone. Not being very well, I remained where I was; but most of the household had already followed Their Majesties.

"On the Royal Family making their appearance, they were received with the most unequivocal shouts of general enthusiasm by the troops. Intoxicated with the pleasure of seeing Their Majesties among them, and overheated with the juice of the grape, they gave themselves up to every excess of joy, which the circumstances and the situation of Their Majesties were so well calculated to inspire. '*Oh, Richard! oh mon roi!*' was sung, as well as many other loyal songs. The healths of the King, Queen, and Dauphin were drunk, till the regiments were really inebriated with the mingled influence of wine and shouting *vivas!*

"When the royal party retired, they were followed by all the military to the very palace doors, where they sung, danced, embraced each other, and gave way to all the frantic demonstrations of devotedness to the royal cause which the excitement of the scene and the table could produce. Throngs, of course, collected to get near the Royal Family. Many persons in the rush were trampled on, and one or two men, it was said, crushed to death. The Dauphin and the king were delighted; but the Queen, in giving the Princess Elizabeth and myself an account of the festival, foresaw the fatal result which would ensue; and deeply deplored the marked enthusiasm with which they had been greeted and followed by the military.

"There was one more military spectacle, a public breakfast, which took place on the 2d of October. Though none of the Royal Family appeared at it, it was no less injurious to their interests than the former. The enemies of the crown spread reports all over Paris, that the King and Queen had maneuvered to pervert the minds of the troops so far as to make them declare against the measures of the national assembly. It is not likely that the assembly, or politics, were even spoken of at the breakfast; but the report did as much mischief as the reality would have done. This was quite sufficient to encourage the Orleans and Mirabeau faction in the assembly to the immediate execution of their long-meditated scheme, of overthrowing the monarchy.

"On the very day following, Dupont, Lameth, and Barnave sent their confidential agent to apprise the Queen that certain deputies had already fully matured a plot to remove the King, nay, to confine Her Majesty from him in a distant part of France, that her influence over his mind might no further thwart their premeditated establishment of a constitution.*

"But others of this body, and the more powerful and subtle portion, had a deeper object, so depraved that, even when forewarned, the Queen could not deem it possible; but of which she was soon convinced by their infernal acts.

"The riotous faction, for the purpose of accelerating this *dénouement*, had contrived, by buying up all the corn and sending it out of the country, to reduce the

---

* The dinner of the Flanders regiment is generally supposed to have been the immediate cause of the massacres of the 5th and 6th of October. But it is obvious that it was only the immediate pretext. The great alarm seems to have been taken after the first introduction of the officers to the Queen; although the conversation of Dumourier shows that the whole affair was entirely concerted some time before.

populace to famine, and then to make it appear that the King and Queen had been the monopolizers, and the extravagance of Maria Antoinette and her largesses to Austria and her favorites, the cause. The plot was so deeply laid that the wretches who undertook to effect the diabolical scheme were metamorphosed in the Queen's livery, so that all the odium might fall on her unfortunate Majesty. At the head of the commission of monopolizers was Luckner, who had taken a violent dislike to the Queen, in consequence of his having been refused some preferment, which he attributed to her influence. Mirabeau, who was still in the background, and longing to take a more prominent part, helped it on as much as possible. Pinet, who had been a confidential agent of the Duke of Orleans, himself told the Duke de Penthièvre that Orleans had monopolized all the corn. This communication, and the activity of the Count de Fersen, saved France, and Paris in particular, from perishing for the want of bread. Even at the moment of the abominable masquerade, in which Her Majesty's agents were made to appear the enemies who were starving the French people, out of revenge for the checks imposed by them on the royal authority, it was well known to all the Court that both Her Majesty and the King were grieved to the soul at their piteous want, and distributed immense sums for the relief of the poor sufferers, as did the Duke de Penthièvre, the Duchess of Orleans, the Prince of Condé, the Duke and Duchess de Bourbon, and others;* but these acts were done privately, while he who had created the necessity took to himself the exclusive credit of the relief, and employed thousands daily to propagate reports of his generosity, Mirabeau, then the factotum agent of the operations of the Palais Royal and its demagogues, greatly added to the support of this impression. Indeed, till undeceived afterward, he believed it to be really the Duke of Orleans who had succored the people.

"I dispensed two hundred and twenty thousand livres

* The Princess should have included her own name, for she was most munificent, though secretly so, on the occasion.

LAST DAYS OF LOUIS XVI, AND FAMILY
Photogravure after a painting by Benczur

merely to discover the names of the agents who had been employed to carry on this nefarious plot to exasperate the people against the throne by starvation imputed to the sovereign.* Though money achieved the discovery in time to clear the characters of my royal mistress and the King, the detection only followed the mischief of the crime. But even the rage thus wickedly excited was not enough to carry through the plot. In the fauxbourgs of Paris, where the women became furies, two hundred thousand livres were distributed ere the horror could be completely exposed.

"But it is time for me to enter upon the scenes to which all the intrigues I have detailed were intended to lead — the removal of the Royal Family from Versailles.

"My heart sickens when I retrace these moments of anguish. The point to which they are to conduct us yet remains one of the mysteries of fate.

---

* Whether the Duke of Orleans had or had not any private motives of rancor against his sister-in-law, the Princess Lamballe, for her attachment to the Queen, he, from this moment, when she so completely unmasked him, never ceased to exercise his vengeance against her.

CHAPTER XV.

"HER Majesty had been so thoroughly lulled into security by the enthusiasm of the regiments at Versailles that she treated all the reports from Paris with contempt. Nothing was apprehended from that quarter, and no preparations were consequently made for resistance or protection. She was at Little Trianon when the news of the approach of the desolating torrent arrived. The King was hunting. I presented to her the commandant of the troops at Versailles, who assured Her Majesty that a murderous faction, too powerful, perhaps, for resistance, was marching principally against her royal person, with La Fayette at their head, and implored her to put herself and valuables in immediate safety; particularly all her correspondence with the princes, emigrants, and foreign Courts, if she had no means of destroying them.

"Though the Queen was somewhat awakened to the truth by this earnest appeal, yet she still considered the extent of the danger as exaggerated, and looked upon the representation as partaking, in a considerable degree, of the nature of all reports in times of popular commotion.

"Presently, however, a more startling omen appeared, in a much milder but ambiguous communication from General La Fayette. He stated that he was on his march from Paris with the national guard, and part of the people, coming to make remonstrances; but he begged Her Majesty to rest assured that no disorder would take place, and that he himself would vouch that there should be none.

"The King was instantly sent for to the heights of Meudon, while the Queen set off from Little Trianon, with me, for Versailles.

"The first movements were commenced by a few women, or men in women's clothes, at the palace gates of Versailles. The guards refused them entrance, from an order they had received to that effect from La Fayette. The consternation produced by their resentment was a mere prelude to the horrid tragedy that succeeded.

"The information now pouring in from different quarters increased Her Majesty's alarm every moment. The order of La Fayette, not to let the women be admitted, convinced her that there was something in agitation, which his unexplained letter made her sensible was more to be feared than if he had signified the real situation and danger to which she was exposed.

"A messenger was forthwith dispatched for M. la Fayette, and another, by order of the Queen, for M. de St. Priest, to prepare a retreat for the Royal Family, as the Parisian mob's advance could no longer be doubted. Everything necessary was accordingly got ready.

"La Fayette now arrived at Versailles in obedience to the message, and, in the presence of all the Court and ministers, assured the King that he could answer for the Paris army, at the head of which he intended to march, to prevent disorders; and advised the admission of the women into the palace, who, he said, had nothing to propose but a simple memorial relative to the scarcity of bread.

"The Queen said to him, 'Remember, sir, you have pledged your honor for the King's safety.'

"'And I hope, madam, to be able to redeem it.'

"He then left Versailles to return to his post with the army.

"A limited number of the women were at length admitted; and so completely did they seem satisfied with the reception they met with from the King, as, in all appearance, to have quieted their riotous companions. The language of menace and remonstrance had changed into shouts of '*Vive le roi!*' The apprehensions of Their Majesties were subdued; and the whole system of operation, which had been previously adopted for the Royal Family's quitting Versailles, was, in consequence, unfortunately changed.

"But the troops, that had been hitherto under arms for the preservation of order, in going back to their hotel, were assailed and fired at by the mob.

"The return of the bodyguards, thus insulted in going to and coming from the palace, caused the Queen and the Court to resume the resolution of instantly retiring from Versailles; but it was now too late. They were stopped by the municipality and the mob of the city, who were animated to excess against the Queen by one of the bass singers of the French opera.*

"Every hope of tranquillity was now shaken by the hideous howlings which arose from all quarters. Intended flight had become impracticable. Atrocious expressions were leveled against the Queen, too shocking for repetition. I shudder when I reflect to what a degree of outrage the *poissardes* of Paris were excited, to express their abominable designs on the life of that most adored of sovereigns.

"Early in the evening Her Majesty came to my apartment, in company with one of her female attendants. She was greatly agitated. She brought all her jewels and a considerable quantity of papers, which she had begun to collect together immediately on her

* "*La Haise.*"

arrival from Trianon, as the commandant had recommended.*

"Notwithstanding the fatigue and agitation which the
Queen must have suffered during the day, and the continued threats, horrible howlings, and discharge of fire-
arms during the night, she had courage enough to visit
the bedchambers of her children and then to retire to
rest in her own.

"But her rest was soon fearfully interrupted. Horrid
cries at her chamber door of 'SAVE THE QUEEN! SAVE THE
QUEEN! OR SHE WILL BE ASSASSINATED!' aroused her. The
faithful guardian who gave the alarm was never heard
more. He was murdered in her defense! Her Majesty herself only escaped the poignards of immediate death by flying
to the King's apartment, almost in the same state as she
lay in bed, not having had time to screen herself with
any covering but what was casually thrown over her by
the women who assisted her in her flight; while one well
acquainted with the palace is said to have been seen
busily engaged in encouraging the regicides who thus
sought her for midnight murder. The faithful guards
who defended the entrance to the room of the intended
victim of these desperadoes took shelter in the room itself

---

*Neither Her Majesty nor the Princess ever returned to Versailles,
after the 6th of that fatal October! Part of the papers, brought by the
Queen to the apartment of the Princess, were tacked by me on two of
my petticoats; the under one three fold, one on the other, and outside;
and the upper one, three or four fold double on the inside; and thus I
left the room with this paper under garment, which put me to no inconvenience. Returning to the Princess, I was ordered to go to Lisle, there
take the papers from their hiding place, and deliver them, with others,
to the same person who received the box, of which mention will be
found in another part of this work. I was not to take any letters, and
was to come back immediately.

As I was leaving the apartment Her Majesty said something to her
highness which I did not hear. The Princess turned round very quickly,
and, kissing me on the forehead, said in Italian, "*Cara mia Inglesina,
per carità guardatevi bene. Io non mi perdonerò giammai se t'arri-
vasse qualche disgrazia!* My dear little Englishwoman, for Heav-
en's sake be careful of yourself, for I should never forgive myself if any
misfortune were to befall you." "Nor I," said Her Majesty.

upon her leaving it, and were alike threatened with instant
death by the grenadier assassins for having defeated
them in their fiendlike purpose; they were, however,
saved by the generous interposition and courage of two
gentlemen, who, offering themselves as victims in their
place, thus brought about a temporary accommodation
between the regular troops and the national guard.

"All this time General La Fayette never once appeared.
It is presumed that he himself had been deceived as to
the horrid designs of the mob, and did not choose to
show himself, finding it impossible to check the impetuosity of the horde he had himself brought to action, in
concurring to countenance their first movements from
Paris. Posterity will decide how far he was justified in
pledging himself for the safety of the Royal Family,
while he was heading a riotous mob, whose atrocities were
guaranteed from punishment or check by the sanction of
his presence and the faith reposed in his assurance. Was
he ignorant, or did he only pretend to be so, of the incalculable mischief inevitable from giving power and a
reliance on impunity to such an unreasoning mass? By
any military operation, as commander-in-chief, he might
have turned the tide. And why did he not avail himself
of that authority with which he had been invested by the
national assembly, as the delegates of the nation, for
the general safety and guardianship of the people? for
the people, of whom he was the avowed protector, were
themselves in peril: it was only the humanity (or rather,
in such a crisis, the imbecility) of Louis XVI. that prevented them from being fired on; and they would inevitably have been sacrificed, and that through the want of
policy in their leader, had not this mistaken mercy of
the King prevented his guards from offering resistance to
the murderers of his brave defenders!

"The cry of 'QUEEN! QUEEN!' now resounded from
the lips of the cannibals stained with the blood of her
faithful guards. She appeared, shielded by filial affection,
between her two innocent children, the threatened orphans! But the sight of so much innocence and heroic

courage paralyzed the hands uplifted for their massacre!

"A tiger voice cried out, 'No CHILDREN!' The infants
were hurried away from the maternal side, only to witness the author of their being offering up herself, eagerly
and instantly, to the sacrifice, an ardent and delighted
victim to the hoped-for preservation of those, perhaps,
ORPHANS, dearer to her far than life! Her resignation
and firm step in facing the savage cry that was thunder-
ing against her, disarmed the ferocious beasts that were
hungering and roaring for their prey!

"Mirabeau, whose immense head and gross figure
could not be mistaken, is said to have been the first
among the mob to have sonorously chanted, 'To PARIS!'
His myrmidons echoed and re-echoed the cry upon the
signal. He then hastened to the assembly to contravene
any measures the King might ask in opposition. The
riots increasing, the Queen said to His Majesty:

"'Oh, sire! why am I not animated with the courage
of Maria Theresa? Let me go with my children to the
national assembly, as she did to the Hungarian Senate,
with my imperial brother, Joseph, in her arms and
Leopold in her womb, when Charles the Seventh of Bavaria had deprived her of all her German dominions, and
she had already written to the Duchess of Lorraine to
prepare her an asylum, not knowing where she should
be delivered of the precious charge she was then bearing; but I, like the mother of the Gracchi, like Cornelia,
more esteemed for my birth than for my marriage, am
the wife of the King of France, and I see we shall be
murdered in our beds for the want of our own exertions!'

"The King remained as if paralyzed and stupefied, and
made no answer. The Princess Elizabeth then threw
herself at the Queen's feet, imploring her to consent to
go to Paris.

"'To Paris!' exclaimed Her Majesty.

"'Yes, madame,' said the King. 'I will put an end
to these horrors, and tell the people so.'

14

"On this, without waiting for the Queen's answer, he opened the balcony, and told the populace he was ready to depart with his family.

"This sudden change caused a change equally sudden in the rabble mob. All shouted, '*Vive le roi! Vive la nation!*'

"Re-entering the room from the window, the King said, 'It is done. This affair will soon be terminated.'

"'And with it,' said the Queen, 'the monarchy!'

"'Better that, madame, than running the risk, as I did some hours since, of seeing you and my children sacrificed!'

"'That, sire, will be the consequence of our not having left Versailles. Whatever you determine, it is my duty to obey. As to myself, I am resigned to my fate.' On this she burst into a flood of tears. 'I only feel for your humiliated state, and for the safety of our children.'

"The Royal Family departed without having consulted any of the ministers, military or civil, or the national assembly, by whom they were followed:*

* The cruel procession is not mentioned in this journal. The descriptions of it are so numerous that they must be fresh in the recollection of all readers. To save the trouble of reference, however, I quote a few words from the accounts of Campan and Bertrand de Moleville.

"The (King's) carriage was preceded by the heads of two murdered bodyguards, carried upon pikes. It was surrounded by ruffians, who contemplated the royal personages with a brutal curiosity. A few of the bodyguards, on foot and unarmed, covered by the ancient French guards, followed dejectedly; and, to complete the climax, after six or seven hours spent in traveling from Versailles to Paris, Their Majesties were led to the Hotel de Ville as if to make the *amende honorable.*"—*Campan*, vol. ii., 313.

"The King did not leave Versailles till one o'clock. The hundred deputies in their carriages followed. A detachment of brigands, bearing the heads of two bodyguards in triumph, formed the advanced guard, and set out two hours earlier. These cannibals stopped a moment at Serres, and carried their cruelty to the length of forcing an unfortunate hairdresser to dress the gory heads; the bulk of the Parisian army followed them closely. The King's carriage was preceded by the *poissardes* who had arrived the day before from Paris and a whole rabble of prostitutes, the vile refuse of their sex, still drunk with fury and wine. Several of them rode astride upon cannon, boasting in the most horrible

"Scarcely had they arrived at Paris when the Queen recollected that she had taken with her no change of dress, either for herself or her children, and they were obliged to ask permission of the national assembly to allow them to send for their different wardrobes.

"What a situation for an absolute King and Queen, which, but a few hours previous, they had been!

"I now took up my residence with Their Majesties at the Tuileries: that odious Tuileries which I cannot name but with horror, where the malignant spirit of rebellion has, perhaps, dragged us to an untimely death!

"Monsieur and Madame had another residence. Bailly, the Mayor of Paris, and La Fayette became the royal jailers.

"The Princess Elizabeth and myself could not but deeply deplore, when we saw the predictions of Dumourier so dreadfully confirmed by the result, that Her Majesty should have so slighted his timely information, and scorned

songs, all the crimes they had committed themselves or seen others commit. Those who were nearest the King's carriage sang ballads, the allusions of which by means of their vulgar gestures they applied to the Queen. Wagons, full of corn and flour which had been brought into Versailles, formed a train escorted by grenadiers and surrounded by women and bullies, some armed with pikes and some carrying long branches of poplar. At some distance this part of the procession had a most singular effect: it looked like a moving forest, amidst which shone pike heads and gun barrels. In the paroxysms of their brutal joy the women stopped passengers, and, pointing to the King's carriage, howled in their ears: 'Cheer up, friends; we shall no longer be in want of bread: we bring you the baker, the baker's wife, and the litte baker boy!' Behind His Majesty's carriage were several of his faithful guards, some on foot and some on horseback, most of them uncovered, all unarmed and worn out with hunger and fatigue; the dragoons, the Flanders regiment, the hundred Swiss of the national guards preceded, accompanied, or followed the file of carriages. I witnessed this heartrending spectacle; I saw the ominous procession. In the midst of all the tumult, clamor, and singing, interrupted by frequent discharges of musketry, which the hand of a monster or a bungler might so easily render fatal, I saw the Queen preserving the most courageous tranquillity of soul and an air of nobleness and inexpressible dignity, and my eyes were suffused with tears of admiration and grief."— *Bertrand de Moleville.*

With this procession ended the sovereignty of Louis XVI. and Maria Antoinette!

his penitence. But delicacy bade us lament in silence; and, while we grieved over her present sufferings, we could not but mourn the loss of a barrier against future aggression, in the rejection of this general's proffered services.

"It will be remembered, that Dumourier in his disclosure declared that the object of this commotion was to place the Duke of Orleans upon the throne, and that Mirabeau, who was a prime mover, was to share in the profits of the usurpation.

"But the heart of the traitor duke failed him at the important crisis. Though he was said to have been recognized through a vulgar disguise, stimulating the assassins to the attempted murder of Her Majesty, yet, when the moment to show himself had arrived, he was nowhere to be found. The most propitious moment for the execution of the foul crime was lost, and with it the confidence of his party. Mirabeau was disgusted. So far from wishing longer to offer him the crown, he struck it forever from his head, and turned against him. He openly protested he would no longer set up traitors who were cowards.

"Soon after this event, Her Majesty, in tears, came to tell me that the King, having had positive proof of the agency of the Duke of Orleans in the riots of Versailles, had commenced some proceedings, which had given the Duke the alarm, and exiled him to Villers Coteretz. The Queen added, that the King's only object had been to assure the general tranquillity, and especially her own security, against whose life the conspiracy seemed most distinctly leveled.

"'Oh, Princess!' continued Her Majesty, in a flood of tears, 'the King's love for me, and his wish to restore order to his people, have been our ruin! He should have struck off the head of Orleans, or overlooked his crime!* Why did he not consult me before he took a

---

* The Queen was right. The Duke did not lose sight of his purpose during his stay at Villers Coteretz. He remained active in his designs against the royal authority, and his hostile spirit still prowled there, in darkness, though he himself was apparently inactive.

step so important? I have lost a friend also in his wife! For, however criminal he may be, she loves him.'

"I assured Her Majesty that I could not think the Duchess of Orleans would be so inconsiderate as to withdraw her affection on that account.

"'She certainly will,' replied Maria Antoinette. 'She is the affectionate mother of his children, and cannot but hate those who have been the cause of his exile. I know it will be laid to my charge, and, added to the hatred the husband has so long borne me, I shall now become the object of the wife's resentment.'

"In the midst of one of the paroxysms of Her Majesty's agonizing agitation after leaving Versailles, for the past, the present, and the future state of the Royal Family, when the Princess Elizabeth and myself were in vain endeavoring to calm her, a deputation was announced from the national assembly and the City of Paris, requesting the honor of the appearance of the King and herself at the theater.

"'Is it possible, my dear Princess,' cried she, on the announcement, 'that I can enjoy any public amusement while I am still chilled with horror at the blood these people have spilled, the blood of the faithful defenders of our lives? I can forgive them, but I cannot so easily forget it.'

"Count de Fersen and the Austrian ambassador now entered, both anxious to know Her Majesty's intentions with regard to visiting the theater, in order to make a party to insure her a good reception; but all their persuasions were unavailing. She thanked the deputation for their friendship; but at the same time told them that her mind was still too much agitated from recent scenes to receive any pleasure but in the domestic cares of her family, and that, for a time, she must decline every other amusement.

"At this moment the Spanish and English ambassadors came to pay their respects to Her Majesty on the same subject as the others. As they entered, Count de Fersen observed to the Queen, looking around:

"'Courage, madam! We are as many nations as persons in this room: English, German, Spanish, Italian, Swedish, and French; and all equally ready to form a rampart around you against aggression. All these nations will, I believe, admit that the French (bowing to the Princess Elizabeth) are the most volatile of the six; and Your Majesty may rely on it, that they will love you, now that you are more closely among them, more tenderly than ever.'

"'Let me live to be convinced of that, sir, and my happiness will be concentrated in its demonstration.'

"'Indeed, gentlemen,' said the Princess Elizabeth, 'the Queen has yet had but little reason to love the French.'

"'Where is our ambassador,' said I, 'and the Neapolitan?'

"'I have had the pleasure of seeing them early this morning,' replied the Queen; 'but I told them, also, that indisposition prevented my going into public. They will be at our card party in your apartment this evening, where I hope to see these gentlemen. The only parties,' continued Her Majesty, addressing herself to the Princess Elizabeth and the ambassadors, 'the only parties I shall visit in future will be those of the Princess Lamballe, my superintendent; as, in so doing, I shall have no occasion to go out of the palace, which, from what has happened, seems to me the only prudent course.'

"'Come, come, madam,' exclaimed the ambassadors; 'do not give way to gloomy ideas. All will yet be well.'

"'I hope so,' answered Her Majesty; 'but till that hope is realized, the wounds I have suffered will make existence a burden to me!'

"The Duchess de Luynes, like many others, had been a zealous partisan of the new order of things, and had expressed herself with great indiscretion in the presence of the Queen. But the Duchess was brought to her senses, when she saw herself, and all the mad, democratical nobility, under the overpowering weight of Jacobinism, deprived of every privileged prerogative and leveled and stripped of hereditary distinction.

"She came to me one day, weeping, to beg I would make use of my good offices in her favor with the Queen, whom she was grieved that she had so grossly offended by an unguarded speech.

"'On my knees,' continued the Duchess, 'am I ready to supplicate the pardon of Her Majesty. I cannot live without her forgiveness. One of my servants has opened my eyes, by telling that the Revolution can make a Duchess a beggar, but cannot make a beggar a Duchess.'

"'Unfortunately,' said I, 'if some of these faithful servants had been listened to, they would still be such, and not now our masters; but I can assure you, Duchess that the Queen has long since forgiven you. See! Her Majesty comes to tell you so herself.'

"The Duchess fell upon her knees. The Queen, with her usual goodness of heart, clasped her in her arms, and, with tears in her eyes, said:

"'We have all of us need of forgiveness. Our errors and misfortunes are general. Think no more of the past; but let us unite in not sinning for the future.'

"'Heaven knows how many sins I have to atone for,' replied the Duchess, 'from the follies of youth; but now, at an age of discretion and in adversity, oh, how bitterly do I reproach myself for my past levities! But,' continued she, 'has Your Majesty really forgiven me?'

"'As I hope to be forgiven!' exclaimed Maria Antoinette. 'No penitent in the sight of God is more acceptable than the one who makes a voluntary sacrifice by confessing error. Forget and forgive is the language of our Blessed Redeemer. I have adopted it in regard to my enemies, and surely my friends have a right to claim it. Come, Duchess, I will conduct you to the King and Elizabeth, who will rejoice in the recovery of one of our lost sheep; for we sorely feel the diminution of the flock that once surrounded us!'

"At this token of kindness, the Duchess was so much overcome that she fell at the Queen's feet motionless, and it was some time before she recovered.*

"From the moment of Her Majesty's arrival at Paris from Versailles, she solely occupied herself with the education of her children; excepting when she resorted to my parties, the only ones, as she had at first determined, which she ever honored with her attendance. In order to discover, as far as possible, the sentiments of certain persons, I gave almost general invitations, whereby, from her amiable manners and gracious condescension, she became very popular. By these means I hope to replace Her Majesty in the good estimation of her numerous visitors; but, notwithstanding every exertion, she could not succeed in dispelling the gloom with which the Revolution had overcast all her former gayety. Though treated with ceremonious respect, she missed the cordiality to which she had been so long accustomed, and which she so much prized. From the great emigration of the higher classes of the nobility, the societies themselves were no longer what they had been. Madame Necker and Madame de Staël were pretty regular visitors. But the most agreeable company had lost its zest for Maria Antoinette; and she was really become afraid of large assemblies, and scarcely ever saw a group of persons collected together without fearing some plot against the King.

"Indeed, it is a peculiarity which has from the first marked, and still continues to distinguish the whole conduct and distrust of my royal mistress, that it never

---

* Ever after, the Duchess remained one of the most sincere friends of that unfortunate Queen. The manner in which Madame Campan speaks of her grief at the murder of Her Majesty proves the sincerity of her professed penitence.

The Princess Lamballe was so uniformly eager in contributing to the peace of mind and happiness of every individual who sought her mediation that she was as well known by the appellation of "the peacemaker" as she was by her title.

operates to create any fears for herself but invariably refers to the safety of His Majesty.

"I had enlarged my circle and made my parties extensive, solely to relieve the oppressed spirits of the Queen; but the very circumstance which induced me to make them so general soon rendered them intolerable to her; for the conversations at last became soly confined to the topics of the Revolution, a subject frequently the more distressing from the presence of the sons of the Duke of Orleans. Though I loved my sister-in-law and my nephews I could not see them without fear, nor could my royal mistress be at ease with them, or in the midst of such distressing indications as perpetually intruded upon her, even beneath my roof, of the spirit which animated the great body of the people for the propagation of antimonarchical principles.

"My parties were, consequently, broken up; and the Queen ceased to be seen in society. Then commenced the unconquerable power over her of those forebodings which have clung to her with such pertinacity ever since.

"I observed that Her Majesty would often indulge in the most melancholy predictions long before the fatal discussion took place in the assembly respecting the King's abdication. The daily insolence with which she saw His Majesty's authority deprived forever of the power of accomplishing what he had most at heart for the good of his people gave her more anguish than the outrages so frequently heaped upon herself; but her misery was wrought up to a pitch altogether unutterable, whenever she saw those around her suffer for their attachment to her in her misfortunes.

" The Princess Elizabeth has been from the beginning an unwavering comforter. She still flatters Maria Antoinette that Heaven will spare her for better times to reward our fidelity and her own agonies. The pious consolations of her highness have never failed to make the most serious impression on our wretched situation. Indeed, each of us strives to pour the balm of comfort into the wounded hearts of the others, while not one of us, in reality, dares to flatter herself with what we all so ardently wish for in regard to our fellow-sufferers. Delusions even sustained by facts, have long since been exhausted. Our only hope on this side of the grave is in our all-merciful Redeemer!"

CHAPTER XVI.

THE reader will not, I trust, be dissatisfied at reposing for a moment from the sad story of the Princess Lamballe to hear some ridiculous circumstances which occurred to me individually; and which, though they form no part of the history, are sufficiently illustrative of the temper of the times.

I had been sent to England to put some letters into the post office for the Prince of Condé and had just returned. The fashion then in England was a black dress, Spanish hat, and yellow satin lining, with three ostrich feathers forming the Prince of Wales's crest, and bearing his inscription, "*Ich dien,** I serve." I also brought with me a white satin cloak, trimmed with white fur.

In this dress, I went to the French opera. Scarcely was I seated in the box, when I heard shouts of, "*En bas les couleurs de l'empereur! En bas!*"

I was very busy talking to a person in the box, and, having been accustomed to hear and see partial riots in the pit, I paid no attention; never dreaming that my poor hat and feathers, and cloak, were the cause of the commotion, till an officer in the national guard very politely knocked at the door of the box, and told me I must either take them off or leave the theater.

There is nothing I more dislike than the being thought particular, or disposed to attract attention by dress. The moment, therefore, I found myself thus unintentionally

*This crest and motto date as far back, I believe, as the time of Edward, the Black Prince.

the object of a whole theater's disturbance, in the first impulse of indignation, I impetuously caught off the cloak and hat, and flung them into the pit, at the very faces of the rioters.

The theater instantly rang with applause. The obnoxious articles were carefully folded up and taken to the officer of the guard, who, when I left the box, at the end of the opera, brought them to me and offered to assist me in putting them on; but I refused them with true cavalier-like loftiness, and entered my carriage without either hat or cloak.

There were many of the audience collected round the carriage at the time, who, witnessing my rejection of the insulted colors, again loudly cheered me; but insisted on the officer's placing the hat and cloak in the carriage, which drove off amid the most violent acclamations.

Another day, as I was going to walk in the Tuileries (which I generally did after riding on horseback), the guards crossed their bayonets at the gate and forbade my entering. I asked them why. They told me no one was allowed to walk there without the national ribbon.

Now, I always had one of these national ribbons about me, from the time they were first worn; but I kept it in the inside of my riding habit: and on that day, in particular, my supply was unusually ample, for I had on a new riding habit, the petticoat of which was so very long and heavy that I bought a large quantity to tie round my waist, and fasten up the dress, to prevent it from falling about my feet.

However, I was determined to plague the guards for their impudence. My English beau, who was as pale as death, and knew I had the ribbon, kept pinching my arm, and whispering, "Show it, show it; zounds, madam, show it! We shall be sent to prison! show it! show it!" But I took care to keep my interrupters in parley till a sufficient mob was collected, and then I produced my colors.

The soldiers were consequently most gloriously hissed, and would have been maltreated by the mob, and sent to the guardhouse by their officer, but for my intercession; on which I was again applauded all through the gardens as *La Brave Anglaise*. But my beau declared he would never go out with me again unless I wore the ribbon on the outside of my hat, which I never did and never would do

At that time the Queen used to occupy herself much in fancy needle works. Knowing, from arrangements, that I was every day in a certain part of the Tuileries, Her Majesty, when she heard the shout of *La Brave Anglaise!* immediately called the Princess Lamballe to know if she had sent me on any message. Being answered in the negative, one of the pages was dispatched to ascertain the meaning of the cry. The Royal Family lived in so continual a state of alarm that it was apprehended I had got into some scrape; but I had left the Tuileries before the messenger arrived, and was already with the Princess Lamballe, relating the circumstances. The Princess told Her Majesty, who graciously observed, "I am very happy that she got off so well; but caution her to be more prudent for the future. A cause, however bad, is rather aided than weakened by unreasonable displays of contempt for it. These unnecessary excitements of the popular jealousy do us no good."

I was, of course, severely reprimanded by the Princess for my frolic, though she enjoyed it of all things, and afterward laughed most heartily.

The Princess told me, a few days after these circumstances of the national ribbon and the Austrian colors had taken place at the theater, that some one belonging to the private correspondence at the palace had been at the French opera on the night the disturbance took place there, and, without knowing the person to whom it related, had told the whole story to the King.

The Queen and the Princesses Elizabeth and Lamballe being present, laughed very heartily. The two latter knew it already from myself, the fountain head, but the Princess Elizabeth said:

"Poor lady! what a fright she must have been in, to have had her things taken away from her at the theater."

"No fright at all," said the King; "for a young woman who could act thus firmly under such an insolent outrage will always triumph over cowards, unmanly enough to abuse their advantages by insulting her. She was not a Frenchwoman, I'll answer for it."

"Oh, no, sire. She is an Englishwoman," said the Princess Lamballe.

"I am glad of it," exclaimed the King; "for when she returns to England this will be a good personal specimen for the information of some of her countrymen, who have rejoiced at what they call the regeneration of of the French nation; a nation once considered the most polished in Europe, but now become the most uncivil, and I wish I may never have occasion to add, the most barbarous! An insult offered, wantonly, to either sex, at any time, is the result of insubordination; but, when offered to a female, it is a direct violation of civilized hospitality, and an abuse of power which never before tarnished that government now so much the topic of abuse by the enemies of order and legitimate authority. The French Princes, it is true, have been absolute; still I never governed despotically, but always by the advice of my counselors and cabinet ministers. If THEY have erred, MY conscience is void of reproach. I wish the national assembly may govern for the future with equal prudence, equity and justice; but they have given a poor earnest in pulling down one fabric before they have laid the solid foundation of another. I am very happy that their agents, who, though they call themselves the guardians of public order have hitherto destroyed its course, have, in the courage of this English lady, met with some resistance to their insolence, in foolishly occupying themselves with petty matters, while those of vital import are totally neglected."

It is almost superfluous to mention that, at the epoch of which I am speaking in the Revolution, the Royal Family were in so much distrust of everyone about them, and very necessarily and justly so, that none were ever confided in for affairs, however trifling, without first having their fidelity repeatedly put to the test. I was myself under this probation long before I knew that such had ever been imposed.

With the private correspondence I had already been for some time intrusted; and it was only previous to employing me on secret missions of any consequence that I was subject to the severer scrutiny. Even before I was sent abroad, great art was necessary to elude the vigilance of prying eyes in the royal circle; and, in order to render my activity available to important purposes, my connection with the Count was long kept secret. Many stratagems were devised to mislead the Arguses of the police. To this end, after the disorders of the Revolution began, I never entered the palaces but on an understood signal for which I have been often obliged to attend many hours in the gardens of Versailles, as I had subsequently done in that of the Tuileries.

To pass the time unnoticed, I used generally to take a book, and seat myself, occupied in reading, sometimes in one spot, sometimes in another; but with my man and maid servant always within call, though never where they could be seen.

On one of these occasions, a person, though not totally masked yet sufficiently disguised to prevent my recognizing his features, came behind my seat, and said he wished to speak to me. I turned round and asked his business.

"That's coming to .the point!" he answered. "Walk a little way with me, and I will tell you."

Not to excite suspicion, I walked into a more retired part of the garden, after a secret signal to my man servant, who followed me unperceived by the stranger.

"I am commissioned," said my mysterious companion, "to make you a very handsome present, if you will tell me what you are waiting for."

I laughed, and was turning from him, saying, " Is this all your business ? "

"No," he replied.

"Then keep it to yourself. I am not waiting here for

anyone or anything; but am merely occupied in reading and killing time to the best advantage."

"Are you a poetess?"

"No."

"And scarcely a female; for your answers are very short."

"Very likely."

"But I have something of importance to communicate "——

"That is impossible."

"But listen to me "——

"You are mistaken in your person."

"But surely you will not be so unreasonable as not to hear what I have to say?"

"I am a stranger in this country, and can have nothing of importance with one I do not know."

"You have quarreled with your lover and are in an ill-humor."

"Perhaps so. Well! come! I believe you have guessed the cause."

"Ah! it is the fate of us all to get into scrapes! But you will soon make it up; and now let me entreat your attention to what I have to offer."——

I became impatient, and called my servant.

"Madam," resumed the stranger, "I am a gentleman, and mean no harm. But I assure you, you stand in your own light. I know more about you than you think I do."

"Indeed!"

"Yes, madam, you are waiting here for an august personage."

At this last sentence, my lips laughed, while my heart trembled.

"I wish to caution you," continued he, "how you embark in plans of this sort."

"Sir, I repeat, you have taken me for some other person. I will no longer listen to one who is either a maniac or an officious intruder."

Upon this, the stranger bowed and left me; but I could perceive that he was not displeased with my answers, though I was not a little agitated, and longed to see her highness to relate to her this curious adventure.

In a few hours I did so. The Princess was perfectly satisfied with my manner of proceeding, only she thought it singular, she said, that the stranger should suspect I was there in attendance for some person of rank; and she repeated, three or four times, "I am heartily glad that you did not commit yourself by any decided answer. What sort of a man was he?"

"Very much of the gentleman; above the middle stature; and, from what I could see of his countenance, rather handsome than otherwise."

"Was he a Frenchman?"

"No. I think he spoke good French and English, with an Irish accent."

"Then I know who it is," exclaimed she. "It is Dillon: I know it from some doubts which arose between Her Majesty, Dillon, and myself, respecting sending you upon a confidential mission. Oh, come hither! come hither!" continued her highness, overwhelming me with kisses. "How glad, how very glad I am, that the Queen will be convinced I was not deceived in what I told Her Majesty respecting you. Take no notice of what I am telling you; but he was sent from the Queen, to tempt you into some imprudence, or to be convinced, by your not falling into the snare, that she might rely on your fidelity."

"What! doubt my fidelity?" said I.

"Oh, my dear, you must excuse Her Majesty. We live in critical times. You will be the more rewarded, and much more esteemed, for this proof of your firmness. Do you think you should know him, if you were to see him again?"

"Certainly, I should, if he were in the same disguise."

"That, I fear, will be rather difficult to accomplish. However, you shall go in your carriage and wait at the door of his sister, the Marchioness of Desmond, where I will send for him to come to me at four o'clock to-morrow. In this way, you will have an opportunity of

15

seeing him on horseback, as he always pays his morning visits riding.

I would willingly have taken a sleeping draught, and never did I wait more anxiously than for the hour of four.

I left the Princess, and in crossing from the Carousal to go to the Place Vendôme, it rained very fast, and there glanced by me, on horseback, the same military cloak in which the stranger had been wrapped. My carriage was driving so fast that I still remained in doubt as to the wearer's person.

Next day, however, as appointed, I repaired to the place of rendezvous; and I could almost have sworn from the height of the person who alighted from his horse that he was my mysterious questioner.

Still, I was not thoroughly certain. I watched the Princess coming out, and followed her carriage to the Champs Elysées and told her what I thought.

"Well," replied she, "we must think no more about it; nor must it ever be mentioned to him, should you by any chance meet him."

I said I should certainly obey her highness.

A guilty conscience needs no accuser. A few days after I was riding on horseback in the Bois de Boulogne, when Lord Edward Fitzgerald came up to speak to me. Dillon was passing at the time, and, seeing Lord Edward, stopped, took off his hat, and observed, "A very pleasant day for riding, madam!" Then, looking me full in the face, he added, "I beg your pardon, madam, I mistook you for another lady with whom Lord Edward is often in company."

I said there was no offense; but the moment I heard him speak I was no longer in doubt of his being the identical person.

When I had learned the ciphering and deciphering, and was to be sent to Italy, the Queen acknowledged to the Princess Lamballe that she was fully persuaded I might be trusted, as she had good reason to know that my fidelity was not to be doubted or shaken.

Dear, hapless Princess! She said to me, in one of her confidential conversations on these matters, "The Queen has been so cruelly deceived and so much watched that she almost fears her own shadow; but it gives me great pleasure that Her Majesty had been herself confirmed by one of her own emissaries in what I never for a moment doubted.

"But do not fancy," continued the Princess, laughing, "that you have had only this spy to encounter. Many others have watched your motions and your conversations, and all concur in saying you are the devil, and they could make nothing of you. But that, *mia cara piccola diavolina*, is just what we want!"

CHAPTER XVII.

Editor in Continuation — Extraordinary Expedients Necessary to Evade Espionage — Anecdote of Boxes Sent by the Editor from Paris — Curious Occurrence Respecting Gamin, the King's Locksmith — Consternation of the Princess Lamballe When Apprised of It — Scheme to Avoid the Consequences — Kind and Interesting Conduct of the Queen and Royal Family.

I AM compelled, with reluctance, to continue personally upon the stage, and must do so for the three ensuing chapters, in order to put my readers in possession of circumstances explanatory of the next portion of the Journal of the Princess Lamballe.

Even the particulars I am about to mention can give but a very faint idea of the state of alarm in which the Royal Family lived, and the perpetual watchfulness and strange and involved expedients that were found necessary for their protection. Their most trifling communications were scrutinized with so much jealousy, that when any of importance were to be made it required a dexterity almost miraculous to screen them from the ever-watchful eye of espionage.

I was often made instrumental to evading the curiosity of others, without ever receiving any clue to the gratification of my own, even had I been troubled with such impertinence. The anecdote I am about to mention will show how cautious a game it was thought necessary to play; and the result of my half-information will evince that over caution may produce evils almost equal to total carelessness.

Some time previous to the flight of the Royal Family from Paris, the Princess Lamballe told me she wanted some repairs made to the locks of certain dressing and writing desks; but she would prefer having them done at my apartments, and by a locksmith who lived at a distance from the palace.

When the boxes were repaired, I was sent with one of them to Lisle, where another person took charge of it for the Archduchess at Brussels.

There was something which strongly marked the kind-heartedness of the Princess Lamballe in a part of this transaction. I had left Paris without a passport, and her highness, fearing it might expose me to inconvenience, sent an express after me. The express arrived three hours before I did, and the person to whom I have alluded came out of Brussels in his carriage to meet me and receive the box. At the same time, he gave me a sealed letter, without any address. I asked him from whom he received it, and to whom it was to be delivered. He said he was only instructed to deliver it to the lady with the box, and he showed me the Queen's cipher. I took the letter; and, after partaking of some refreshments, returned with it, according to my orders.

On my arrival at Paris, the Princess Lamballe told me her motive for sending the express, who, she said, informed her, on his return, that I had a letter for the Queen. I said it was more than I knew. "Oh, I suppose that is because the letter bears no address," replied she; "but you were shown the cipher, and that is all which is necessary."

She did not take the letter, and I could not help remarking how far, in this instance, the rigor of etiquette was kept up, even between these close friends. The Princess, not having herself received the letter, could not take it from my hands to deliver without Her Majesty's express command. This being obtained, she asked me for it, and gave it to Her Majesty. The circumstance convinced me that the Princess exercised much less influence over the Queen, and was much more directed by Her Majesty's authority, than has been imagined.

Two or three days after my arrival at Paris, my servant lost the key of my writing desk, and, to remedy the evil, he brought me the same locksmith I had

employed on the repairs just mentioned. As it was necessary I should be present to remove my papers when the
lock was taken off, of course I saw the man. While I
was busy clearing the desk, with an air of great familiarity he said, "I have had jobs to do here before now,
my girl, as your sweetheart there well knows."

I humored his mistake in taking me for my own maid
and my servant's sweetheart, and I pertly answered,
"Very likely."

"O yes, I have," said he; "it was I who repaired the
Queen's boxes in this very room."

Knowing I had never received anything of the sort
from Her Majesty, and utterly unaware that the boxes
the Princess sent to my apartments had been the Queen's,
I was greatly surprised. Seeing my confusion, he said,
"I know the boxes as well as I know myself. I am the
King's locksmith, my dear, and I and the King worked
together many years. Why, I know every creek and
corner of the palace, aye, and I know everything that's
going on in them too:—queer doings! Lord, my pretty
damsel, I made a secret place in the palace to hide the
King's papers, where the devil himself would never find
them out, if I or the King didn't tell!"

Though I wished HIM at the devil every moment, he
detained me from disclosing his information at the palace,
yet I played off the *soubrette* upon him till he became so
interested I thought he never would have gone. At last,
however, he took his departure, and the moment he disappeared, out of the house I flew.

The agitation and surprise of the Princess at what I
related were extreme. "Wait," cried she; "I must go
and inform the Queen instantly." In going out of the
room, "*Gran Dio, qual scoperta!* Great God, what a
discovery!" exclaimed her highness.

It was not long before she returned. Luckily, I was
dressed for dinner. She took me by the hand and, unable to speak, led me to the private closet of the Queen.

Her Majesty graciously condescended to thank me for
the letter I had taken charge of. She told me that for

the future all letters to her would be without any super-scription; and desired me, if any should be given to me by persons I had not before seen, and the cipher were shown at the same time, to receive and deliver them my-self into her hands, as the production of the cipher would be a sufficient pledge of their authenticity.

Being desired to repeat the conversation with Gamin, "There, Princess!" exclaimed Her Majesty, "*Non son io il corvo delle cative notizie?* am I not the crow of evil forebodings? I trust the King will never again be cred-ulous enough to employ this man. I have long had an extreme aversion to His Majesty's familiarity with him; but he shall hear his impudence himself from your own lips, my good little Englishwoman; and then he will not think it is prepossession or prejudice."

A few evenings elapsed, and I thought no more of the subject, till one night I was ordered to the palace by the Princess, which never happened but on very particu-lar occasions, as she was fearful of exciting suspicion by any appearance of close intimacy with one so much about Paris upon the secret embassies of the Court.

When I entered the apartment, the King, the Queen, and the Princess Elizabeth were, as if by accident, in an adjoining room; but, from what followed, I am certain they all came purposely to hear my deposition. I was presently commanded to present myself to the august party.

The King was in deep conversation with the Princess Elizabeth. I must confess I felt rather embarrassed. I could not form an idea why I was thus honored. The Princess Lamballe graciously took me by the hand.

"Now tell His Majesty, yourself, what Gamin said to you."

I began to revive, perceiving now wherefore I was sum-moned. I accordingly related, in the presence of the royal guests assembled, as I had done before Her Maj-esty and the Princess Lamballe, the scene as it occurred.

When I came to that part where he said, "where the devil himself could never find them out," His Majesty approached from the balcony, at which he had been talking with the Princess Elizabeth, and said, "Well! he is very right — but neither he nor the devil SHALL find them out, for they shall be removed this very night."*

The King, the Queen and the Princess Elizabeth most graciously said, "*Nous sommes bien obligés, ma petite anglaise!*" and Her Majesty added, "Now, my dear, tell me all the rest about this man, whom I have long suspected for his wickedness."

I said he had been guilty of no hostile indications, and that the chief fault I had to find with him was his exceeding familiarity in mentioning himself before the King, saying, "I and the King."

"Go on," said Her Majesty; "give us the whole as it occurred, and let us form our own conclusions."

"Yes," cried the Princess, "*parlate sciolto.*" "*Si, si,*" rejoined the Queen, "*parlate tutto* — yes, yes, speak out and tell us all."

I then related the remainder of the conversation, which very much alarmed the royal party, and it was agreed that to avoid suspicion I should next day send for the locksmith and desire him, as an excuse, to look at the locks of my trunks and traveling carriage, and set off in his presence to take up my pretended mistress on the road to Calais, that he might not suspect I had any connection with anyone about the Court. I was strictly enjoined by Her Majesty to tell him that the man servant had had the boxes from some one to get them repaired, without either my knowledge or that of my mistress, and, by her pretended orders, to give him a discharge upon the spot for having dared to use her apartments as a workshop for the business of other people.

"Now," said the Princess Lamballe, "*fate la buffona come avete fatta col servo vostro e Gamin* — now play the comic part you acted between your servant and Gamin:" which I did, as well as I could recollect it, and the royal

* Which was done; and these are, therefore, no doubt, the papers and portfolio of which Madame Campan speaks, vol. ii., p. 142, as having been intrusted to her care after being taken from their hiding place by the King himself.

audience were so much amused, that I had the honor to
remain in the room and see them play at cards. At
length, however, there came three gentle taps at the
outer door. "*Ora è tempo perche vene andata,*" exclaimed her highness at the sound, having ordered a person to call with this signal to see me out of the palace
to the Rue Nicaise, where my carriage was in waiting
to conduct me home.

It is not possible for me to describe the gracious condescension of the Queen and the Princess Elizabeth, in
expressing their sentiments for the accidental discovery
I had made. Amid their assurances of tender interest
and concern, they both reproved me mildly for my imprudence in having, when I went to Brussels, hurried
from Paris without my passport. They gave me prudential cautions with regard to my future conduct and residence at Paris; and it was principally owing to the
united persuasions and remonstrances of these three angels in human form that I took six or seven different
lodgings, where the Princess Lamballe used to meet me
by turns; because had I gone often to the palace, as
many others did, or waited for her highness regularly in
any one spot, I should, infallibly, have been discovered.

"Gracious God!" exclaimed Her Majesty in the course
of this conversation, "am I born to be the misfortune of
everyone who shows an interest in serving me? Tell my
sister, when you return to Brussels again — and do not
forget to say I desired you to tell her, our cruel situation! She does not believe that we are surrounded by
enemies, even in our most private seclusions! in our
prison! that we are even thrown exclusively upon
foreigners in our most confidential affairs; that in France
there is scarcely an individual to whom we can look!
They betray us for their own safety, which is endangered
by any exertions in our favor. Tell her this," repeated
the Queen three or four times.

The next day I punctually obeyed my orders. Gamin
was sent for to look at the locks, and received six francs
for his opinion. The man servant was reproved by me

on behalf of my supposed mistress, and, in the presence
of Gamin, discharged for having brought suspicious things
into the house. The man being tutored in his part,
begged Gamin to plead for my intercession with our
mistress. I remained inexorable, as he knew I should.
While Gamin was still by I discharged the bill at the
house, got into my carriage, and took the road toward
Calais.

At Saint Denis, however, I feigned to be taken ill, and
in two days returned to Paris.

Even this simple act required management. I contrived it in the following manner: I walked out on the
high road leading to the capital for the purpose of meeting my servant at a place which had been fixed for the
meeting before I left Paris. I found him on horseback
at his post, with a carriage prepared for my return. As
soon as I was out of sight he made the best of his way
forward, went to the inn with a note from me, and returned with my carriage and baggage to lodgings I had
at Passy.

The joy of the Princess on seeing me safe again brought
tears into her eyes; and when I related the scene I
played off before Gamin against my servant, she laughed
most heartily. "But surely," said she, "you have not
really discharged the poor man?" "Oh, no," replied
I; "he acted his part so well before the locksmith, that
I should be very sorry to lose such an apt scholar."

"You must perform this *buffa scena*," observed her
highness, "to the Queen. She has been very anxious to
know the result; but her spirits are so depressed that I
fear she will not come to my party this evening. However, if she do not, I will see her to-morrow, and you
shall make her laugh. It would be a charity, for she
has not done so from the heart for many a day!"

CHAPTER XVIII.

EVERYONE who has read at all, is familiar with the immortal panegyric of the great Edmund Burke upon
Maria Antoinette. It is known that this illustrious
man was not mean enough to flatter; yet his eloquent
praises of her as a princess, a woman, and a beauty, in-
spiring something beyond what any other woman could
excite, have been called flattery by those who never knew
her; those who DID, must feel them to be, if possible,
even below the truth. But the admiration of Mr. Burke was
set down even to a baser motive, and, like everything else,
converted into a source of slander for political purposes,
long before that worthy palladium of British liberty had
even thought of interesting himself for the welfare of
France, which his prophetic eye saw plainly was the common cause of all Europe.

But, keenly as that great statesman looked into futurity,
little did he think, when he visited the Queen in all her
splendor at Trianon, and spoke so warmly of the cordial
reception he had met with at Versailles from the Duke

and Duchess de Polignac, that he should have so soon to deplore their tragic fate!

Could his suggestions to Her Majesty, when he was in France, have been put in force, there is scarcely a doubt that the Revolution might have been averted, or crushed. But he did not limit his friendship to personal advice. It is not generally known that the Queen carried on, through the medium of the Princess Lamballe, a very extensive correspondence with Mr. Burke. He recommended wise and vast plans; and these, if possible, would have been adopted. The substance of some of the leading ones I can recall from the journal of her highness and letters which I have myself frequently deciphered. I shall endeavor, succinctly, to detail such of them as I remember.

Mr. Burke recommended the suppression of all superfluous religious institutions, which had not public seminaries to support. Their lands, he advised, should be divided, without regard to any distinction but that of merit, among such members of the army and other useful classes of society, as, after having served the specified time, should have risen, through their good conduct, to either civil or military preferment. By calculations upon the landed interest, it appeared that every individual under the operation of this bounty would, in the course of twenty years, possess a yearly income of from five to seven hundred francs.

Another of the schemes suggested by Mr. Burke was to purge the kingdom of all the troops which had been corrupted from their allegiance by the intrigues growing out of the first meeting of the Notables. He proposed that they should sail at the same time, or nearly so, to be colonized in the different French islands and Madagascar; and, in their place, a new national guard created, who should be bound to the interest of the legitimate Government by receiving the waste crown lands to be shared among them, from the common soldier to its generals and field marshals. Thus would the whole mass of rebellious blood have been reformed. To insure an effectual change,

Mr. Burke advised the enrollment, in rotation, of sixty thousand Irish troops,* twenty thousand always to remain in France, and forty thousand in reversion for the same service. The lynx-eyed statesman saw clearly, from the murders of the Marquis de Launay and M. Flesselles, and from the destruction of the Bastille, and of the ramparts of Paris, that party had not armed itself against Louis, but against the throne. It was therefore necessary to produce a permanent revolution in the army.

There was another suggestion to secure troops around the throne of a more loyal temper. It was planned to incorporate all the French soldiers, who had not voluntarily deserted the royal standard, with two-thirds of Swiss, German, and Low Country forces, among whom were to be divided, after ten years' service, certain portions of the crown lands, which were to be held by presenting every year a flag of acknowledgment to the King and Queen; with the preference of serving in the civil or military departments, according to the merit or capacity

---

* Mr. Burke was too great a statesman not to be the friend of his country's interest. He also saw that from the destruction of the monarchy in France, England had more to fear than to gain. He well knew that the French Revolution was not, like that of the Americans, founded on grievances and urged in support of a great and disinterested principle. He was aware that so restless a people, when they had overthrown the monarchy, would not limit the overthrow to their own country. After Mr. Burke's death, Mr. Fox was applied to, and was decidedly of the same opinion. Mr. Sheridan was interrogated, and, at the request of the Princess Lamballe, he presented, for the Queen's inspection, plans nearly equal to those of the above two great statesmen; and what is most singular and scarcely credible is that one and all of the opposition party in England strenuously exerted themselves for the upholding of the monarchy in France. Many circumstances which came to my knowledge before and after the death of Louis XVI. prove that Mr. Pitt himself was averse to the republican principles being organized so near a constitutional monarchy as France was to Great Britain. Though the conduct of the Duke of Orleans was generally reprobated, I firmly believe that if he had possessed sufficient courage to have usurped the crown and re-established the monarchy, he would have been treated with in preference to the republicans. I am the more confirmed in this opinion by a conversation between the Princess Lamballe and Mirabeau, in which he said a republic in France would never thrive.

of the respective individuals. Messieurs de Broglio, Bouillé, Luxembourg, and others, were to have been commanders. But this plan, like many others, was foiled in its birth, and, it is said, through the intrigues of Mirabeau.

However, all concurred in the necessity of ridding France, upon the most plausible pretexts, of the foment-ers of its ruin. Now arose a fresh difficulty. Transports were wanted, and in considerable numbers.

A navy agent in England was applied to for the sup-ply of these transports. So great was the number re-quired, and so peculiar the circumstances, that the agent declined interfering without the sanction of his Govern-ment.

A new dilemma succeeded. Might not the King of England place improper constructions on this extensive shipment of troops from the different ports of France for her West India possessions! Might it not be fancied that it involved secret designs on the British settlements in that quarter?

All these circumstances required that some communica-tion should be opened with the Court of St. James's, and the critical posture of affairs exacted that such communi-cation should be less diplomatic than confidential.

It will be recollected, that, at the very commencement of the reign of Louis XVI., there were troubles in Britanny, which the severe governorship of the Duke d'Aiguillon augmented. The Britons took privileges with them, when they became blended with the kingdom of France, by the marriage of Anne of Brittany with Charles VIII , beyond those of any other of its provinces. These privileges they seemed rather disposed to extend than relinquish, and were by no means reserved in the expression of their resolution. It was considered expedi-ent to place a firm, but conciliatory, governor over them, and the Duke de Penthièvre was appointed to this dif-ficult trust. The Duke was accompanied to his vice-royalty by his daughter-in-law, the Princess Lamballe, who, by her extremely judicious management of the female part of the province, did more for the restoration of order than could have been achieved by armies. The remembrance of this circumstance induced the Queen to regard her highness as a fit person to send secretly to England at this very important crisis; and the purpose was greatly encouraged by a wish to remove her from a scene of such daily increasing peril.

For privacy, it was deemed expedient that her highness should withdraw to Aumale, under the plea of ill health, and thence proceed to England; and it was also by way of Aumale that she as secretly returned, after the fatal disaster of the stoppage, to discourage the impression of her ever having been out of France.

The mission was even unknown to the French minister at the Court of St. James's.

The Princess was ordered by Her Majesty to cultivate the acquaintance of the late Duchess of Gordon, who was supposed to possess more influence than any woman in England — in order to learn the sentiments of Mr. Pitt relative to the revolutionary troubles. The Duchess, however, was too much of an Englishwoman, and Mr. Pitt too much interested in the ruin of France, to give her the least clue to the truth.

In order to fathom the sentiments of the opposition party, the Princess cultivated the society also of the late Duchess of Devonshire, but with as little success. The opposition party foresaw too much risk in bringing anything before the house to alarm the prejudices of the nation.

The French ambassador, too, jealous of the unexplained purpose of the Princess, did all he could to render her expedition fruitless.

Nevertheless, though disappointed in some of her main objects with regard to influence and information, she became so great a favorite at the British Court * that she

---

* The Princess visited Bath, Windsor, Brighton, and many other parts of England, and associated with all parties. She managed her conduct so judiciously that the real object of her visit was never suspected. In all these excursions I had the honor to attend her confiden-

obtained full permission of the King and Queen of England to signify to her royal mistress and friend, that the specific request she came to make would be complied with.

In the meantime, however, the troubles in France were so rapidly increasing from hour to hour, that it became impossible for the Government to carry any of their plans into effect. This particular one, on the very eve of its accomplishment, was marred, as it was imagined, by the secret intervention of the friends of Mirabeau. The Government became more and more infirm and wavering in its purposes; the Princess was left without instructions, and under such circumstances as to expose her to the supposition of having trifled with the good will of Their Majesties of England.

In this dilemma, I was sent off from England to the Queen of France. I left her highness at Bath, but when I returned she had quitted Bath for Brighton. I am unacquainted with the nature of all the papers she received, but I well remember the agony they seemed to inflict on her. She sent off a packet by express that very night to Windsor.

tially. I was the only person intrusted with papers from her highness to Her Majesty. I had many things to copy, of which the originals went to France.

Twice during the term of her highness's residence in England I was sent by Her Majesty with papers communicating the result of the secret mission to the Queen of Naples. On the second of these two trips, being obliged to travel night and day, I could only keep my eyes open by means of the strongest coffee. When I reached my destination I was immediately compelled to decipher the dispatches with the Queen of Naples in the office of the Secretary of State. That done, General Acton ordered some one, I know not whom, to conduct me, I know not where, but it was to a place where, after a sound sleep of twenty-four hours, I awoke thoroughly refreshed, and without a vestige of fatigue either of mind or body. On waking, lest anything should transpire, I was desired to quit Naples instantly, without seeing the British minister. To make assurance doubly sure, General Acton sent a person from his office to accompany me out of the city on horseback; and, to screen me from the attack of robbers, this person went on with me as far as the Roman frontier.

The Princess immediately began the preparations for her return. Her own journal is explicit on this point of her history, and therefore I shall leave her to speak for herself. I must not, however, omit to mention the remark she made to me upon the subject of her reception in Great Britain. With these, let me dismiss the present chapter.

"The general cordiality with which I have been received in your country," said her highness, "has made a lasting impression upon my heart. In particular, never shall I forget the kindness of the Queen of England, the Duchess of Devonshire, and her truly virtuous mother, Lady Spencer. It gave me a cruel pang to be obliged to undervalue the obligations with which they overwhelmed me by leaving England as I did, without giving them an opportunity of carrying their good intentions, which I had myself solicited, into effect. But we cannot command fate. Now that the King has determined to accept the constitution (and you know my sentiments upon the article respecting ecclesiastics), I conceive it my duty to follow Their Majesties' example in submitting to the laws of the nation. Be assured, *Inglesina*, it will be my ambition to bring about one of the happiest ages of French history. I shall endeavor to create that confidence so necessary for the restoration to their native land of the Princes of the blood, and all the emigrants who abandoned the King, their families, and their country, while doubtful whether His Majesty would or would not concede this new charter; but now that the doubt exists no longer, I trust we shall all meet again the happier for the privation to which we have been doomed from absence. As the limation of the monarchy removes every kind of responsibility from the monarch, the Queen will again taste the blissful sweets she once enjoyed during the reign of Louis XV. in the domestic tranquillity of her home at Trianon. Often has she wept those times in which she will again rejoice. Oh, how I long for their return! I fly to greet the coming period of future happiness to us all!"

16

Postscript.

Although I am not making myself the historian of France, yet it may not be amiss to mention that it was during this absence of her highness that Necker finally retired from power and from France.

The return of this minister had been very much against the consent of Her Majesty and the King. They both feared what actually happened soon afterward. They foresaw that he would be swept away by the current of popularity from his deference to the royal authority. It was to preserve the favor of the mob that he allowed them to commit the shocking murders of M. de Foulon (who had succeeded him on his first dismission as minister of Louis XVI.) and of Berthier, his son-in-law. The union of Necker with Orleans, on this occasion, added to the cold indifference with which Barnave in one of his speeches expressed himself concerning the shedding of human blood, certainly animated the factious assassins to methodical murder, and frustrated all the efforts of La Fayette to save these victims from the enraged populace, to whom both unfortunately fell a sacrifice.

Necker, like La Fayette, when too late, felt the absurdity of relying upon the idolatry of the populace. The one fancied he could command the Parisian *poissardes* as easily as his own battalions; and the other persuaded himself that the mob which had been hired to carry about his bust, would as readily promulgate his theories.

But he forgot that the people in their greatest independence are only the puppets of demagogues; and he lost himself by not gaining over that class, which, of all others, possesses most power over the million, I mean the men of the bar, who, arguing more logically than the rest of the world, felt that from the new constitution the long robe was playing a losing game, and therefore discouraged a system which offered nothing to their personal ambition or private emolument. Lawyers, like priests, are never overripe for any changes or innovations, except such as tend to their personal interest. The more perplexed the state of public and private affairs, the better for them. Therefore in revolutions, as a body, they remain neuter, unless it is made for their benefit to act. Individually, they are a set of necessary evils; and, for the sake of the bar, the bench, and the gibbet, require to be humored. But any legislator who attempts to render laws clear, concise, and explanatory, and to divest them of the quibbles whereby these expounders — or confounders — of codes, fatten on the credulity of states and the miseries of unfortunate millions, will necessarily encounter opposition, direct or indirect, in every measure at all likely to reduce the influence of this most abominable horde of human depredators. It was Necker's error to have gone so directly to the point with the lawyers that they at once saw his scope; and thus he himself defeated his hopes of their support, the want of which utterly baffled all his speculations.*

When Necker undertook to re-establish the finances, and to reform generally the abuses in the Government, he was the most popular minister (Lord Chatham, when the great Pitt, excepted) of any in Europe. Yet his errors were innumerable, though possessing such sound knowledge and judgment, such a superabundance of political contrivance, diplomatic coolness, and mathematical calculation, the result of deep thought aided by great practical experience.

But how futile he made all these appear when he declared the national bankruptcy. Could anything be more absurd than the assumption, by the individual, of a personal instead of a national guarantee of part of a national debt? an undertaking too hazardous and by far too ambiguous, even for a monarch who is not backed by his kingdom — how doubly frantic, then, for a subject! Necker imagined that the above declaration and his own

---

* The great Frederick of Prussia, on being told of the numbers of lawyers there were in England, said he wished he had them in his country. "Why?" some one inquired. "To do the greatest benefit in my power to society." "How so?" "Why to hang one-half as an example to the other!"

quixotic generosity would have opened the coffers of the great body of rich proprietors, and brought them forward to aid the national crisis. But he was mistaken. The nation then had no interest in his financial system. The effect it produced was the very reverse of what was expected. Every proprietor began to fear the ambition of the minister, who undertook impossibilities. The being bound for the debts of an individual, and justifying bail in a court of law in commercial matters, affords no criterion for judging of, or regulating, the pecuniary difficulties of a nation. Necker's conduct in this case was, in my humble opinion, as impolitic as that of a man who, after telling his friends that he is ruined past redemption, asks for a loan of money. The conclusion is, if he obtains the loan, that "the fool and his money are soon parted."*

It was during the same interval of her highness's stay in England, that the discontent ran so high between the people and the clergy.

I have frequently heard the Princess Lamballe ascribe the King's not sanctioning the decrees against the clergy to the influence of his aunt, the Carmelite nun, Madame Louise. During the life of her father, Louis XV., she nearly engrossed all the Church benefices by her intrigues. She had her regular conclaves of all orders of the Church. From the bishop to the sexton, all depended on her for preferment; and, till the Revolution, she maintained equal power over the mind of Louis XVI. upon similar matters. The Queen would often express her disapprobation; but the King was so scrupulous, whenever the discussion fell on the topic of religion, that she made it a point not to contrast her opinion with his, from a conviction that she was unequal to cope with him on that head, upon which he was generally very animated.

---

* I prognosticate that all money concerns which may take place in Spain, unless guaranteed by the nation to the nation whose individuals undertake the supply, will end in the ruin of those who may credulously be led, for a momentary advantage, to assist in its promulgation; that, in short, it will terminate, as the French paper did, from the million to one.

It is perfectly certain that the French clergy, by refusing to contribute to the exigencies of the state, created some of the primary horrors of the Revolution. They enjoyed one-third of the national revenues, yet they were the first to withhold their assistance from the national wants. I have heard the Princess Lamballe say, "The Princess Elizabeth and myself used our utmost exertions to induce some of the higher orders of the clergy to set the example and obtain for themselves the credit of offering up a part of the revenues, the whole of which we knew must be forfeited if they continued obstinate; but it was impossible to move them."

The characters of some of the leading dignitaries of the time sufficiently explain their selfish and pernicious conduct; when churchmen trifle with the altar, be their motives what they may, they destroy the faith they profess, and give examples to the flock intrusted to their care, of which no foresight can measure the baleful consequences. Who that is false to his God can be expected to remain faithful to his sovereign? When a man, as a Catholic bishop, marries; and, under the mask of patriotism, becomes the declared tool of all-work to every faction, and is the weathercock, shifting to any quarter according to the wind; such a man can be of no real service to any party; and yet has a man of this kind been by turns the *primum mobile* of them all, even to the present times, and was one of those great Church fomenters of the troubles of which we speak, who disgraced the virtuous reign of Louis XVI.

CHAPTER XIX.

A MID the perplexities of the Royal Family it was perfectly unavoidable that repeated proposals should have been made at various times for them to escape these dangers by flight. The Queen had been frequently and most earnestly entreated to withdraw alone; and the King, the Princess Elizabeth, the Princess Lamballe, the royal children, with their little hands uplifted, and all those attached to Maria Antoinette, after the horrid business at Versailles, united to supplicate her to quit France and shelter herself from the peril hanging over her existence. Often and often have I heard the Princess Lamballe repeat the words in which Her Majesty uniformly rejected the proposition. "I have no wish," cried the Queen, "for myself. My life or death must be encircled by the arms of my husband and my family. With them, and with them only, will I live or die."

It would have been impossible to have persuaded her to leave France without her children. If any woman on earth could have been justified in so doing, it would have been Maria Antoinette. But she was above such unnatural selfishness, though she had so many examples to encourage her; for, even among the members of her own family, self-preservation had been considered paramount to every other consideration.

I have heard the Princess say that Pope Pius VI. was the only one of all the sovereigns who offered the slightest condolence or assistance to Louis XVI. and his family. "The Pope's letter," added she, "when shown to me by the Queen, drew tears from my eyes. It really was in a style of such Christian tenderness and princely feeling as could only be dictated by a pious and illuminated head of the Christian Church. He implored not only all the family of Louis XVI., but even extended his entreaties to me (the Princess Lamballe) to leave Paris, and save themselves, by taking refuge in his dominions, from the horrors which so cruelly overwhelmed them. The King's aunts were the only ones who profited by the invitation. Madame Elizabeth was to have been of the party, but could not be persuaded to leave the King and Queen."

As the clouds grew more threatening, it is scarcely to be credited how many persons interested themselves for the same purpose, and what numberless schemes were devised to break the fetters which had been imposed on the Royal Family by their jailers, the assembly.

A party, unknown to the King and Queen, was even forming under the direction of the Princess Elizabeth; but as soon as Their Majesties were apprized of it, it was given up as dangerous to the interests of the Royal Family, because it thwarted the plans of the Marquis de Bouillé. Indeed, Her Majesty could never be brought to determine on any plan for her own or the King's safety until their royal aunts, the Princesses Victoria and Adelaide, had left Paris.

The first attempt to fly was made early in the year 1791, at St. Cloud, where the horses had been in preparation nearly a fortnight; but the scheme was abandoned in consequence of having been intrusted to too many persons. This the Queen acknowledged. She had it often in her power to escape alone with her son, but would not consent.

The second attempt was made in the spring of the same year at Paris. The guards shut the gates of the Tuileries, and would not allow the King's carriage to pass. Even though a large sum of money had been expended to form a party to overpower the mutineers, the treacherous mercenaries did not appear. The expedition was, of course, obliged to be relinquished. Many of the

royal household were very ill-treated, and some lives unfortunately lost.

At last, the deplorable journey did take place. The intention had been communicated by Her Majesty to the
Princess Lamballe before she went abroad, and it was
agreed that, whenever it was carried into effect, the
Queen should write to her highness from Montmédi, where
the two friends were once more to have been reunited.

Soon after the departure of the Princess, the arrangements for the fatal journey to Varennes were commenced,
but with blamable and fatal carelessness.

Mirabeau was the first person who advised the King to
withdraw; but he recommended that it should be alone,
or, at most, with the Dauphin only. He was of opinion
that the overthrow of the constitution could not be
achieved while the Royal Family remained in Paris. His
first idea was that the King should go to the seacoast,
where he would have it in his power instantly to escape
to England, if the assembly, through his (Mirabeau's)
means, did not comply with the royal propositions. Though
many of the King's advisers were for a distinct and open
rejection of the constitution, it was the decided impression of Mirabeau that he ought to stoop to conquer, and
temporize by an instantaneous acceptance, through which
he might gain time to put himself in an attitude to
make such terms as would at once neutralize the act and
the faction by which it was forced upon him. Others
imagined that His Majesty was too conscientious to avail
himself of any such subterfuge, and that, having once
given his sanction, he would adhere to it rigidly. This
third party of the royal counselors were therefore for a
cautious consideration of the document, clause by clause,
dreading the consequences of an *ex abrupto* signature
in binding the sovereign, not only against his policy,
but his will.

In the midst of all these distracting doubts, however,
the departure was resolved upon. Mirabeau had many
interviews with the Count de Fersen upon the subject.
It was his great object to prevent the flight from being

encumbered. But the King would not be persuaded to separate himself from the Queen and the rest of the family, and intrusted the project to too many advisers. Had he been guided by Fersen only, he would have succeeded.

The natural consequence of a secret being in so many hands was felt in the result. Those whom it was most important to keep in ignorance were the first on the alert. The weakness of the Queen in insisting upon taking a re- markable dressing case with her, and, to get it away unobserved, ordering a facsimile to be made under the pretext of intending it as a present to her sister at Brussels, awakened the suspicion of a favorite, but false female attendant, then intriguing with the aid-de-camp of La Fayette. The rest is easily to be conceived. The assembly were apprised of all the preparations for the departure a week or more before it occurred. La Fayette himself, it is believed, knew and encouraged it, that he might have the glory of stopping the fugitive himself; but he was overruled by the assembly.

When the secretary of the Austrian ambassador came publicly, by arrangement, to ask permission of the Queen to take the model of the dressing case in question, the very woman to whom I have alluded was in attendance at Her Majesty's toilet. The paramour of the woman was with her, watching the motions of the Royal Family on the night they passed from their own apartments to those of the Duke de Villequie in order to get into the carriage; and by this paramour was La Fayette instantly informed of the departure. The traitress discovered that Her Majesty was on the eve of setting off by seeing her diamonds packed up. All these things were fully known to the assembly, of which the Queen herself was afterward apprised by the Mayor of Paris.*

In the suite of the Count de Fersen,† there was a

* See Madame Campan's work, p. 146, vol. ii.

† Alvise de Pisani, the last Venetian ambassador to the King, who was my husband's particular friend, and with whom I was myself long acquainted, and have been ever since to this day, as well as with all his

young Swede who had an intrigue purposely with one of the Queen's women, from whom he obtained many important disclosures relative to the times. The Swede mentioned this to his patron, who advised Her Majesty to discharge a certain number of these women, among whom was the one who afterward proved her betrayer. It was suggested to dismiss a number at once, that the guilty person might not suspect the exclusion to be leveled against her in particular. Had the Queen allowed herself to be directed in this affair by Fersen, the chain of communication would have been broken, and the Royal Family would not have been stopped at Varennes, but have got clear out of France, many hours before they could have been perceived by the assembly; but Her Majesty never could believe that she had anything to fear from the quarter against which she was warned.

It is not generally known that a very considerable sum had been given to the head recruiting sergeant, Mirabeau, to enlist such of the constituents as could be won with gold to be ready with a majority in favor of the royal fugitives. But the death of Mirabeau, previous to this event, leaves it doubtful how far he distributed the bribes conscientiously; indeed, it is rather to be questioned whether he did not retain the money, or much of it, in his own hands, since the strongly hoped for and dearly paid majority never gave proof of existence, either before or after the journey to Varennes. Immense bribes were also given to the Mayor of Paris, which proved equally ineffective.

Had Mirabeau lived till the affair of Varennes, it is not impossible that his genius might have given a different complexion to the result. He had already treated with the Queen and the Princess for a reconciliation; and in the apartments of her highness, disguised in a monk's

noble family, during my many years' residence at Venice, told me this circumstance while walking with him at his country seat at Strà, which was subsequently taken from him by Napoleon, and made the imperial palace of the viceroy, and is now that of the German reigning prince.

dress, had frequent evening, and early morning, audiences of the Queen.

It is pretty certain, however, that the recantation of Mirabeau, from avowed democracy to aristocracy and royalty, through the medium of enriching himself by a *salva regina*, made his friends prepare for him that just retribution, which ended in a *de profundis*. At a period when all his vices were called to aid one virtuous action, his thread of vicious life was shortened, and he, no doubt, became the victim of his insatiable avarice. That he was poisoned is not to be disproved; though it was thought necessary to keep it from the knowledge of the people.

I have often heard her highness say, " When I reflect on the precautions which were taken to keep the interviews with Mirabeau profoundly secret — that he never conversed but with the King, the Queen, and myself — his untimely death must be attributed to his own indiscreet enthusiasm, in having confidentially intrusted the success with which he flattered himself, from the ascendancy he had gained over the Court, to some one who betrayed him. His death, so very unexpectedly, and at that crisis, made a deep impression on the mind of the Queen. She really believed him capable of redressing the monarchy, and he certainly was the only one of the turncoat constitutionalists in whom she placed any confidence. Would to Heaven that she had had more in Barnave, and that she had listened to Dumourier! These I would have trusted more, far more readily than the mercenary Mirabeau! "

I now return, once more, to the Journal of the Princess.

CHAPTER XX.

"IN THE midst of the perplexing debates upon the course most advisable with regard to the constitution after the unfortunate return from Varennes, I sent off my little English amanuensis to Paris to bring me, through the means of another trusty person I had placed about the Queen, the earliest information concerning the situation of affairs. On her return she brought me a ring, which Her Majesty had graciously condescended to send me, set with her own hair, which had whitened like that of a person of eighty, from the anguish the Varennes affair had wrought upon her mind, and bearing the inscription, 'Bleached by sorrow.' This ring was accompanied by the following letter:

"'MY DEAREST FRIEND:

"'The King has made up his mind to the acceptance of the constitution, and it will ere long be proclaimed publicly. A few days ago I was secretly waited upon and closeted in your apartment with many of our faithful friends — in particular, Alexander Lameth, Duport, Barnave, Montmorin, Bertrand de Moleville, et cætera. The two latter opposed the King's council, the ministers, and the numerous other advisers of an immediate and unscrutinizing acceptance. They were a small minority, and could not prevail with me to exercise my influence with His Majesty in support of their opinion, when all the rest seemed so confident that a contrary course must re-establish the tranquillity of the nation and our own happiness, weaken the party of the Jacobins against us, and greatly increase that of the nation in our favor.

" 'Your absence obliged me to call Elizabeth to my aid in managing the coming and going of the deputies to and from the Pavilion of Flora, unperceived by the spies of our enemies. She executed her charge so adroitly, that the visitors were not seen by any of the household. Poor Elizabeth! little did I look for such circumspection in one so unacquainted with the intrigues of Court, or the dangers surrounding us, which they would now fain persuade us no longer exist. God grant it may be so! and that I may once more freely embrace and open my heart to the only friend I have nearest to it. But though this is my most ardent wish, yet, my dear, dearest Lamballe, I leave it to yourself to act as your feelings dictate. Many about us profess to see the future as clear as the sun at noonday. But, I confess, my vision is still dim. I cannot look into events with the security of others who confound logic with their wishes. The King, Elizabeth, and all of us, are anxious for your return. But it would grieve us sorely for you to come back to such scenes as you have already witnessed. Judge and act from your own impressions. If we do not see you, send me the result of your interview at the precipice.* *Vostra cara picciola Inglesina* † will deliver you many letters. After looking over the envelopes, you will either send her with them as soon as possible or forward them as addressed, as you may think most advisable at the time you receive them.

" 'Ever, ever, and forever,
" ' Your affectionate,
" ' MARIA ANTOINETTE.'

"There was another hurried and abrupt note from Her Majesty among these papers, obviously written later than the first. It lamented the cruel privations to which she was doomed at the Tuileries, in consequence of the impeded flight, and declared, that what the Royal Family were forced to suffer from being totally deprived of every individual of their former friends and attendants to condole with, excepting the equally oppressed and unhappy Princess Elizabeth, was utterly insupportable.

"On the receipt of these much esteemed epistles, I returned, as my duty directed, to the best of Queens, and

---

* The name the Queen gave to Mr. Pitt.
† The appellation by which the Princess and Her Majesty always condescended to distinguish me.

most sincere of friends. My arrival at Paris, though so much wished for, was totally unexpected.

"At our first meeting, the Queen was so agitated that she was utterly at a loss to explain the satisfaction she felt in beholding me once more near her royal person. Seeing the ring on my finger, which she had done me the honor of sending me, she pointed to her hair, once so beautiful, but now, like that of an old woman, not only gray, but deprived of all its softness, quite stiff and dried up.

"Madame Elizabeth, the King, and the rest of our little circle, lavished on me the most endearing caresses. The dear Dauphin said to me, 'You will not go away again, I hope, Princess? Oh, mamma has cried so since you left us!'

"I had wept enough before, but this dear little angel brought tears into the eyes of us all.

"When I mentioned to Her Majesty the affectionate sympathy expressed by the King and Queen of England in her sufferings, and their regret at the state of public affairs in France, 'It is most noble and praiseworthy in them to feel thus,' exclaimed Maria Antoinette; 'and the more so considering the illiberal part imputed to us against those sovereigns in the rebellion of their ultramarine subjects, to which, Heaven knows, I never gave my approbation. Had I done so, how poignant would be my remorse at the retribution of our own sufferings, and the pity of those I had so injured! No. I was, perhaps, the only silent individual among millions of infatuated enthusiasts at General La Fayette's return to Paris, nor did I sanction any of the *fêtes* given to Dr. Franklin, or the American ambassadors at the time. I could not conceive it prudent for the Queen of an absolute monarchy to countenance any of their new-fangled philosophical experiments with my presence. Now, I feel the reward in my own conscience. I exult in my freedom from a self-reproach, which would have been altogether insupportable under the kindness of which you speak.'

"As soon as I was settled in my apartment, which was on the same floor with that of the Queen, she condescended to relate to me every particular of her unfortunate journey. I saw the pain it gave her to retrace the scenes, and begged her to desist till time should have, in some degree, assuaged the poignancy of her feelings. 'That,' cried she, embracing me, 'can never be! Never, never will that horrid circumstance of my life lose its vividness in my recollection. What agony, to have seen those faithful servants tied before us on the carriage, like common criminals! All, all may be attributed to the King's goodness of heart, which produces want of courage, nay, even timidity, in the most trying scenes. As poor King Charles the First, when he was betrayed in the Isle of Wight, would have saved himself, and perhaps thousands, had he permitted the sacrifice of one traitor, so might Louis XVI. have averted calamities so fearful, that I dare not name, though I distinctly forsee them, had he exerted his authority where he only called up his compassion.'

"'For Heaven's sake,' replied I, 'do not torment yourself by these cruel recollections!'

"'These are gone by,' continued Her Majesty, 'and greater still than even these. How can I describe my grief at what I endured in the assembly, from the studied humiliation to which the King and the royal authority were there reduced in the face of the national representatives! from seeing the King on his return choked with anguish at the mortifications to which I was doomed to behold the majesty of a French sovereign humbled! These events bespeak clouds, which, like the horrid waterspout at sea, nothing can dispel but cannon! The dignity of the crown, the sovereignty itself, is threatened; and this I shall write this very night to the Emperor. I see no hope of internal tranquillity without the powerful aid of foreign force.* The King has allowed himself to be too

* The only difference of any moment which ever existed between the Queen and the Princess Lamballe as to their sentiments on the Revolution was on this subject. Her highness wished Maria Antoinette to rely on the many persons who had offered and promised to serve the cause of the monarchy with their internal resources, and not depend on the

much led to attempt to recover his power through any
sort of mediation. Still, the very idea of owing our
liberty to a foreign army distracts me for the consequences.'

"My reinstatement in my apartments at the Pavilion
of Flora seemed not only to give universal satisfaction to
every individual of the Royal Family, but it was hailed
with much enthusiasm by many deputies of the constituent assembly. I was honored with the respective visits of
all who were in any degree well disposed to the royal cause.

"One day, when Barnave and others were present with
the Queen, 'Now,' exclaimed one of the deputies, 'now
that this good Princess is returned to her adopted country, the active zeal of her highness, coupled with Your
Majesty's powerful influence over the mind of the King
for the welfare of his subjects, will give fresh vigor to
the full execution of the constitution.'

"My visitors were earnest in their invitations for me
to go to the assembly to hear an interesting discussion,
which was to be brought forward upon the King's
spontaneous acceptance of the constitution.

"I went; and amid the plaudits for the good King's
condescension, how was my heart lacerated to hear
Robespierre denounce three of the most distinguished of
the members, who had requested my attendance as traitors to their country!

"This was the first and only assembly discussion I ever
attended; and how dearly did I pay for my curiosity! I

Princes and foreign armies. This salutary advice she never could en-
force on the Queen's mind, though she had to that effect been importuned
by upward of two hundred persons, all zealous to show their penitence
for former errors by their present devotedness.

"Whenever," observed her highness, "we came to that point, the
Queen (upon seriously reflecting that these persons had been active instruments in promoting the first changes in the monarchy, for which she
never forgave them from her heart) would hesitate and doubt; and never
could I bring Her Majesty definitely to believe the profferers to be sincere. Hence, they were trifled with, till one by one she either lost them,
or saw them sacrificed to an attachment, which her own distrust and
indecision rendered fruitless."

was accompanied by my *cara Inglesina*, who, always on the alert, exclaimed, 'Let me entreat your highness not to remain any longer in this place. You are too deeply moved to dissemble.'

"I took her judicious advice, and the moment I could leave the assembly unperceived, I hastened back to the Queen to beg her, for God's sake, to be upon her guard; for, from what I had just heard at the assembly, I feared the Jacobins had discovered her plans with Barnave, Lameth, Duport, and others of the royal party. Her countenance, for some minutes, seemed to be the only sensitive part of her. It was perpetually shifting from a high florid color to the paleness of death. When her first emotions gave way to nature, she threw herself into my arms, and, for some time, her feelings were so overcome by the dangers which threatened these worthy men, that she could only in the bitterness of her anguish exclaim, 'Oh! this is all on my account!' And I think she was almost as much alarmed for the safety of these faithful men, as she had been for that of the King on the 17th of July, when the Jacobins in the Champ de Mars called out to have the King brought to trial — a day of which the horrors were never effaced from her memory!

"The King and the Princess Elizabeth fortunately came in at the moment; but even our united efforts were unavailable. The grief of Her Majesty at feeling herself the cause of the misfortunes of these faithful adherents, now devoted victims of their earnestness in foiling the machinations against the liberty and life of the King and herself, made her nearly frantic. She too well knew that to be accused was to incur instant death. That she retained her senses under the convulsion of her feelings can only be ascribed to that wonderful strength of mind, which triumphed over every bodily weakness, and still sustains her under every emergency.

"The King and the Princess Elizabeth, by whom Barnave had been much esteemed ever since the journey from Varennes, were both inconsolable. I really believe the Queen entirely owed her instantaneous recovery from

that deadly lethargic state in which she had been thrown
by her grief for the destined sacrifice, to the exuberant
goodness of the King's heart, who instantly resolved to
compromise his own existence, to save those who had
forfeited theirs for him and his family.

"Seeing the emotion of the Queen, 'I will go myself
to the assembly,' said Louis XVI. 'and declare their innocence !'

"The Queen sprang forward, as if on the wings of an
angel, and grasping the King in her arms, cried, 'Will
you hasten their deaths by confirming the impression of
your keeping up an understanding with them? Gracious
Heaven! Oh, that I could recall the acts of attachment
they have shown us, since to these they are now falling
victims! I would save them,' continued Her Majesty,
'with my own blood; but, sire, it is useless. We should
only expose ourselves to the vindictive spirit of the Jacobins without aiding the cause of our devoted friends.

"''Who,' asked she, 'was the guilty wretch that accused our unfortunate Barnave?'

"' 'Robespierre.'

"''Robespierre!' echoed Her Majesty. 'Oh God! then
he is numbered with the dead! This fellow is too fond
of blood to be tempted with money. But you, sire, must
not interfere!'

"Notwithstanding these doubts, however, I undertook,
at the King and Queen's most earnest desire, to get
some one to feel the pulse of Robespierre, for the salvation of these our only palladium to the constitutional
monarchy. To the first application, though made through
the medium of one of his earliest college intimates, Carrier, the wretch was utterly deaf and insensible. Of this
failure I hastened to apprize Her Majesty. 'Was any sum,'
asked she, 'named as a compensation for suspending this
trial?' 'None,' replied I; 'I had no commands to that
effect.' 'Then let the attempt be renewed, and back it
with the argument of a check for a hundred thousand
livres on M. Laborde. He has saved my life and the
King's, and, as far as is in my power, I am determined

to save his. Barnave has exposed his life more than any of our unfortunate friends, and if we can but succeed in saving him, he will speedily be enabled to save his colleagues. Should the sum I name be insufficient, my jewels shall be disposed of to make up a larger one. Fly to your agent, dear Princess! Lose not a moment to intercede in behalf of these our only true friends!'

"I did so, and was fortunate enough to gain over to my personal entreaties one who had the courage to propose the business; and a hundred and fifty thousand livres procured them a suspension of accusation. All, however, are still watched with such severity of scrutiny that I tremble, even now, for the result.*

"It was in the midst of such apprehensions, which struck terror into the hearts of the King and Queen, that the Tuileries resounded with cries of multitudes hired to renew those shouts of '*Vive le roi! vive la famille royale!*' which were once spontaneous.

"In one of the moments of our deepest affliction, multitudes were thronging the gardens and enjoying the celebration of the acceptance of the constitution. What a contrast to the feelings of the unhappy inmates of the palace! We may well say, that many an aching heart rides in a carriage, while the pedestrian is happy!

"The *fêtes* on this occasion were very brilliant. The King, the Queen, and the Royal Family were invited to take part in this first national festival. They did so, by appearing in their carriage through the streets of Paris and the Champs Elysées, escorted only by the Parisian guard, there being no other at the time. The mob was so great, that the royal carriage could only keep pace with the foot passengers.

* And with reason; for all, eventually, were sacrificed upon the scaffold. Carrier was the factotum in all the cool, deliberate, sanguinary operations of Robespierre; when he saw the check, he said to the Princess Lamballe: "Madam, though your personal charms and mental virtues had completely influenced all the authority I could exercise in favor of your *protégé*, without this interesting argument I should not have had courage to have renewed the business with the principal agent of life and death."

"Their Majesties were in general well received. The only exceptions were a few of the Jacobin members of the assembly, who, even on this occasion, sought every means to afflict the hearts, and shock the ears of Their Majesties, by causing republican principles to be vociferated at the very doors of their carriage.

"The good sense of the King and Queen prevented them from taking any notice of these insults while in public; but no sooner had they returned to the castle, than the Queen gave way to her grief at the premeditated humiliation she was continually witnessing to the majesty of the constitutional monarchy; an insult less to the King himself than to the nation, which had acknowledged him their sovereign.

"When the royal party entered the apartment, they found M. de Montmorin with me, who had come to talk over these matters, secure that at such a moment we should not be surprised.

"On hearing the Queen's observation, M. de Montmorin made no secret of the necessity there was of Their Majesties dissembling their feelings; the avowal of which, he said, would only tend to forward the triumph of Jacobinism, 'which,' added he, 'I am sorry to see predominates in the assembly, and keeps in subordination all the public and private clubs.' *

---

* I recollect a letter from the Princess Lamballe to the Queen upon the subject of the constitution and its supporters, in which her highness observes that she believed Barnave, Duport, Lameth, and the sixty-two other deputies detached by them from the left side of the assembly, to be the only members who entered *bona fide* into the spirit of the times. The Princess was persuaded that they, and they only, were sincerely disposed to uphold the constitutional monarchy; and she earnestly advised Her Majesty to profit by their counsel and warned her against all the rest, whom she deemed actuated by private motives, personal resentments, or ambition — treacherous conspirators, looking to their own aggrandizement, building *châteaux en Espagne*, or from more criminal motives injuring alike the royal authority and the progress of the constitutional system by disunion among themselves, notwithstanding the immense, the incalculable sums expended by the Court for its promulgation.

One-tenth of the money thus impotently lavished would have been more than sufficient to have secured the assistance of the most effective

" 'What!' exclaimed the Princess Elizabeth, 'can that be possible, after the King has accepted the constitution ?'

" 'Yes,' said the Queen; 'these people, my dear Elizabeth, wish for a constitution which sanctions the overthrow of him by whom it has been granted.'

" 'In this, observed M. de Montmorin, 'as on some other points, I perfectly agree with Your Majesty and the King, notwithstanding I have been opposed by the whole council and many other honest constituent members, as well as the cabinet of Vienna. And it is still, as it has ever been, my firm opinion, that the King ought, previous to the acceptance of the constitution, to have been allowed, for the security of its future organization, to have examined it maturely; which, not having been the case, I foresee the dangerous situation in which His Majesty stands, and I foresee, too, the non-promulgation of this charter. Malouet, who is an honest man, is of my opinion. Duport, Lameth, Barnave, and even La Fayette are intimidated at the prevailing spirit of the Jacobins. They were all with the best intentions for Your Majesty's present safety, for the acceptance *in toto*, but without reflecting

mercenary military force which, well directed, would have established the national tranquillity and the constitutional monarchical authority; but the first rational proposers of limited monarchy were considered so criminal in their ideas by all those who have unfortunately suffered on the scaffold for their folly in rejecting it, that they were not only never listened to, but never forgiven; and had a change taken place in favor of the executive royal authority no measures would have been observed, and one and all would have been exiled from France. This I have heard repeatedly asserted by the Princess Lamballe, who disapproved of it as a maxim, and often told the Queen so; but it was adopted by all the Princes of the blood, who uniformly counseled the King to adhere rather to the Jacobin party than to the constitutional, from an idea that they would be much more easily got rid of.

These sentiments were never generally known. They were circumscribed to those immediately concerned. But if we take a retrospective view of the different stages and maneuvers of the Revolution, it will clearly appear, from the total desertion of the royal party, that there must have been well-founded circumstances of premeditated vengeance. so thoroughly to have paralyzed every operation they attempted.

on the consequences which must follow should the nation be deceived. But I, who am, and ever shall be, attached to royalty, regret the step, though I am clear in my impression as to the only course which ought to succeed it. The throne can now only be made secure by the most unequivocal frankness of proceeding on the part of the crown. It is not enough to have conceded, it is necessary also to show that the concession has some more solid origin than mere expediency. It should be made with a good grace. Every motive of prudence, as well as of necessity, requires that the monarch himself, and all those most interested for his safety, should, neither in looks, manners, or conversation, seem as if they felt a regret for what has been lost, but rather appear satisfied with what has been bestowed.'

" ' In that case,' said the Queen, ' we should lose all the support of the royalists.'

" ' Every royalist, madam,' replied he, ' who, at this critical crisis, does not avow the sentiments of a constitutionalist, is a nail in the King's untimely coffin.'

" ' Gracious God! ' cried the Queen; ' that would destroy the only hope which still flatters our drooping existence. Symptoms of moderation, or any conciliatory measures we might be inclined to show, of our free will, to the constitutionalists, would be immediately considered as a desertion of our supporters, and treachery to ourselves, by the royalists.'

" ' It would be placed entirely out of my power, madam,' replied M. de Montmorin, ' to make my attachment to the persons of Your Majesties available for the maintenance of your rights, did I permit the factious, overbearing party which prevails, to see into my real zeal for the restoration of the royal authority, so necessary for their own future honor, security, and happiness. Could they see this, I should be accused as a national traitor, or even worse, and sent out of the world by a sudden death of ignominy, merely to glut their hatred of monarchy; and it is therefore I dissemble.'

" ' I perfectly agree with you,' answered the Queen.

'That cruel moment when I witnessed the humiliating state to which royalty had been reduced by the constituents, when they placed the President of their assembly upon a level with the King; gave a plebeian, exercising his functions *pro tempore*, prerogatives in the face of the nation to trample down hereditary monarchy and legislative authority — that cruel moment discovered the fatal truth. In the anguish of my heart, I told His Majesty that he had outlived his kingly authority.' Here she burst into tears, hiding her face in her handkerchief.

"With the mildness of a saint, the angelic Princess Elizabeth exclaimed, turning to the King, 'Say something to the Queen, to calm her anguish!'

"'It will be of no avail,' said the King; 'her grief adds to my affliction. I have been the innocent cause of her participating in this total ruin, and as it is only her fortitude which has hitherto supported me, with the same philosophical and religious resignation we must await what fate destines!'

"'Yes,' observed M. de Montmorin; 'but Providence has also given us the rational faculty of opposing imminent danger, and by activity and exertion obviating its consequences.'

"'In what manner, sir?' cried the Queen; 'tell me how this is to be effected, and, with the King's sanction, I am ready to do anything to avert the storm, which so loudly threatens the august head of the French nation.'

"'Vienna, madam,' replied he; 'Vienna! Your Majesty's presence at Vienna would do more for the King's safety and the nation's future tranquillity, than the most powerful army.'

"'We have long since suggested,' said the Princess Elizabeth, 'that Her Majesty should fly from France and take refuge——'

"'Pardon me, Princess,' interrupted M. de Montmorin, 'it is not for refuge solely I would have Her Majesty go thither. It is to give efficacy to the love she bears the King and his family, in being there the powerful advocate to check the fallacious march of a foreign army to invade us for the subjection of the French nation. All these external attempts will prove abortive, and only tend to exasperate the French to crime and madness. Here I coincide with my coadjutors, Barnave, Duport, Lameth, etc. The principle on which the re-establishment of the order and tranquillity of France depends, can only be effected by the non-interference of foreign powers. Let them leave the rational resources of our own internal force to re-establish our real interests, which every honest Frenchman will strive to secure, if not thwarted by the threats and menaces of those who have no right to interfere. Besides, madam, they are too far from us to afford immediate relief from the present dangers, internally surrounding us. These are the points of fearful import. It is not the threats and menaces of a foreign army which can subdue a nation's internal factions. These only rouse them to prolong disorders. National commotions can only be quelled by national spirit, whose fury, once exhausted on those who have aroused it, leave it free to look within, and work a reform upon itself.'

" M. de Montmorin, after many other prudent exhortations and remarks, and some advice with regard to the King and Queen's household, took his leave. He was no sooner gone than it was decided by the King that Maria Antoinette, accompanied by myself and some other ladies, and the gentlemen of the bedchamber, couriers, etc., should set out forthwith for Vienna.*

---

* The Princess Lamballe sent me directions that very evening, some time after midnight, to be at our place of rendezvous early in the morning. I was overjoyed at the style of the note. It was the least mysterious I had ever received from her highness. I inferred that some fortunate event had occurred, with which, knowing how deeply I was interested in the fate of her on whom my own so much depended, she was eager to make me acquainted.

But what was my surprise, on entering the church fixed on for the meeting, to see the Queen's unknown confessor beckoning me to come to him. I approached. He bade me wait till after mass, when he had something to communicate from the Princess.

This confessor officiated in the place of the one whom Mirabeau had seduced to take the constitutional oath. The Queen and Princess con-

"To say why this purpose was abandoned is unnecessary. The same fatality, which renders every project unattainable, threw insuperable impediments in the way of
this.

fessed to him in the private apartment of her highness on the ground
floor; though it was never known where, or to whom they confessed,
after the treachery of the royal confessor. This faithful and worthy successor was only known as "THE UNKNOWN." I never heard who he was,
or what was his name.

The mass being over, I followed him into the sacristy. He told me
that the Princess, by Her Majesty's command, wished me to set off immediately for Strasburg, and there await the arrival of her highness, to
be in readiness to follow her and Her Majesty for the copying of the
cipher, as they were going to Vienna.

When everything, however, had been settled for their departure,
which it was agreed was to take place from the house of Count de Fersen, the resolution was suddenly changed; but I was desired to hold myself in readiness for another journey.

CHAPTER XXI.

Journal Continued — Effect on the Queen of the Death of Her Broth-
ers, the Emperors Joseph and Leopold — Change in the Queen's
Household During the Absence of the Princess — Causes and Con-
sequences — Course Pursued by the Princess — Communication from
M. Laporte, Head of the King's Police, of a Plot to Poison the
Queen and Royal Family — Plans to Prevent Its Accomplishment —
Conversations between the Queen and the Princess, and between
the King and the Queen upon the Subject.

"THE news of the death of the Emperor Leopold, in
the midst of the other distresses of Her Majesty,
afflicted her very deeply; the more so because
she had every reason to think he fell a victim to the active part he took in her favor. Externally, this monarch
certainly demonstrated no very great inclination to become a member of the coalition of Pilnitz. He judged,
very justly, that his brother Joseph had not only defeated his own purposes by too openly and violently as-
serting the cause of their unfortunate sister, but had
destroyed himself, and, therefore, selected what he deemed
the safer and surer course of secret support. But all
his caution proved abortive. The assembly knew his maneuvers as well as he himself did. He died an untimely
death; and the Queen was assured, from undoubted
authority, that both Joseph and Leopold were poisoned
in their medicines.

"During my short absence in England, the King's
household had undergone a complete change. When the
emigration first commenced, a revolution in the officers of the
Court took place, but it was of a nature different from this
last; and, by destroying itself, left the field open to those who
now made the palace so intolerable. The first change to
which I refer arose as follows:

"The greater part of the high offices being vacated by the

succession of the most distinguished nobility, many places fell to persons who had all their lives occupied very subordinate situations. These, to retain their offices, were indiscreet enough publicly to declare their dissent from all the measures of the assembly; an absurdity, which, at the commencement, was encouraged by the Court, till the extreme danger of encouraging it was discovered too late; and when once the error had been tolerated and rewarded, it was found impossible to check it, and stop these fatal tongues. The Queen, who disliked the character of capriciousness, for a long time allowed the injury to go on, by continuing about her those who inflicted it. The error, which arose from delicacy, was imputed to a very different and less honorable feeling, till the clamor became so great, that she was obliged to yield to it, and dismiss those who had acted with so much indiscretion.

"The King and Queen did not dare now to express themselves on the subject of the substitutes who were to succeed. Consequently they became surrounded by persons placed by the assembly as spies. The most conspicuous situations were filled by the meanest persons — not, as in the former case, by such as had risen, though by accident, still regularly to their places — but by myrmidons of the prevailing power, to whom Their Majesties were compelled to submit, because their rulers willed it. All orders of nobility were abolished. All the Court ladies, not attached to the King and Queen personally, abandoned the Court. No one would be seen at the Queen's card parties, once so crowded, and so much sought after. We were entirely reduced to the family circle. The King, when weary of playing with the Princess Elizabeth and the Queen, would retire to his apartments without uttering a word, not from sullenness, but overcome by silent grief.

"The Queen was occupied continually by the extensive correspondence she had to carry on with the foreign sovereigns, the princes, and the different parties. Her Majesty once gave me nearly thirty letters she had written in the course of two days, which were forwarded by my *cara Inglesina — cara* indeed! for she was of the greatest service.*

"Her Majesty slept very little. But her courage never slackened; and neither her health, nor her general amiableness, was in the least affected. Though few females could be more sensible than herself to poignant mortification at seeing her former splendor hourly decrease, yet she never once complained. She was, in this respect, a real stoic.

"The palace was now become, what it still remains, like a police office. It was filled with spies and runners. Every member of the assembly, by some means or other, had his respective emissary. All the antechambers were peopled by inveterate Jacobins, by those whose greatest pleasure was to insult the ears and minds of all whom they considered above themselves in birth, or rank, or virtue. So completely were the decencies of life abolished, that common respect was withheld even from the Royal Family.

"I was determined to persevere in my usual line of conduct, of which the King and Queen very much approved. Without setting up for a person of importance, I saw all who wished for public or private audiences of Their Majesties. I carried on no intrigues, and only discharged the humble duties of my situation to the best of my ability for the general good, and to secure as far as possible, the comfort of Their Majesties, who really were to be pitied, utterly friendless and forsaken as they were.

"M. Laporte, the head of the King's private police, came to me one day in great consternation. He had discovered that schemes were on foot to poison all the Royal Family, and that in a private committee of the assembly

---

* I here copy the very words of that angelic victim, not from vanity to myself, but merely to do justice to the goodness of her heart, which at the moment she was so deeply engrossed in matters of such importance, could divert her attention to the remembrance of the little services it was my duty and my good fortune to perform.

considerable pensions had been offered for the perpetration of the crime. Its facility was increased, as far as regarded the Queen, by the habit to which Her Majesty had accustomed herself of always keeping powdered sugar at hand, which, without referring to her attendants, she would herself mix with water and drink as a beverage whenever she was thirsty.

"I entreated M. Laporte not to disclose the conspiracy to the Queen till I had myself had an opportunity of apprizing her of his praiseworthy zeal. He agreed, on condition that precautions should be immediately adopted with respect to the persons who attended the kitchen. This, I assured him, should be done on the instant.

"At the period I mention, all sorts of etiquette had been abolished. The custom which prevented my appearing before the Queen except at stated hours, had long since been discontinued; and as all the other individuals who came before or after the hours of service were eyed with distrust, and I remained the only one whose access to Their Majesties was free and unsuspected, though it was very early when M. Laporte called, I thought it my duty to hasten immediately to my royal mistress.

" I found her in bed. ' Has Your Majesty breakfasted? ' said I.

" ' No,' replied she; ' will you breakfast with me? '

" ' Most certainly,' said I, ' if Your Majesty will insure me against being poisoned.'

"At the word POISON Her Majesty started up and looked at me very earnestly, and with a considerable degree of alarm.

" ' I am only joking,' continued I; ' I will breakfast with Your Majesty if you will give me tea.'

"Tea was presently brought. ' In this,' said I, ' there is no danger.'

" ' What do you mean? ' asked Her Majesty.

" ' I am ordered,' replied I, taking up a lump of sugar, ' not to drink chocolate, or coffee, or anything with POWDERED sugar. These are times when caution alone can

prevent our being sent out of the world with all our sins
upon our heads.'

"'I am very glad to hear you say so; for you have
reason to be particular, after what you once so cruelly
suffered from poison. But what has brought that again
into your mind just now?'

"'Well, then, since Your Majesty approves of my circumspection, allow me to say I think it advisable that
we should, at a moment like this especially, abstain from
all sorts of food by which our existence may be endangered. For my own part, I mean to give up all made
dishes, and confine myself to the simplest diet.'

"'Come, come, Princess,' interrupted Her Majesty;
'there is more in this than you wish me to understand.
Fear not. I am prepared for anything that may be perpetrated against my own life, but let me preserve from
peril my King, my husband, and my children!'

"My feelings prevented me from continuing to dissemble. I candidly repeated all I had heard from M. Laporte.

"Her Majesty instantly rang for one of her confidential women. 'Go to the King,' said Her Majesty to the
attendant, 'and if you find him alone, beg him to come
to me at once; but if there are any of the guards or
other persons within hearing, merely say that the Princess
Lamballe is with me and is desirous of the loan of a
newspaper.'

"The King's guard, and indeed most of those about
him, were no better than spies, and this caution in the
Queen was necessary to prevent any jealousy from being
excited by the sudden message.

"When the messenger left us by ourselves, I observed
to Her Majesty that it would be imprudent to give the
least publicity to the circumstance, for were it really
mere suspicion in the head of the police, its disclosure
might only put this scheme into some miscreant's head,
and tempt him to realize it. The Queen said I was perfectly right, and it should be kept secret.

"Our ambassadress was fortunate enough to reach the
King's apartment unobserved, and to find him unattended,

so he received the message forthwith. On leaving the apartment, however, she was noticed and watched. She immediately went out of the Tuileries as if sent to make purchases, and some time afterward returned with some trifling articles in her hand.*

"The moment the King appeared, 'Sire,' exclaimed Her Majesty, 'the assembly, tired of endeavoring to wear us to death by slow torment, have devised an expedient to relieve their own anxiety and prevent us from putting them to further inconvenience.'

"'What do you mean?' said the King. I repeated my conversation with M. Laporte. 'Bah! bah!" resumed His Majesty, 'They never will attempt it. They have fixed on other methods of getting rid of us. They have not POLICY enough to allow our deaths to be ascribed to accident. They are too much initiated in great crimes already.'

"'But,' asked the Queen, 'do you not think it highly necessary to make use of every precaution, when we are morally sure of the probability of such a plot?'

"'Most certainly! otherwise we should be, in the eyes of God, almost guilty of suicide. But how prevent it? surrounded as we are by persons, who, being seduced to believe that we are plotting against them, feel justified in the commission of any crime under the false idea of self-defense!'

---

* This incident will give the reader an idea of the cruel situation in which the first sovereigns of Europe then stood; and how much they appreciated the few subjects who devoted themselves to thwart and mitigate the tyranny practiced by the assembly over these illustrious victims. I can speak from my own experience on these matters. From the time I last accompanied the Princess Lamballe to Paris till I left it in 1792, what between milliners, dressmakers, flower girls, fancy toy sellers, perfumers, hawkers of jewelry, purse and gaiter makers, etc., I had myself assumed twenty different characters, besides that of a drummer boy, sometimes blackening my face to enter the palace unnoticed, and often holding conversations analogous to the sentiments of the wretches who were piercing my heart with the remarks circumstances compelled me to encourage. Indeed, I can safely say I was known, in some shape or other, to almost everybody, but to no one in my real character, except the Princess by whom I was so graciously employed.

" 'We may prevent it,' replied Her Majesty, 'by abstaining from everything in our diet wherein poison can be introduced; and that we can manage without making any stir by the least change either in the kitchen arrangements or in our own, except, indeed, THIS ONE. Luckily, as we are restricted in our attendants, we have a fair excuse for dumb waiters, whereby it will be perfectly easy to choose or discard without exciting suspicion.

" This, consequently, was the course agreed upon; and every possible means, direct and indirect, was put into action to secure the future safety of the Royal Family and prevent the accomplishment of the threat of poison.*

* On my seeing the Princess next morning, her highness condescended to inform me of the danger to which herself and the Royal Family were exposed. She requested I would send my man servant to the persons who served me, to fill a moderate-sized hamper with wine, salt, chocolate, biscuits, and liquors, and take it to her apartment, at the Pavilion of Flora, to be used as occasion required. All the fresh bread and butter which was necessary I got made for nearly a fortnight by persons whom I knew at a distance from the palace, whither I always conveyed it myself.

Much greater precautions were adopted by the Queen's confidential woman, Madame Campan, who, in her work, speaks more at large upon the subject.

When the Princess apprized me of the plot, " We have escaped, however," she observed, " the horrid plots of the 20th of June and of the 14th of July. If they do not attempt another attack on the Tuileries we may possibly still escape assassination — BUT THIS I MUCH DOUBT."

I was greatly affected at hearing this observation from her highness; and especially at the cool and resigned manner in which it was made, as if she considered it a matter of course. I took the liberty of saying, in answer, that whatever might have been the effect of past calamities, I hoped she had no reasons for her melancholy apprehensions of the future.

" *Sia quel ch' Iddio voglia!* Let the will of God be done," cried she. " My religion has hitherto strengthened me; but I have still the most cruel forebodings for the fate of the King, the Queen, and their innocent offspring. May God continue to protect them, as he has hitherto done, against their unnatural enemies! As for myself, I am a foreigner; and if ever a foreign army enters France, I shall be the first to be sacrificed — and I am prepared!"

This heroic resignation resembles what Bertrand de Molleville describes of the martyred Louis XVI. after his escape from the dangers of the 20th of June.

CHAPTER XXII.

I AM again, for this and the following chapter, compelled to resume the pen in my own person, and quit the more agreeable office of a transcriber for my illustrious patroness.

I have already mentioned that the Princess Lamballe, on first returning from England to France, anticipated great advantages from the recall of the emigrants. The desertion of France by so many of the powerful could not but be a deathblow to the prosperity of the monarchy. There was no reason for these flights at the time they began. The fugitives only set fire to the four quarters of the globe against their country. It was natural enough that the servants whom they had left behind to keep their places should take advantage of their masters' pusillanimity, and make laws to exclude those who had, uncalled for, resigned the sway into bolder and more active hands.

I do not mean to impeach the living for the dead; but when we see those bearing the lofty titles of brothers of kings and princesses, escaping, with their wives and families, from an only brother and sister with helpless infant children, at the hour of danger, we cannot help wishing for a little plebeian disinterestedness in exalted minds.

I have traveled Europe twice, and I have never seen any woman with that indescribable charm of person, manner, and character, which distinguished Maria Antoinette. This is in itself a distinction quite sufficient to detach friends from its possessor through envy. Besides, she was Queen of France; the first female of a most capricious, restless, and libertine nation. The two princesses placed nearest to her, and who were the first to desert her, though both very much inferior in personal and mental qualifications, no doubt, though not directly, may have entertained some anticipations of her place. Such feelings are not likely to decrease the distaste, which results from comparisons to our own disadvantage. It is, therefore, scarcely to be wondered at, that those nearest to the throne should be least attached to those who fill it. How little do such persons think that the grave they are thus insensibly digging may prove their own! In this case it only did not by a miracle. What the effect of the royal brothers' and the nobility's remaining in France would have been we can only conjecture. That their departure caused great and irreparable evils we know; and we have good reason to think they caused the greatest. Those who abandon their houses on fire, silently give up their claims to the devouring element. Thus the first emigration kindled the French flame, which, though for a while it was got under by a foreign stream, was never completely extinguished till subdued by its native current.

The unfortunate Louis XVI. and Maria Antoinette ceased to be sovereigns from the period they were ignominiously dragged to their jail at the Tuileries. From this moment they were abandoned to the vengeance of miscreants, who were disgracing the nation with unprovoked and useless murders. But from this moment also the zeal of the Princesses Elizabeth and Lamballe became redoubled. Out of one hundred individuals and more, male and female, who had been exclusively occupied about the person of Maria Antoinette, few, excepting this illustrious pair, and the inestimable Clery, remained devoted to the last. The saintlike virtues of these Princesses, malice itself has not been able to tarnish. Their love and unalterable friendship became the shield of their unfortunate sovereigns, and their much injured relatives. till the dart struck their own faithful bosoms.

Princes of the earth! here is a lesson of greatness FROM the great.

Scarcely had the Princess Lamballe been reinstated in the Pavilion of Flora at the Tuileries, than, by the special royal command, and in Her Majesty's presence, she wrote to most of the nobility, entreating their return to France. She urged them, by every argument, that there was no other means of saving them or their country from the horrors impending over them and France, should they persevere in their pernicious absence. In some of these letters, which I copied, there was written on the margin, in the Queen's hand, "I am at her elbow, and repeat the necessity of your returning, if you love your King, your religion, your government, and your country. MARIA ANTOINETTE. Return! Return! Return!"

Among these letters, I remember a large envelope directed to the Duchess de Brisac, then residing alternately at the baths of Albano and the mineral waters at Valdagno, near Vicenza, in the Venetian states. Her Grace was charged to deliver letters addressed to Her Majesty's royal brothers, the Count de Provence, and the Count d'Artois, who were then residing, I think, at Strà, on the Brenta, in company with Madame Polcatre, Diana Polignac, and others.

A few days after, I took another envelope, addressed to the Count Dufour,* who was at Turin. It contained

---

* The Count Dufour is the father of the gentleman who was the French ambassador at Florence, under the reign of Louis XVI. who afterward married at Padova a lady of my acquaintance, Miss Seymour, niece of the late Lord Cooper, and sister to Mrs. Bennett. During the residence of the late King Louis XVIII. at Verona, I was present at Venice when this gentleman had all his plate sent to the mint at Venice, to be melted down for the use of Louis. The daughters of the late ambassador of whom I speak are now at Paris. They also are acquaintances of mine. One of them married one of my oldest friends, General Bournonville, who was long in prison with General La Fayette and Alexander Lameth, so treacherously given up by Dumourier to the Austrians, who sent them to Olmutz, where they remained till exchanged for her royal highness the present Dauphiness of France.

General Bournonville I had the pleasure to see in the character of ambassador under the government of Bonaparte at Berlin; and some time letters for M. and Madame de Polignac, M. and Madame de Guiche Grammont, the King's aunts at Rome, and the two Princesses of Piedmont, wives of His Majesty's brothers.

If, therefore, a judgment can be formed from the impressions of the Royal Family, who certainly must have had ample information with respect to the spirit which predominated at Paris at that period, could the nobility have been prevailed on to have obeyed the mandates of the Queen and prayers and invocations of the Princess, there can be no doubt that much bloodshed would have been spared, and the page of history never have been sullied by the atrocious names which now stand there as beacons of human infamy.

The storms were now so fearfully increasing that the King and Queen, the Duke de Penthièvre, the Count de Fersen, the Princess Elizabeth, the Duchess of Orleans, and all the friends of Princess Lamballe, once more united in anxious wishes for her to quit France. Even the Pope himself endeavored to prevail upon her highness to join the royal aunts at Rome. To all these applications she replied, " I have nothing to reproach myself with. If my inviolable duty and unalterable attachment to my sovereigns, who are my relations and my friends; if love for my dear father and for my adopted country are crimes, in the face of God and the world I confess my guilt, and shall die happy if in such a cause! "

The Duke de Penthièvre, who loved her as well as his own child, the Duchess of Orleans, was too good a man, and too conscientious a prince, not to applaud the disinterested firmness of his beloved daughter-in-law; yet, foreseeing and dreading the fatal consequences which must result from so much virtue, at a time when vice alone predominated, unknown to the Princess Lamballe, interested the Court of France to write to the Court of

afterward in the same capacity in Spain. He was very much attached to the English. He procured passports for Lord Holland's family and myself, to travel through France, at a time when no English subjects were allowed to enter the French territories.

Sardinia to entreat that the King, as head of her family, would use his good offices in persuading the Princess to leave the scenes of commotion, in which she was so much exposed, and return to her native country. The King of Sardinia, her family, and her particular friend, the Princess of Piedmont, supplicated ineffectually. The answer of her highness to the King, at Turin, was as follows:

"SIRE, AND MOST AUGUST COUSIN:

"I do not recollect that any of our illustrious ancestors of the house of Savoy, before or since the great hero Charles Emanuel, of immortal memory, ever dishonored or tarnished their illustrious names with cowardice. In leaving the Court of France at this awful crisis, I should be the first. Can Your Majesty pardon my presumption in differing from your royal counsel? The King, Queen, and every member of the Royal Family of France, both from the ties of blood and policy of states, demand our united efforts in their defense. I cannot swerve from my determination of never quitting them, especially at a moment when they are abandoned by every one of their former attendants, except myself. In happier days Your Majesty may command my obedience; but, in the present instance, and given up as is the Court of France to their most atrocious persecutors, I must humbly insist on being guided by my own decision. During the most brilliant period of the reign of Maria Antoinette, I was distinguished by the royal favor and bounty. To abandon her in adversity, Sire, would stain my character, and that of my illustrious family, for ages to come, with infamy and cowardice, much more to be dreaded than the most cruel death."

Similar answers were returned to all those of her numerous friends and relatives, who were so eager to shelter her from the dangers threatening her highness and the Royal Family.

Her highness was persuaded, however, to return once more to England, under the pretext of completing the mission she had so successfully begun; but it is very clear that neither the King nor Queen had any serious idea of her succeeding, and that their only object was to get her away from the theater of disaster.* Circum-

* The Princess set off from Paris and went to England by the way of Calais, not as has been repeatedly supposed by the way of Dieppe. This may be refuted, even at this distant period, by the heir of the late M. Dessin, M. Quillac, the present proprietor of the hotel at Calais, where the Princess and her suite alighted.

stances had so completely changed for the worst, that, though her highness was received with great kindness, her mission was no longer listened to. The policy of England shrunk from encouraging twenty thousand French troops to be sent in a body to the West Indies, and France was left to its fate. A conversation with Mr. Burke, in which the disinclination of England to interfere was distinctly owned, created that deep-rooted grief and apprehension in the mind of the Queen, from which Her Majesty never recovered. The Princess Lamballe was the only one in her confidence. It is well known that the King of England greatly respected the personal virtues of Their French Majesties; but upon the point of business, both King and ministers were now become ambiguous and evasive. Her highness, therefore, resolved to return. It had already been whispered that she had left France, only to save herself, like the rest; and she would no longer remain under so slanderous an imputation. She felt, too, the necessity of her friendship to her royal mistress. Though the Queen of England, by whom her highness was very much esteemed, and many other persons of the first consequence in the British nation, foreseeing the inevitable fate of the Royal Family, and of all their faithful adherents, anxiously entreated her not to quit England, yet she became insensible to every consideration as to her own situation, and only felt the isolated one of her august sovereign, her friend, and benefactress.

CHAPTER XXIII.

E VENTS seemed molded expressly to produce the state of feeling which marked that disastrous day, the 20th of June, 1792. It frequently happens that nations, like individuals, rush wildly upon the very dangers they apprehend, and select such courses as invite what they are most solicitous to avoid. So it was with everything preceding this dreadful day.

By a series of singular occurrences I did not witness its horrors, though in some degree their victim. Not to detain my readers unnecessarily, I will proceed directly to the accident which withdrew me from the scene.

The apartment of the Princess Lamballe in the Pavilion of Flora, looked from one side upon the Pont Royal. On the day of which I speak, a considerable quantity of combustibles had been thrown from the bridge into one of her rooms. The Princess, in great alarm, sent instantly for me. She desired to have my English man servant, if he were not afraid, secreted in her room, while she herself withdrew to another part of the palace, till the extent of the intended mischief could be ascertained. I assured her highness that I was not only ready to answer for my servant, but would myself remain with him, as he always went armed, and I was so certain of his courage and fidelity, that I could not hesitate even to trust my life in his hands.

"For God's sake, *mia cara*," exclaimed the Princess, "do not risk your own safety, if you have any value for my friendship. I desire you not to go near the Pavilion of Flora. Your servant's going is quite sufficient. Never again let me hear such a proposition. What! after having hitherto conducted yourself so punctually, would you, by one rash act, devote yourself to ruin, and deprive us of your valuable services?"

I begged her highness would pardon the ardor of the dutiful zeal I felt for her in the moment of danger.

"Yes, yes," continued she; "that is all very well; but this is not the first time I have been alarmed at your too great intrepidity; and if ever I hear of your again attempting to commit yourself so wantonly, I will have you sent to Turin immediately, there to remain till you have recovered your senses. I always thought English heads cool; but I suppose your residence in France has changed the national character of your's."

Once more, with tears in my eyes, I begged her forgiveness, and on my knees implored that she would not send me away in the hour of danger. After having so long enjoyed the honor of her confidence, I trusted she would overlook my fault, particularly as it was the pure emanation of my resentment at any conspiracy against one I so dearly loved; and to whom I had been under so many obligations, that the very idea of my being deprived of such a benefactress drove me frantic.

Her highness burst into tears. "I know your heart," exclaimed she; "but I also know too well our situation, and it is that which makes me tremble for the consequences which must follow your overstepping the bounds so necessary to be observed by all of us at this horrid period." And then she called me again her *cara Inglesina*, and graciously condescended to embrace me, and bathed my face with her tears, in token of her forgiveness, and bade me sit down and compose myself, and weep no more.

Scarcely was I seated, when we were both startled by deafening shouts for the head of MADAME VETO, the name they gave the poor unfortunate Queen. An immense crowd of cannibals and hired ruffians were already in the Tuileries, brandishing all sorts of murderous weapons, and howling for blood! My recollections from this moment are very indistinct. I know that in an instant the apartment was filled; that the Queen, the Princess Elizabeth, all the attendants, even the King, I believe, appeared there. I myself received a wound upon my hand in warding a blow from my face; and in the turmoil of the scene, and of the blow, I fainted, and was conveyed by some humane person to a place of safety, in the upper part of the palace.

Thus deprived of my senses for several hours, I was spared the agony of witnessing the scenes of horror which succeeded. For two or three days I remained in a state of so much exhaustion and alarm, that when the Princess came to me I did not know her, nor even where I was.

As soon as I was sufficiently recovered, places were taken for me and another person in one of the common diligences, by which I was conveyed to Passy, where the Princess came to me in the greatest confusion. My companion from the palace was the widow of one of the Swiss guards, who had been murdered on the 6th of October, in defending the Queen's apartment at Versailles. The poor woman had been herself protected by Her Majesty, and accompanied me by the express order of the Princess Lamballe. What the Princess said to her on departing, I know not, for I only caught the words "general insurrection," on hearing which the afflicted woman fell into a fit. To me, her highness merely exclaimed, "Do not come to Paris till you hear from me;" and immediately set off to return to the Tuileries.

However, as usual, my courage soon got the better of my strength, and of every consideration of personal safety. On the third day, I proposed to the person who took care of me, that we should both walk out together; and, if there appeared no symptoms of immediate danger, it was agreed, that we might as well get into one of the common conveyances, and proceed forthwith to Paris; for I could no longer repress my anxiety to learn what was going on there, and the good creature who was with me was no less impatient.

When we got into a diligence, I felt the dread of another severe lecture like the last, and thought it best not to incur fresh blame by new imprudence. I therefore told the driver to set us down on the high road near Paris leading to the Bois de Boulogne. But before we got so far, the woods resounded with the howling of mobs, and we heard, "*Vive le roi*" vociferated, mingled with "Down with the King," "Down with the Queen;" and, what was still more horrible, the two parties were in actual bloody strife, and the ground was strewed with the bodies of dead men, lying like slaughtered sheep.

It was fortunate that we were the only persons in the vehicle. The driver, observing our extreme agitation, turned round to us. "Nay, nay," cried he; "do not alarm yourselves. It is only the constitutionalists and the Jacobins fighting againt each other. I wish the devil had them both."

It was evident, however, that though the man was desirous of quieting our apprehensions, he was considerably disturbed by his own; for though he acknowledged he had a wife and children in Paris, who he hoped were safe, still he dared not venture to proceed, but said, if we wished to be driven back, he would cake us to any place we liked, out of Paris.

Our anxiety to know what was going forward at the Tuileries was now become intolerable; and the more so, from the necessity we felt of restraining our feelings. At last, however, we were in some degree relieved from this agony of reserve.

"God knows," exclaimed the driver, "what will be the consequence of all this bloodshed! The poor King and Queen are greatly to be pitied!"

This ejaculation restored our courage, and we said he might drive us wherever he chose out of the sight of those horrors; and it was at length settled that he should take us to Passy. "Oh," cried he, "if you will allow me, I will take you to my father's house there; for you seem more dead than alive, both of you, and ought to go where you can rest in quiet and safety."

My companion, who was a German, now addressed me in that language.

"German!" exclaimed the driver on hearing her. "German! Why I am a German myself, and served the good King, who is much to be pitied, for many years; and when I was wounded, the Queen, God bless her! set me right up in the world, as I was made an invalid; and I have ever since been enabled to support my family respectably. D—— the assembly! I shall never be a farthing the better for them!"

"Oh," replied I, "then I suppose you are not a Jacobin?"

The driver, with a torrent of curses, then began execrating the very name of Jacobin. This emboldened me to ask him how long he had left Paris. He replied, "Only this very morning," and added, that the assembly had shut the gates of the Tuileries under the pretense of preventing the King and Queen from being assassinated. "But that is all a confounded lie," continued he, "invented to keep out the friends of the Royal Family. But, God knows, they are now so fallen, they have few such left to be turned away!"

"I am more enraged," pursued he, "at the ingratitude of the nobility than I am at these hordes of bloodthirsty plunderers, for we all know that the nobility owe everything to the King. Why do they not rise *en masse* to shield the Royal Family from these bloodhounds? Can they imagine they will be spared if the King should be murdered? I have no patience with them!"

I then asked him our fare. "Two livres is the fare, but you shall not pay anything. I see plainly, ladies, that you are not what you assume to be."

"My good man," replied I, "we are not; and there-fore, pray take this *louis d'or* for your trouble."

He caught my hand and pressed it to his lips, ex-claiming, "I never in my life knew a man who was faithful to his King, that God did not provide for."

He then took us to Passy, but advised us not to re-main at the place where we had been staying; and for-tunate enough it was for us that we did not, for the house was set on fire and plundered by a rebel mob very soon after.

I told the driver how much I was obliged to him for his services, and he seemed delighted when I promised to give him proofs of my confidence in his fidelity.

"If," said I, "you can find out my servant whom I left in Paris, I will give you another *louis d'or*." I was afraid, at first, to mention where he was to look for him.

"If he be not dead," replied the driver, "I WILL find him out."

"What!" cried I, "even though he should be at the Tuileries ?"

"Why, madam, I am one of the national guard. I have only to put on my uniform to be enabled to go to any part of the palace I please. Tell me his name, and where you think it likely he may be found, and depend upon it I will bring him to you."

"Perhaps," continued he, "it is your husband dis-guised as a servant; but no matter. Give me a clue, and I'll warrant you he shall tell you the rest himself by this time to-morrow."

"Well, then," replied I, "he is in the Pavilion of Flora."

"What, with the Princess Lamballe ? Oh, I would go through fire and water for that good Princess! She has done me the honor to stand godmother to one of my children, and allows her a pension."

"I took him at his word. We changed our quarters to his father's house, a very neat little cottage, about a quarter of a mile from the town. He afterward rendered me many services in going to and fro from Passy to Paris; and, as he promised, brought me my servant.

When the poor fellow arrived, his arm was in a sling. He had been wounded by a musket shot, received in defense of the Princess. The history of his disaster was this:

On the night of the riot, as he was going from the Pont Royal to the apartment of her highness, he detected a group of villains under her windows. Six of them were attempting to enter by a ladder. He fired, and two fell. While he was reloading, the others shot at him. Had he not, in the flurry of the moment, fired both his pistols at the same time, he thinks he should not have been wounded, but might have punished the assailant. One of the men, he said, could have been easily taken by the national guard, who so glaringly encouraged the escape that he could almost swear the guard was a party concerned. The loss of blood had so exhausted him that he could not pursue the offender himself, whom otherwise he could have taken without any difficulty.

As the employing of my servant had only been proposed, and the sudden interruption of my conversation with her highness by the riot had prevented my ever communicating the project to him, I wondered how he got into the business, or ascertained so soon that the apartment of the Princess was in danger. He explained that he never had heard of its being so; but my own coachman having left me at the palace that day, and not hearing of me for some time, had driven home, and, fearing that my not returning arose from something which had happened, advised him to go to the Pont Royal and hear what he could learn, as there was a report of many persons having been murdered and thrown over the bridge.

My man took the advice, and armed himself to be ready in case of an attack. It was between one and two o'clock after midnight when he went. The first objects he perceived were these miscreants attempting to scale the palace.

He told me that the Queen had been most grossly insulted; that the gates of the Tuileries had been shut in consequence; that a small part alone remained open to the public, who were kept at their distance by a national ribbon, which none could pass without being instantly arrested. This had prevented his apprizing the Princess of the attempt which he had accidentally defeated, and which he wished me to communicate to her immediately. I did so by a letter, which my good driver carried to Paris, and delivered safe into the hands of our benefactress.

The surprise of the Princess on hearing from me, and her pleasure at my good fortune in finding by accident such means, baffles all description. Though she was at the time overwhelmed with the imminent dangers which threatened her, yet she still found leisure to show her kindness to those who were doing their best, though in vain, to serve her. The following letter, which she sent me in reply, written amid all the uneasiness it describes, will speak for her more eloquently than my praises:

"I can understand your anxiety. It was well for you that you were unconscious of the dreadful scenes which were passing around you on that horrid day. The Princess de Tarente, Madame de Tourzel, Madame de Mockau, and all the other ladies of the household owed the safety of their lives to one of the national guards having given his national cockade to the Queen. Her Majesty placed it on her head, unperceived by the mob. One of the gentlemen of the King's wardrobe provided the King and the Princess Elizabeth with the same impenetrable shield. Though the cannibals came for murder, I could not but admire the enthusiastic deference that was shown to this symbol of authority, which instantly paralyzed the daggers uplifted for our extermination.

"Merlin de Thionville was the stoic head of this party. The Princess Elizabeth having pointed him out to me, I ventured to address him respecting the dangerous situation to which the Royal Family were daily exposed. I flattered him upon his influence over the majority of the fauxbourgs, to which only we could look for the extinction of these disorders. He replied, that the despotism of the Court had set a bad example to the people; that he felt for the situation of the royal party as individuals, but he felt much more for the safety of the French nation, who were in still greater danger than Their Majesties had to dread, from the Austrian faction, by which a foreign army had been encouraged to invade the territory of France, where they were now waiting the opportunity of annihilating French liberty forever!

"To this Her Majesty replied, 'When the deputies of the assembly have permitted, nay, I may say, encouraged this open violation of the King's asylum, and, by their indifference to the safety of all those who surround us, have sanctioned the daily insults to which we have been, and still are, exposed, it is not to be wondered at, that all sovereigns should consider it their interest to make common cause with us, to crush internal commotions, leveled, not only against the throne, and the persons of the sovereign and his family, but against the very principle of monarchy itself.'

"Here the King, though much intimidated for the situation of the Queen and his family, for whose heads the wretches were at that very moment howling in their ears, took up the conversation.

"'These cruel facts,' said he, 'and the menacing situation you even now witness, fully justify our not rejecting foreign aid, though God knows how deeply I deplore the necessity of such a cruel resource! But when all internal measures of conciliation have been trodden under foot, and the authorities, who ought to check it and protect us from these cruel outrages, are only occupied in daily fomenting the discord between us and our subjects; though a forlorn hope, what other hope is there of safety? I foresee the drift of all these commotions, and am resigned; but what will become of this misguided nation, when the head of it shall be destroyed?'

"Here the King, nearly choked by his feelings, was compelled to pause for a moment, and he then proceeded.

" ' I should not feel it any sacrifice to give up the guardianship of the nation, could I, in so doing, insure its future tranquillity: but I foresee that my blood, like that of one of my unhappy brother sovereigns,* will only open the floodgates of human misery, the torrent of which, swelled with the best blood of France, will deluge this once peaceful realm.'

" This, as well as I can recollect, is the substance of what passed at the castle on this momentous day. Our situation was extremely doubtful, and the noise and horrid riots were at times so boisterous, that frequently we could not, though so near them, distinguish a word the King and Queen said; and yet, whenever the leaders of these organized ruffians spoke or threatened, the most respectful stillness instantly prevailed.

" I weep in silence for misfortunes, which I fear are inevitable! The King, the Queen, the Princess Elizabeth, and myself, with many others under this unhappy roof, have never ventured to undress or sleep in bed, till last night. None of us any longer reside on the ground floor.

" By the very manly exertions of some of the old officers incorporated in the national army, the awful riot I have described was overpowered, and the mob, with difficulty, dispersed. Among these, I should particularize Generals Vomenil,† Mandate, and Rôederer. Principally by their means the interior of the Tuileries was at last cleared, though partial mobs, such as you have often witnessed, still subsist.

* Charles the First of England.

† This general, the last time I came from Italy to England, on my way through Vienna, I had the pleasure of seeing at the house of a particular friend of mine, Madame Peschie, the wife of a banker of that name. I think, also, I saw him once afterward in company, at the house of the Count de Fries, from whom I received the most marked and cordial attention during my different visits to that truly hospitable city.

While I am on the subject of the hospitalities of this city I must not omit to mention some families in particular, such as the Prince Odescalchi, the family of Baron Arentium, Eskeless, Pierera, and Hanenstein; Gondart, Curzbeck the famous Haydn, Baron Brown, the late Prince

"I am thus particular in giving you a full account of this last revolutionary commotion, that your prudence may still keep you at a distance from the vortex. Continue where you are, and tell your man servant how much I am obliged to him, and, at the same time, how much I am grieved at his being wounded! I knew nothing of the affair but from your letter and your faithful messenger. He is an old pensioner of mine, and a good honest fellow. You may depend on him. Serve yourself, through him, in communicating with me. Though he has had a limited education, he is not wanting in intellect. Remember that honesty, in matters of such vital import, is to be trusted before genius.

"My apartment appears like a barrack, like a bear garden, like anything but what it was! Numbers of valuable things have been destroyed, numbers carried off. Still, notwithstanding all the horrors of these last days, it delights me to be able to tell you, that no one in the service of the Royal Family failed in duty at this dreadful crisis. I think we may firmly rely on the inviolable attachment of all around us. No jealousy, no considerations of etiquette, stood in the way of their exertions to show themselves worthy of the situations they hold. The Queen showed the greatest intrepidity during the whole of these trying scenes.

"At present, I can say no more. Petion, the mayor

Lobkowitz, Count de Sauron, Prince Throumansdorf, the Prince and Princess Colalto Station, and others too numerous to be particularized here, for whose kindness, though not mentioned, I shall ever retain the most lively gratitude.

General de Vomenil was private secretary of the late Queen of Naples, who was the sister of Napoleon, and wife of that ill-fated King of Naples, Murat, and who, it is said, has since become the wife of Marshal Macdonald, and lives retired at Hamburg, near Vienna. Her brother, the late King of Westphalia, now Prince Rumford, lives also in retirement, at a country seat he purchased from the friend I have just mentioned, Baron Brown. Neither the deposed brother or sister have any but ancient nobility in their suite. The Countess of Athmis, sister to Mrs. Spencer Smith, wife of the late British Ambassador at Constantinople, is one of the ex-queen's ladies of honor.

of Paris, has just been announced; and, I believe, he wishes for an audience of Her Majesty, though he never made his appearance during the whole time of the riots in the palace. Adieu, *mia cara Inglesina!*"

The receipt of this letter, however it might have affected me to hear what her highness suffered, in common with the rest of the unfortunate royal inmates of the Tuileries, gave me extreme pleasure from the assurance it contained of the firmness of those nearest to the sufferers. I was also sincerely gratified in reflecting on the probity and disinterested fidelity of this worthy man, which contrasted him, so strikingly and so advantageously to himself, with many persons of birth and education, whose attachment could not stand the test of the trying scenes of the Revolution, which made them abandon and betray, where they had sworn an allegiance, to which they were doubly bound by gratitude.

My man servant was attended, and taken the greatest care of. The Princess never missed a day in sending to inquire after his health; and, on his recovery, the Queen herself not only graciously condescended to see him, but, besides making him a valuable present, said many flattering and obliging things of his bravery and disinterestedness.

I should scarcely have deemed these particulars — honorable as they are to the feelings of the illustrious personages from whom they proceeded — worth mentioning in a work of this kind, did they not give indications of character rarely to be met with (and, in their case, how shamefully rewarded!), from having occurred at a crisis when their minds were occupied in affairs of such deep importance, and amid the appalling dangers which hourly threatened their own existence.

Her Majesty's correspondence with foreign courts had been so much increased by these scenes of horror, especially her correspondence with her relations in Italy, that ere long, I was sent for back to Paris.

Why dost thou intrude, O memory, to tear asunder wounds, to cause them to bleed afresh! It is now thirty long years since I beheld these scenes, yet still my blood curdles in my veins when I recall the heart-rending picture which presented itself on my first return to the Princess's apartment at the Pavilion of Flora from Passy! My pen cannot depict my agony. My readers must imagine what I felt, and they will readily pardon my want of ability to describe those feelings, when I refer them to what met my view — a royal palace nearly razed to the ground, gutted apartments, costly furniture in fragments amid the ruins, three of the most august personages in Europe standing amid the wreck, totally unmoved by the surrounding desolation, and solely occupied in fervent prayers, invoking God for the safety of the journey of an insignificant individual like myself! I was thrilled with horror, with pity, with shame at their sufferings. If there be a soul within the human breast, no human eye could look on such a scene and not be moved. Fallen majesty, under any circumstances, must be an object of uncommon sensation to any reflecting mind; but there were distinctions in this case, to give it peculiar poignancy. A Queen of the brightest prospects, the gentlest and noblest heart, bereaved of her rights, and execrated by her people; a royal virgin, nipped in the bloom of youth; and an illustrious widowed princess, denied kindness from those whom she had fostered, and now seeking relief from the humble whom she had succored — what an accumulation of misfortune! Human vicissitude! what a school art thou for reflection! what a lesson to the follies of earthly grandeur! But we do not see it, we do not feel it, nor do we even believe it, till the hour of danger, when, alas! it is too late; and we only awake from torpor to be convinced that we are mere mortals, and may not be heedless with impunity.

God forbid I should insinuate that these saintlike, martyred victims, ever in the slightest degree deserved that ignominious, unceasing persecution, of which history presents no parallel. But we are apt to be blind to circumstances, by confounding our calculations with our wishes; and, though death stared them in the face, yet no energy was called up to resist it, till the very last moment, when the earthquake had shaken the edifice to its foundation, and no human power could prevent their being buried in its ruins. No resource remained. Like lambs, they submitted to the slaughter. The sacrifice was made before it was performed. "I know that my Redeemer liveth" was the only hope to which they clung; and they were dead to the world, long, long before the thread of life was mercifully cut by the bloody hands, which had already despoiled them of all that made life desirable!

CHAPTER XXIV.

"THE insurrection of the 20th of June, and the uncertain state of the safety of the Royal Family, menaced as it was by almost daily riots, induced a number of well-disposed persons to prevail on General La Fayette to leave his army and come to Paris, and there personally remonstrate against these outrages. Had he been sincere, he would have backed the measure by appearing at the head of his army, then well disposed, as Cromwell did, when he turned out the rogues who were seeking the Lord through the blood of their King, and put the keys in his pocket. Violent disorders require violent remedies. With an army and a few pieces of cannon at the door of the assembly, whose members were seeking the aid of the devil, for the accomplishment of their horrors, he might, as was done when the same scene occurred in England in 1668, by good management, have averted the deluge of blood. But, by appearing before the assembly isolated, without ' *voilà mon droit*,' which the King of Prussia had had engraven on his cannon, he lost the opinion of all parties.*

* In this instance the General grossly committed himself, in the opinion of every impartial observer of his conduct. He should never have shown himself in the capital, but at the head of his army. France, circumstanced as it was, torn by intestine commotion, was only to be intimidated by the sight of a popular leader at the head of his forces. Usurped authority can only be quashed by the force of legitimate authority. La Fayette being the only individual in France that in reality possessed

"La Fayette came to the palace frequently, but the King would never see him. He was obliged to return, with the additional mortification of having been deceived in his expected support from the national guard of Paris, whose pay had been secretly trebled by the national assembly, in order to secure them to itself. His own safety, therefore, required that he should join the troops under his command. He left many persons in whom he thought he could confide; among whom were some who came to me one day requesting I would present them to the Queen without loss of time, as a man condemned to be shot had confessed to his captain that there was a plot laid to murder Her Majesty that very night.

"I hastened to the royal apartment, without mentioning the motive; but some such catastrophe was no more than what we incessantly expected, from the almost hourly changes of the national guard, for the real purpose of giving easy access to all sorts of wretches to the very rooms of the unfortunate Queen, in order to furnish opportunities for committing the crime with impunity.

"After I had seen the Queen, the applicants were introduced, and, in my presence, a paper was handed by them to Her Majesty. At the moment she received it, I was obliged to leave her for the purpose of watching an opportunity for their departure unobserved. These precautions were necessary with regard to every person who came to us in the palace, otherwise the jealousy of the assembly and its emissaries and the national guard of the interior might have been alarmed, and we should have been placed under express and open surveillance. The confusion created by the constant change of guard, however, stood us in good stead in this emergency.

such an authority, not having availed himself at a crisis like the one in which he was called upon to act, rendered his conduct doubtful, and all his intended operations suspicious to both parties, whether his feelings were really inclined to prop up the fallen kingly authority, or his newly-acquired republican principles prompted him to become the head of the democratical party, for no one can see into the hearts of men; his popularity from that moment ceased to exist.

Much passing and repassing took place unheeded in the bustle.

"When the visitors had departed, and Her Majesty at one window of the palace, and I at another, had seen them safe over the Pont Royal, I returned to Her Majesty. She then graciously handed me the paper which they had presented.

"It contained an earnest supplication, signed by many thousand good citizens, that the King and Queen would sanction the plan of sending the Dauphin to the army of La Fayette. They pledged themselves, with the assistance of the royalists, to rescue the Royal Family They urged that if once the King could be persuaded to show himself at the head of his army, without taking any active part, but merely for his own safety and that of his family, everything might be accomplished with the greatest tranquillity.

"The Queen exclaimed, 'What! send my child! No! never while I breathe!'* Yet were I an independent queen, or the regent of a minority, I feel that I should be inclined to accept the offer, to place myself at the head of the army as my immortal mother did, who,

---

*Little did this unfortunate mother think, that they, who thus pretended to interest themselves for this beautiful, angelic prince only a few months before, would, when she was in her horrid prison after the butchery of her husband, have required this only comfort to be violently torn from her maternal arms!

Little, indeed, did she think, when her maternal devotedness thus repelled the very thought of his being trusted to myriads of sworn defenders, how soon he would be barbarously consigned by the infamous assembly as the footstool of the inhuman savage cobbler, SIMON, to be the night-boy of the excrements of the vilest of the works of human nature!

Is it possible, that such facts — facts known to all the world! — can be retraced with coolness or in any tone of moderation by one, who, like me, had the honor of knowing this most innocent of all victims.

Unhappy mother! your religious resignation has made you the heroine of all martyrs! My hand refuses its functions, my pen drops from my fingers, and my paper is bathed with useless tears! Memory rests on the wounded mind, which has never been healed, and which bleeds afresh at the recollection!

by that step, transmitted the crown of our ancestors
to its legitimate descendants. It is the monarchy itself
which now requires to be asserted. Though Orleans is
actively engaged in attempting the dethronement of His
Majesty, I do not think the nation will submit to such a
prince, or to any other monarchical government, if the
present be decidedly destroyed.'

"'All these plans, my dear Princess,' continued she,
'are mere castles in the air. The mischief is too deeply
rooted. As they have already frantically declared for
the King's abdication, any strong measure now, in-
competent as we are to assure its success, would at once
arm the advocates of republicanism to proclaim the King's
dethronement.'

"'The cruel observations of Petion to His Majesty, on
our ever memorable return from Varennes, have made a
deeper impression than you are aware of. When the
King observed to him, "What do the French nation want?"
—"A republic," replied he. And though he has been the
means of already costing us some thousands, to crush
this unnatural propensity, yet I firmly believe, that he
himself is at the head of all the civil disorders fomented
for its attainment. I am the more confirmed in this
opinion from a conversation I had with the good old man,
M. de Malesherbes, who assured me the great sums we
were lavishing on this man were thrown away, for he
would be certain, eventually, to betray us: and such an
inference could only have been drawn from the lips of
the traitor himself. Petion must have given Malesherbes
reason to believe this. I am daily more and more convinced it will be the case. Yet, were I to show the
least energy or activity in support of the King's authority,
I should be accused of undermining it. All France would
be up in arms against the danger of female influence.
The King would only be lessened in the general opinion
of the nation, and the kingly authority still more weakened. Calm submission to His Majesty is, therefore, the
only safe course for both of us, and we must wait events.'

"While Her Majesty was thus opening her heart to

me, the King and Princess Elizabeth entered, to inform her, that M. Laporte, the head of the private police, had discovered, and caused to be arrested, some of the wretches who had maliciously attempted to fire the palace of the Tuileries.

"'Set them at liberty!' exclaimed Her Majesty; 'or, to clear themselves and their party, they will accuse us of something worse.'

"'Such, too, is my opinion, sire,' observed I; 'for however I abhor their intentions, I have here a letter from one of these miscreants which was found among the combustibles. It cautions us not to inhabit the upper part of the Pavilion. My not having paid the attention which was expected to the letter, has aroused the malice of the writer, and caused a second attempt to be made from the Pont Royal upon my own apartment; in preventing which, a worthy man* has been cruelly wounded in the arm.'

"'Merciful Heaven!' exclaimed the poor Queen and the Princess Elizabeth, 'not dangerously I hope!'†

"'I hope not,' added I; 'but the attempt, and its escaping unpunished, though there were guards all around, is a proof how perilous it will be, while we are so weak, to kindle their rancor by any show of impotent resentment; for I have reason to believe it was to THAT, the want of attention to the letter of which I speak was imputed.'

The Queen took this opportunity of laying before the King the above-mentioned plan. His Majesty, seeing it in the name of La Fayette, took up the paper, and, after he had attentively perused it, tore it in pieces, exclaiming, "What! has not M. La Fayette done mischief enough yet, but must he even expose the names of so many worthy men by committing them to paper at a critical period like this, when he is fully aware that we are in immediate danger of being assailed by a banditti of

* My man servant, as elsewhere described.
† Thus were these unfortunate princesses always more anxious for the safety and welfare of others, than for their own.

inhuman cannibals, who would sacrifice every individual attached to us, if, unfortunately, such a paper should be found? I am determined to have nothing to do with his ruinous plans. Popularity and ambition made him the principal promoter of republicanism. Having failed of becoming a Washington, he is mad to become a Cromwell. I have no faith in these turncoat constitutionalists."

"I know that the Queen heartily concurred in this sentiment concerning General La Fayette, as soon as she escertained his real character, and discovered that he considered nothing paramount to public notoriety. To this he had sacrificed the interest of his country, and trampled under foot the throne; but finding he could not succeed in forming a Republican Government in France as he had in America, he, like many others, lost his popularity with the demagogues, and, when too late, came to offer his services, through me, to the Queen, to recruit a monarchy which his vanity had undermined to gratify his chimerical ambition. Her Majesty certainly saw him frequently, but never again would she put herself in the way of being betrayed by one whom she considered faithless to all." *

Here ends the Journal of my lamented benefactress. I have continued the history to the close of her career,

---

* Thus ended the proffered services of General La Fayette, who then took the command of the national army, served against that of the Prince Condé, and the princes of his native country, and was given up with General Bournonville, Lameth, and others by General Dumourier, on the first defeat of the French, to the Austrians, by whom they were sent to the fortress of Olmutz in Hungary, where they remained till after the death of the wretch Robespierre, when they were exchanged for the Duchess d'Angoulême, now Dauphiness of France.

From the retired life led by General La Fayette on his return to France, there can be but little doubt that he spent a great part of his time in reflecting on the fatal errors of his former conduct, as he did not coincide with any of the revolutionary principles which preceded the short-lived reign of imperialism. But though Napoleon too well knew him to be attached from principle to republicanism — every vestige of which he had long before destroyed — to and that of the Royal Family, especially as her highness herself acted so important a part in many of the scenes, which are so strongly illustrated by her conversation and letters.   It is only necessary to add that the papers which I have arranged were received from her highness amid the disasters which were now thickening around her and her royal friends.

employ him in any military capacity, still he recalled him from his hiding place, in order to prevent his doing mischief, as he politically did every other royalist whom he could bring under the banners of his imperialism.

Had Napoleon made use of his general knowledge of mankind in other respects, as he politically did in France over his conquered subjects, in respecting ancient habits, and gradually weaned them from their natural prejudices instead of violently forcing all men to become Frenchmen, all men would have fought for him, and not against him.   These were the weapons by which his power became annihilated, and which, in the end, will be the destruction of all potentates who presume to follow his fallacious plan of forming individuals to a system instead of accommodating systems to individuals.   The fruits from southern climes have been reared in the north, but without their native virtue or vigor.   It is more dangerous to attack the habits of men than their religion.

The British constitution, though a blessing to Englishmen, is very ill-suited to nations not accustomed to the climate and its variations.   Every country has peculiarities of thought and manners resulting from the physical influence of its sky and soil.   Whenever we lose sight of this truth, we naturally lose the affections of those whose habits we counteract.

CHAPTER XXV.

The Editor Attends Debates, and Executes Confidential Employments in Various Disguises — Becomes Intimate with a Reporter — Adventure with Danton in the Tuileries, Disguised as a Milliner's Apprentice — Horrid Scene in the Gardens — Consternation of the Royal Party on Seeing Her with Danton — She Contrives to be Taken by Him to the Palace — Delight of the Princess Lamballe at Her Return — Conversation with the Princess upon the State of Public Affairs and Hopelessness of the Royal Cause.

FROM the time I left Passy till my final departure from Paris for Italy, which took place on the 2d of August, 1792, my residence was almost exclusively at the capital. The faithful driver, who had given such proofs of probity, continued to be of great service, and was put in perpetual requisition. I was daily about on the business of the Queen and the Princess, always disguised, and most frequently as a drummer boy; on which occasions the driver and my man servant were my companions. My principal occupation was to hear and take down the debates of the assembly,* and to convey and receive letters from the Queen to the Princess Lamballe, to and from Barnave, Bertrand de Moleville, Alexandre de Lameth, Duport de Fertre, Duportail, Montmorin, Turbé, Mandate,

* I was by no means a novice in this species of masquerading, as, I believe, I have mentioned before.

I remember one day, long previous to the time I now allude to, the Princess Lamballe told me the Queen had been informed by Mirabeau that the Abbé Maury was to make a motion in the assembly, which, by a private understanding between the two, Mirabeau was to oppose, for the purpose of the better carrying on the deception of their plans, and thereby ascertaining " HOW THE LAND LAY " with respect to some of the deputies, whom Mirabeau had not yet been able to secure to the interest of the monarchy. "I wish," said the Princess, "you would go in boy's clothes with your servant in the gallery to hear the discussions." I said I would most willingly, as I was desirous of seeing Mirabeau's impetuosity contrasted with the phlegmatic propositions of the Abbé Maury. It was on that very day, and in consequence of that very argument, that the Duke de Brissac, etc., with whom my illustrious patronesses kept up a continued correspondence, to which I believe all of them fell a sacrifice; for, owing to the imprudence of the King in not removing their communications when he removed the rest of his papers from the Tuileries, the exposure of their connection with the Court was necessarily consequent upon the plunder of the palace on the 10th of August, 1792.

In my masquerade visits to the assembly, I got acquainted with an editor of one of the papers; I think he

---

when the Abbé came from the assembly, the mob cried out, "*a la lanterne, M. l'Abbé!*" The Abbé, turning round, replied, with the greatest *sang froid*, "Will your hanging me to the lamp-post make you see the clearer?"

A similar story is related of Mr. Pitt. He was once coming across the park from the King's levee, followed by an immense mob, who were pelting his carriage and abusing him most outrageously, till he reached his house, which was in one of the streets leading out of the park. There, seeing them settling in battle array, he turned round in the politest manner, took off his hat, and made them a low bow. This turned the tide. They instantly became as vehement in their applause as they had been brutally violent in their abuse.

Oh, what a many-headed monster is a plebeian mob! During the French Revolution, how often have I seen this change achieved on most serious occasions, whenever the objects of their malice had courage enough to face their brutal assailants.

A similar circumstance happened to me at my country house near Treviso. I was translating the works of Lady Mary Wortley Montague into Italian. A fellow, after I had accommodated him and his staff with many beds, demanded of me to give up my own bedroom. "Where, then," asked I, "are my husband, my family, and myself to sleep?" "In the stables," replied he. We had nearly five hundred soldiers on our grounds, all their luggage and many fieldpieces, or I would have STABLED him out of the room. I dared not call my husband as he would have stabled him out of the windows in double-quick time, as he had done before in a case of similar violence. However, I told him my mind in language which caused the coward to draw his sword against me. When I saw this, I rose from my seat, advanced toward him, and said, "Give me that weapon, coward, and I will not threaten you, but use it as your unjustifiable insolence deserves!" I cannot say what my countenance betrayed at the moment, but his became like that of a corpse, and he set off in the night, probably from the fear lest I should put my threat in execution, which, I verily believe, I should have done at the moment had I been mistress of the weapon.

told me his name was Duplessie.   Being pleased with the liveliness of my remarks on some of the organized disorders, as I termed them, and with some comments I made upon the meanness of certain disgusting speeches on the patriotic gifts, my new acquaintance suffered me to take copies of his own shorthand remarks and reports. By this means the Queen and the Princess had them before they appeared in print.   M. Duplessie was on other occasions of great service to me, especially as a protector in the mobs, for my man servant and the honest driver * were so much occupied in watching the movements of the various fauxbourg factions, that I was often left entirely unattended.

The horrors of the Tuileries, both by night and day, were now grown appalling beyond description. Almost unendurable as they had been before, they were aggravated by the insults of the national guard to every passenger to and from the palace. I was myself in so much peril, that the Princess thought it necessary to procure a trusty person, of tried courage, to see me through the throngs, with a large bandbox of all sorts of fashionable millinery, as the mode of ingress and egress least liable to excite suspicion.

Thus equipped, and guarded by my *cicisbeo*, I one day found myself, on entering the Tuileries, in the midst of an immense mob of regular trained rioters, who, seeing me go toward the palace, directed their attention entirely to me. They took me for some one belonging to the Queen's milliner, Madame Bertin, who, they said, was fattening upon the public misery, through the Queen's extravagance.   The poor Queen herself they called by names so opprobrious, that decency will not suffer me to repeat them. With a volley of oaths, pressing upon us, they bore us to another part of the garden, for the purpose of compelling us to behold six or eight of the most

* These were two, among the persons in the confidence of the Princess, whose fidelity and attention Madame Campan mentioned to her august mistress, and to which she bears public testimony in her late work.

infamous outcasts, amusing themselves, in a state of exposure, with their accursed hands and arms tinged with blood up to the elbows. The spot they had chosen for this exhibition of their filthy persons was immediately before the windows of the apartments of the Queen and the ladies of the Court. Here they paraded up and down, to the great entertainment of a throng of savage rebels, by whom they were applauded and encouraged with shouts of *"Bis! bis!"* signifying in English, "Again! again!"

The demoniac interest excited by this scene withdrew the attention of those who were enjoying it from me, and gave me the opportunity of escaping unperceived, merely with the loss of my bandbox. Of that the infuriated mob made themselves masters; and the hats, caps, bonnets, and other articles of female attire, were placed on the parts of their degraded carcasses, which, for the honor of human nature, should have been shot.

Overcome with agony at these insults, I burst from the garden in a flood of tears. On passing the gate, I was accosted by a person, who exclaimed in a tone of great kindness, *"Qu'as tu, ma bonne? qu'est ce qui vous afflige?"* Knowing the risk I should run in representing the real cause of my concern, I immediately thought of ascribing it to the loss of the property of which I had been plundered. I told him I was a poor milliner, and had been robbed of everything I possessed in the world by the mob. "Come back with me," said he, "and I will have it restored to you." I knew it was of no avail, but policy stimulated me to comply; and I returned with him into the garden toward the palace.

What should I have felt, had I been aware when this man came up, that I was accosted by the villain Danton! The person who was with me knew him, but dared not speak, and watched a chance of escaping in the crowd for fear of being discovered. When I looked round and found myself alone, I said I had lost my brother in the confusion, which added to my grief.

"Oh, never mind," said Danton; "take hold of my arm;

no one shall molest you. We will look for your brother, and try to recover your things;" and on we went together: I, weeping, I may truly say, for my life, stopped at every step, while he related my doleful story to all whose curiosity was excited by my grief.

On my appearing arm in arm with Danton before the windows of the Queen's apartments, we were observed by Her Majesty and the princesses. Their consternation and perplexity, as well as alarm for my safety, may readily be conceived. A signal from the window instantly apprized me that I might enter the palace, to which my return had been for some time impatiently expected.

Finding it could no longer be of any service to carry on the farce of seeking my pretended brother, I begged to be escorted out of the mob to the apartments of the Princess Lamballe.

"Oh," said Danton, "certainly! and if you had only told the people that you were going to that good princess, I am sure your things would not have been taken from you. But," added he, "are you perfectly certain they were not for that detestable Maria Antoinette?"

"Oh!" I replied, quite, quite certain!" All this while the mob was at my heels.

"Then," said he, "I will not leave you till you are safe in the apartments of the Princess Lamballe, and I will myself make known to her your loss: she is so good," continued he, "that I am convinced she will make you just compensation."

When we entered the palace, he said to the national guard, "*Voilà, mes enfans, une pauvre malheureuse qui a été volée de toutes ses marchandises; mais je vais chez la Lamballe moi même avec elle*" — but he omitted her title of Princess.

I then told him how much I should be obliged by his doing so, as I had been commissioned to deliver the things, and if I was made to pay for them, the loss would be more serious than I could bear.

"Bah! bah!" exclaimed he. "*Laissez moi faire! Laissez moi faire!!*"

When he came to the inner door, which I pretended to know nothing about, he told the gentleman of the chamber his name, and said he wished to see his mistress.

Her highness came in a few minutes, and from her looks and visible agitation at the sight of Danton, I feared she would have betrayed both herself and me. However, while he was making a long preamble, I made signs, from which she inferred that all was safe.

When Danton had finished telling her the story, she calmly said to me: "Do you recollect, child, the things you have been robbed of?"

I replied, that if I had pen and ink, I could even set down the prices.

"Oh, well then, child, come in," said her highness, "and we will see what is to be done!"

"There!" exclaimed Danton. "Did I not tell you this before?" Then giving me a hearty squeeze of the hand, he departed, and thus terminated the millinery speculation, which I have no doubt, cost her highness a tolerable sum.

As soon as he was gone, the Princess said, " For Heaven's sake tell me the whole of this affair candidly; for the Queen has been in the greatest agitation at the bare idea of your knowing Danton, ever since we first saw you walking with him! He is one of our most inveterate enemies."

I said that if they had but witnessed one-half of the scenes that I saw, I was sure their feelings would have been shocked beyond description. "We did not see all, but we heard too much for the ears of our sex."

I then related the particulars of our meeting to her highness, who observed : "This accident, however unpleasant, may still turn out to our advantage. This fellow believes you to be a *merchande de modes*, and the circumstance of his having accompanied you to my apartment, will enable you, in future, to pass to and from the Pavilion unmolested by the national guard."

With tears of joy in her eyes for my safety, she could not, however, help laughing when I told her the farce I

20

kept up respecting the loss of my brother, and my band-box with the millinery, for which I was also soon congratulated most graciously by Her Majesty, who much applauded my spirit and presence of mind, and condescended immediately to intrust me with letters of the greatest importance, for some of the most distinguished members of the assembly, with which I left the palace in triumph, but taking care to be ready with a proper story of my losses.

When I passed the guardroom I was pitied by the very wretches, who, perhaps, had already shared in the spoils; and who would have butchered me, no doubt, into the bargain, could they have penetrated the real object of my mission. They asked me if I had been paid for the loss I sustained. I told them I had not, but I was promised that it should be settled.

"Settled!" said one of the wretches. "Get the money as soon as you can. Do not trust to promises of its being settled. They will all be settled themselves soon!"

The next day, on going to the palace, I found the Princess Lamballe in the greatest agitation, from the accounts the Court had just received of the murder of a man belonging to Arthur Dillon, and of the massacres at Nantes.

"The horrid prints, pamphlets, and caricatures," cried she, "daily exhibited under the very windows of the Tuileries, against His Majesty, the Queen, the Austrian party, and the Coblentz party, the constant thwarting of every plan, and these last horrors at Nantes, have so overwhelmed the King that he is nearly become a mere automaton. Daily and nightly execrations are howled in his ears. Look at our boasted deliverers! The poor Queen, her children, and all of us belonging to the palace, are in danger of our lives at merely being seen; while they by whom we have been so long buoyed up with hope, are quarreling among themselves for the honor and etiquette of precedency, leaving us to the fury of a race of cannibals, who know no mercy, and will have destroyed us long before their disputes of etiquette can be settled."

The utterance of her highness while saying this was rendered almost inarticulate by her tears.

"What support against internal disorganization," continued she, "is to be expected from so disorganized a body as the present army of different nations, having all different interests?"

I said there was no doubt that the Prussian army was on its march, and would soon be joined by that of the princes and of Austria.

"You speak as you wish, *mia cara Inglesina*, but it is all to no purpose. Would to God they had never been applied to, never been called upon to interfere. Oh, that Her Majesty could have been persuaded to listen to Dumourier and some other of the members, instead of rolying on succors which, I fear, will never enter Paris in our lifetime! No army can subdue a nation; especially a nation frenzied by the recent recovery of its freedom and independence from the shackles of a corrupt and weak administration. The King is too good; the Queen has no equal as to heart; but they have both been most grossly betrayed. The royalists on one side, the constitutionalists on the other, will be the victims of the Jacobins, for they are the most powerful, they are the most united, they possess the most talent, and they act in a body, and not merely for the time being. Believe me, my dear, their plans are too well grounded to be defeated, as every one framed by the fallacious constitutionalists and mad-headed royalists has been; and so they will ever be while they continue to form two separate interests. From the very first moment when these two bodies were worked upon separately, I told the Queen that till they were united for the same object the monarchy would be unsafe, and at the mercy of the Jacobins, who, from hatred to both parties, would overthrow it themselves to rule despotically over those whom they no longer respected or feared, but whom they hated, as considering them both equally their former oppressors."

"May the All-seeing Power," continued her highness, "grant, for the good of this shattered state, that I may be mistaken, and that my predictions may prove different in the result; but of this I see no hope, unless in the strength of our own internal resources. God knows how powerful they might prove could they be united at this moment! But from the anarchy and division kept up between them, I see no prospect of their being brought to bear, except in a general overthrow of this, as you have justly observed, organized system of disorders, from which at some future period we may obtain a solid, systematic order of government. Would Charles the Second ever have reigned after the murder of his father had England been torn to pieces by different factions? No! It was the union of the body of the nation for its internal tranquillity, the amalgamation of parties against domestic faction, which gave vigor to the arm of power, and enabled the nation to check foreign interference abroad, while it annihilated anarchy at home. By that means the Protector himself laid the first stone of the Restoration. The division of a nation is the surest harbinger of success to its invaders, the death-blow to its sovereign's authority, and the total destruction of that innate energy by which alone a country can obtain the dignity of its own independence."

CHAPTER XXVI.

Affecting Interview between the Queen, Princess Elizabeth, Princess Lamballe, and the Editor — Princess Lamballe Communicates the Intention of the Queen to Send the Editor on a Mission to Her Royal Relations — Receives the Cipher of the Italian Correspondence — Presents Given to the Editor Previous to Her Departure — Instructions from the Princess — Sees Her for the Last Time — Quits France — Contrast between the Duchess of Parma and the Queen of Naples on the Receipt of Her Majesty's Letters — Conversation of the Queen of Naples with General Acton.

WHILE her highness was thus pondering on the dreadful situation of France, strengthening her arguments by those historical illustrations, which, from the past, enabled her to look into the future, a message came to her from Her Majesty. She left me, and, in a few minutes, returned to her apartment, accompanied by the Queen, and her royal highness the Princess Elizabeth. I was greatly surprised at seeing these two illustrious and august personages bathed in tears. Of course, I could not be aware of any new motive to create any new or extraordinary emotion; yet there was in the countenances of all the party an appearance different from anything I had ever witnessed in them, or any other person before; a something which seemed to say, they no longer had any affinity with the rest of earthly beings. I will therefore endeavor to convey some idea of the impression which each, respectively, made on me at the moment.

The look of the Princess Elizabeth was perfectly celestial; she seemed as if loosened from every mortal tie, and her soul, dwelling far from the polluted state of earthly vegetation, was already consigned to the regions of immortal bliss, with no thought of worldly cares, but aspirations for the happiness and eternal pardon of those who

had made its abode to her and her's so horribly lament-
able!

In the air of Her Majesty the Queen shone all the dignity of that heroic spirit, which even the weight of misfortune, irremovable on this side the grave, could not
overwhelm. Though her heavenly blue eyes no longer
dazzled with those bursts of fire, which once penetrated
into the secret recesses of every heart, and gladdened the
soul of every beholder with sympathetic affection; though
they were sunken in their sockets, never more to emerge
from earthly grief, and turned toward the asylum of future tranquillity beyond the earth, yet they still spoke the
greatness and supernatural strength of her character; and
their splendor, while setting in eternal darkness, was still
the brightness of a setting sun.

The Princess Lamballe seemed a beautiful form animated by some saintlike spirit, with scarcely a consciousness of its own existence, and with no thought but that
of consoling those around, and no desire but that of
smoothing their path to those mansions of eternal peace
to which she had already, by anticipation, consigned herself. She appeared as if, through heavenly revelations,
only solicitous to sustain others by the assurances she
found so consolatory to herself. Her countenance beamed
with a serenity perfectly supernatural, under such circumstances, in one of her weak sex. Her air was elevated
and firm, though not presumptuous. The graces that
played about her bespoke her already the crowned martyr
of Elysium, rather than the exposed victim of earthly
assassins. Her voice was like the tones of angels; her
looks—Oh! never shall I forget the glance which told
me, "I see before me the mansion of peace. If we meet
no more, be it your consolation for my untimely end that
I am happy!"

I am conscious of the faintness of my delineation of
these three heroic princesses when last I had the honor
of seeing them; and even were my powers of description of
the highest order they must have fallen infinitely short
of the indelible impression of that ever lamented day!

After the numberless kindnesses I had received, the infinite condescensions and liberalities, to find them still, in the midst of such miseries of their own, when in hourly peril of their lives, so solicitous to screen me from danger——. But the subject is too painful: let me go on with the interview.

I have already remarked, that the two august personages who accompanied the Princess Lamballe were in tears. I soon discovered the cause. They had all been just writing to their distant friends and relations. A fatal presentiment, alas! too soon verified, told them it was for the last time.

Her highness the Princess Lamballe now approached me.

"Her Majesty," observed the Princess, "wishes to give you a mark of her esteem, in delivering to you, with her own hands, letters to her family, which it is her intention to intrust to your especial care.

"On this step Her Majesty has resolved, as much to send you out of the way of danger, as from the conviction occasioned by the firm reliance your conduct has created in us, that you will faithfully obey the orders you may receive, and execute our intentions with that peculiar intelligence which the emergency of the case requires.

"But even the desirable opportunity which offers, through you, for the accomplishment of the mission, might not have prevailed with Her Majesty to hasten your departure, had not the wretch Danton twice inquired at the palace for the "little milliner," whom he rescued and conducted safe to the apartments of the Pavilion of Flora. This, probably, may be a matter of no real consequence whatever; but it is our duty to avoid danger, and it has been decided that you should, at least for a time, absent yourself from Paris.

"*Per cio, mia cara Inglesina*, speak now freely and candidly: is it your wish to return to England, or go elsewhere? For though we are all sorry to lose you, yet it would be a source of still greater sorrow to us, prizing your services and fidelity as we do, should any plans and purposes of ours lead you into difficulty or embarrassment."

"*Oh, mon Dieu! c'est vrai!*" interrupted Her Majesty, her eyes at the same time filled with tears.

"I should never forgive myself," continued the Princess, "if I should prove the cause of any misfortune to you."

"Nor I!" most graciously subjoined the Queen.

"Therefore," pursued the Princess, "speak your mind without reserve."

I was, however, so completely overwhelmed by my feelings, that notwithstanding frequent attempts, I found myself totally incapable, for some time, even to express the gratitude I naturally felt for such unbounded condescension, which did not fail to produce the greatest sensibility on the illustrious personages who witnessed my embarrassment; and when at last my tears permitted me the faculty of utterance, I could only articulate in broken accents.

The Princess Lamballe approached me. I took her hand; I bathed it with my tears, as she, at the same moment, was bathing my face with hers. Sobbing all the while, I replied, that I was a stranger to fear, except that of incurring their displeasure; that though to quit Paris and their august personages would be a severe sacrifice at a period so critical, yet it must greatly diminish my reluctance to know that I had the honor to be considered as useful elsewhere. I sincerely hoped they had not been influenced in their wish to remove me from any doubt of my fidelity, as their confidence in me formed the pride of my life; and, I added, that the poignant regret I felt at being compelled to withdraw myself, in obedience to their royal commands, could only be diminished by the flattering prospect that the missions which occasioned my absence would tend to console and render them more happy on my return; a wish that would everywhere accompany me, and would never be extinguished but with my existence.

Here my own feelings, and the sobs of the illustrious

party, completely overcame me, and I could not proceed. The Princess Lamballe clasped me in her arms. "Not only letters," exclaimed she, "but my life I would trust to the fidelity of my *vera, verissima, cara Inglesina!* And now," continued her highness, turning round to the Queen, "will it please Your Majesty to give *Inglesina* your commands?"

"Here, then," said the Queen, "is a letter for my dear sister, the Queen of Naples, which you must deliver into her own hands.

"Here is another for my sister, the Duchess of Parma. If she should not be at Parma, you will find her at Colorno.

"This is for my brother, the Archduke of Milan; this for my sister-in-law, the Princess Clotilda Piedmont, at Turin; and here are four others. You will take off the envelope when you get to Turin, and then put them into the post yourself. Do not give them to, or send them by, any person whatsoever.

"Tell my sisters the state of Paris. Inform them of our cruel situation. Describe the riots and convulsions you have seen. Above all, assure them how dear they are to me, and how much I love them."

At the word LOVE, Her Majesty threw herself on a sofa, and wept bitterly.

The Princess Elizabeth gave me a letter for her sister, and two for her aunts, to be delivered to them, if at Rome; but if not, to be put under cover and sent through the post at Rome to whatever place they might have made their residence.

I had also a packet of letters to deliver for the Princess Lamballe at Turin; and another for the Duke de Serbelloni at Milan.

Her Majesty and the Princess Elizabeth not only allowed me the honor to kiss their hands, but they both gave me their blessing and good wishes for my safe return, and then left me with the Princess Lamballe.

Her Majesty had scarcely left the apartment of the Princess, when I recollected she had forgotten to give me the cipher and the key for the letters.* The Princess immediately went to the Queen's apartment, and returned with them shortly after.

"Now that we are alone," said her highness, "I will tell you what Her Majesty has graciously commanded me

* Madame Campan, vol. ii., page 176, alludes to the Queen's cipher, and represents very truly its being impossible to detect it; for should the cipher or even the correspondence be lost or taken, neither could be understood by any but the two persons so corresponding.

The cipher, however, which Madame Campan often assisted Her Majesty in copying, and which was selected from "Paul and Virginia," was merely for the Paris correspondence, and principally for that of Bertrand de Moleville; different altogether from the one I allude to, and which was only used by the Queen in corresponding with her Italian relations. This is still in my possession, and has been so ever since the unfortunate moment I am now describing.

As this cipher may be a subject of some curiosity to my readers, I annex it. It can only be applied to the Italian language, which has no K and no double vowels. It is scarcely necessary to observe that Maria Antoinette corresponded almost exclusively in Italian. If well understood beforehand, with the possession of the key, the deciphering, after a little practice, becomes very easy. For instance, take for a key the word Lodovico; and suppose that you wish to write the ciphers for the words "Maria Antonia, Regina di Francia"; set down the whole line, and immediately over each letter write the separate letters of the key, or word Lodovico, successively, thus —

Key – – L O D O V I C O L O D O V I C O L O D O V I C O L O D
Subject M A R I A - A N T O N I A - R E G I N A - D I - F R A N C I A

Then, in the first alphabet of the large initials of the cipher (see the beginning of the volume), the letter L must be sought, and on the transversal line being traced for M it will be found on the same square with Q, which must be set down; then in the large initials look for O, and A will be found in the small square with T. Put T down, and proceed, in the same manner, with each letter of the key and subject, and the result will be —

QTEQY-RAAIFXT-GXTQHT-QQ-QANFTQN

On receiving this, the person with whom it has been agreed to correspond by the word Lodovico as the key, will apply the separate letters of the word to decipher it, and taking L of the key large initials, will seek on the transversal lines for the cipher Q which will be found with M; in the same manner O and T produce A; D and E — R; O and Q — I; V and Y — A; I and R — A, etc., so that the deciphering will be —

MARIA ANTONIA REGINA DI FRANCIA.

to signify to you in her royal name. The Queen commands me to say that you are provided for for life; and that, on the first vacancy which may occur, she intends fixing you at Court.

"Therefore, *mia cara Inglesina*, take especial care what you are about, and obey Her Majesty's wishes when you are absent, as implicitly as you have hitherto done all her commands during your abode near her. You are not to write to anyone. No one is to be made acquainted with your route. You are not to leave Paris in your own carriage. It will be sent after you by your man servant, who is to join you at Chalons on the Saone.

"I have further to inform you that Her Majesty the Queen, on sending you the cipher, has at the same time graciously condescended to add these presents as further marks of her esteem."

Her highness then showed me a most beautiful gold watch, chain, and seals.*

"These," said she, placing them with her own hands, "Her Majesty desired me to put round your neck in testimony of her regard."

At the same time her highness presented me, on her own part, with a beautiful pocketbook, the covers of which were of gold enameled, with the word "SOUVENIR" in diamonds on one side, and a large cipher of her own initials on the other. The first page contained the names of the Queen and her royal highness the Princess Elizabeth, in their own handwriting. There was a cheque in it on a Swiss banker, at Milan, of the name of Bonny.†

* It was a very handsome repeater, set round with diamonds and pearls; and the chain and seals set with beautiful gems.

† The greater part of the time I resided in Milan I was entertained at the house of this banker, although the cheque was of no use to me. Payment was refused in consequence of what happened in Paris on the 10th of August; but M. Bonny gave me what money I wanted on my own signature, an apartment in his house, and the use of his table, for all of which he was handsomely remunerated on my arrival at Naples, through the means of Sir William Hamilton, upon whose kindness I was thrown

Having given me these invaluable tokens, her highness proceeded with her instructions.

"At Chalons," continued she, "*mia cara*, your man servant will perhaps bring you other letters. Take two places in the stage for yourself and your *femme de chambre*, in her name, and give me the memorandum, that our old friend the driver may procure the passports. You must not be seen; for there is no doubt that Danton has given the police a full description of your person. Now go and prepare: we shall see each other again before your departure."

Only a few minutes afterward, my man servant came to me to say that it would be some hours before the stage would set off, and that there was a lady in her carriage waiting for me in the Bois de Boulogne. I hastened thither. What was my surprise on finding it was the Princess. I now saw her for the last time!

Let me pass lightly over this sad moment. I must not, however, dismiss the subject without noticing the visible changes which had taken place in the short space of a

by the loss of a trunk containing all my valuables and money. This disaster occurred between Acqua Pendenti and Monte Rosi. My servant, who generally had his feet on the carriage box containing the trunk, had been sent on before to order horses, that I might reach Rome in the daytime. It was during this interval that the trunk was cut away, that part of the Roman States from the MALARIA being only inhabited by notorious assassins and common thieves, under the protection of some cardinal or other, as was the practice then. Had it not been for the kindness of the good Duchess de Paoli, who resided at the Fontana de Trevi, I should have been very·much embarrassed, when I arrived at Rome, to have got on to Naples. Indeed, I must do the Italian nobility the justice to say that I generally met with the greatest hospitality from them everywhere; and even the Duchess de Strozzi, of Florence, when she heard of the accident, wrote to me at Naples, offering her assistance, which I declined though very grateful for such testimonies of esteem from a mere letter introduction.

Though Sir William Hamilton used every exertion in his power with the Roman authorities, to regain my property, nothing more was ever heard of the matter, nor did I recover the most trifling article. Yet the two postilions were known as common thieves, having been detected in attempting the same on another English family, only eight days previous.

month, in the appearance of all these illustrious princesses. Their very complexions were no longer the same, as if grief had changed the whole mass of their blood. The Queen, in particular, from the month of July to the 2d of August, looked ten years older. The other two princesses were really worn out with fatigue, anxiety, and the want of rest, as, during the whole month of July, they scarcely ever slept, for fear of being murdered in their beds, and only threw themselves on them, now and then, without undressing. The King, three or four times in the night, would go round to their different apartments, fearful they might be destroyed in their sleep, and ask, "*Etes vous là?*" when they would answer him from within, "*Nous sommes encore ici.*" * Indeed, if when nature was exhausted, sleep by chance came to the relief of their worn out and languid frames, it was only to awaken them to fresh horrors, which constantly threatened the convulsion by which they were finally annihilated.

It would be uncandid in me to be silent concerning the marked difference I found in the feelings of the two royal sisters of Her Majesty.

I had never had the honor before to execute any commissions for her royal highness the Duchess of Parma, and, of course, took that city in my way to Naples.

I did not reach Parma till after the horrors which had taken place at the Tuileries on the 10th of August, 1792. The whole of the unfortunate Royal Family of France were then lodged in the Temple. There was not a feeling heart in Europe unmoved at their afflicting situation.

I arrived at Colorno, the country residence of the Duchess of Parma, just as her royal highness was going out on horseback.

I ordered my servant to inform one of the pages that I came by express from Paris, and requested the honor to know when it would be convenient for her royal highness to allow me a private audience, as I was going, post

---

* This fact was mentioned to me by a confidential person, who often remained in the apartment during the day, while her highness would herself repose upon a couch.

haste, to Rome and Naples. Of course, I did not choose
to tell my business either to my own or her royal highness's servant, being in honor and duty bound to deliver
the letter and the verbal message of her then truly unfortunate sister in person and in privacy.

The mention of PARIS I saw somewhat startled and
confused her. Meantime, she came near enough to my
carriage for me to say to her in German, in order that
none of the servants, French or Italian, might understand,
that I had a letter to deliver into her own hands, without
saying from whom.

She then desired I would alight, and she soon followed
me; and after having very graciously ordered me some
refreshments, asked me from whom I had been sent.

I delivered Her Majesty's letter. Before she opened
it, she exclaimed, "*O Dio! tutto é perduto è troppo tardi!*
Oh, God! all is lost, it is too late!" I then gave her the
cipher and the key. In a few minutes I enabled her to
decipher the letter. On getting through it, she again
exclaimed, "*E tutto inutile!* it is entirely useless! I am
afraid they are all lost. I am sorry you are so situated
as not to allow of your remaining here to rest from your
fatigue. Whenever you come to Parma, I shall be glad
to see you."

She then took out her pocket-handkerchief, shed a few
tears, and said, that as circumstances were now so totally
changed, to answer the letter might only commit her,
her sister, and myself; but that if affairs took the turn
she WISHED, no doubt her sister would write again. She
then mounted her horse, and wished me a good journey;
and I took leave, and set off for Rome.

I must confess that the conduct of the Duchess of
Parma appeared to me rather cold, if not unfeeling.
Perhaps she was afraid of showing too much emotion,
and wished to encourage the idea that princesses ought
not to give way to sensibility, like common mortals.

But how different was the conduct of the Queen of
Naples! She kissed the letter; she bathed it with her
tears! Scarcely could she allow herself time to decipher

it. At every sentence she exclaimed, "Oh, my dear, oh, my adored sister! What will become of her! My brothers are now both no more! Surely she will soon be liberated!" Then, turning suddenly to me, she asked with eagerness, "Do you not think she will ? Oh, Maria, Maria! why did she not fly to Vienna ? Why did she not come to me instead of writing ? Tell me, for God's sake, all you know!"

I said I knew nothing further of what had taken place at Paris, having traveled night and day, except what I had heard from the different couriers, which I had met and stopped on my route; but I hoped to be better informed by Sir William Hamilton, as all my letters were to be sent from France to Turin, and thence on to Sir William at Naples; and if I found no letters with him, I should immediately set off and return to Turin or Milan, to be as near France as possible for my speedy return if necessary. I ventured to add, that it was my earnest prayer that all the European sovereigns would feel the necessity of interesting themselves for the Royal Family of France, with whose fate the fate of monarchy throughout Europe might be interwoven.

"Oh, God of Heaven!" cried the Queen, "all that dear family may ere now have been murdered! Perhaps they are already numbered among the dead! Oh, my poor, dear, beloved Maria! Oh, I shall go frantic! I must send for General Acton."

Wringing her hands, she pulled the bell, and in a few minutes the general came. On his entering the apartment, she flew to him like one deprived of reason.

"There!" exclaimed she. "There! Behold the fatal consequences!" showing him the letter. "Louis XVI. is in the state of Charles the First of England, and my sister will certainly be murdered."

"No, no, no!" exclaimed the general. "Something will be done. Calm yourself, madam." Then turning to me, "When," said he, "did you leave Paris ?"

"When all was lost!" interrupted the Queen.

"Nay," cried the general; "pray let me speak. All is not lost, you will find; have but a little patience."

"Patience!" said the Queen. "For two years I have heard of nothing else. Nothing has been done for these unfortunate beings." She then threw herself into a chair. "Tell him!" cried she to me; "tell him! tell him!"

I then informed the general that I had left Paris on the 2d of August, but did not believe at the time, though the daily riots were horrible, that such a catastrophe could have occurred so soon as eight days after.

The Queen was now quite exhausted, and General Acton rang the bell for the lady-in-waiting, who entered accompanied by the Duchess Curigliano Marini, and they assisted Her Majesty to bed.

When she had retired, "Do not," said the general to me, "do not go to Sir William's to-night. He is at Caserte. You seem too much fatigued."

"More from grief," replied I, "and reflection on the fatal consequences that might result to the great personages I have so lately left, than from the journey."

"Take my advice," resumed he. "You had much better go to bed and rest yourself. You look very ill."

I did as he recommended, and went to the nearest hotel I could find. I felt no fatigue of mind or body till I had gotten into bed, where I was confined for several days with a most violent fever. During my illness I received every attention both from the Court, and our Ambassador and Lady Hamilton, who kindly visited me every day. The Queen of Naples I never again saw till my return in 1793, after the murder of the Queen of France; and I am glad I did not, for her agony would have acted anew upon my disordered frame, and might have proved fatal.

I was certainly somewhat prepared for a difference of feeling between the two princesses, as the unfortunate Maria Antoinette, in the letters to the Queen of Naples, always wrote, "To my much beloved sister, the Queen of the two Sicilies, etc.," and to the other, merely, "To the Duchess of Parma, etc." But I could never have dreamed of a difference so little flattering, under such circumstances, to the Duchess of Parma.

CHAPTER XXVII.

FROM the moment of my departure from Paris on the 2d of August, 1792, the tragedy hastened to its denouement. On the night of the 9th, the tocsin was sounded, and the King and the Royal Family looked upon their fate as sealed. Notwithstanding the personal firmness of His Majesty, he was a coward for others. He dreaded the responsibility of ordering blood to be shed, even in defense of his nearest and dearest interests. Petion, however, had given the order to repel force by force to Mandat, who was murdered upon the steps of the Hotel de Ville. It has been generally supposed that Petion had received a bribe for not ordering the cannon against the Tuileries on the night of the 9th, and that Mandat was massacred by the agents of Petion for the purpose of extinguishing all proof that he was only acting under the instructions of the mayor.

I shall not undertake to judge of the propriety of the King's impression, that there was no safety from the insurgents but in the hall, and under the protection of the assembly. Had the members been well disposed toward him, the event might have proved very different. But there is one thing certain. The Queen would never have consented to this step but to save the King and her innocent children. She would have preferred death to the humiliation of being under obligations to her sworn enemies; but she was overcome by the King declaring, with tears in his eyes, that he would not quit the palace without her. The Princesses Elizabeth and Lamballe fell at her feet — implored Her Majesty to obey the King, and assured her there was no alternative between instant death and refuge from it in the assembly. "Well," said the Queen, "if our lot be death, let us away to receive it with the national sanction."

I need not expatiate on the succession of horrors which now overwhelmed the royal sufferers. Their confinement at the Feuillans, and their subsequent transfer to the Temple, are all topics sufficiently enlarged upon by many who were actors in the scenes to which they led. The Princess Lamballe was, while it was permitted, the companion of their captivity. But the consolation of her society was considered too great to be continued. Her fate had no doubt been predetermined; and, unwilling to await the slow proceedings of a trial, which it was thought politic should precede the murder of her royal mistress, it was found necessary to detach her from the wretched inmates of the Temple, in order to have her more completely within the control of the miscreants, who hated her for her virtues. The expedient was resorted to of casting suspicion upon the correspondence which her highness kept up with the exterior of the prison, for the purpose of obtaining such necessaries as were required, in consequence of the utter destitution in which the Royal Family retired from the Tuileries. Two men, of the name of Devin and Priquet, were bribed to create a suspicion, by their informations against the Queen's female attendant. The first declared that on the 18th of August, while he was on duty near the cell of the King, he saw a female about eleven o'clock in the day come from a room in the center, holding in one hand three letters, and with the other cautiously opening the door of the right-hand chamber, whence she presently came back without the letters and returned into the center chamber. He further asserted that twice, when this female opened the door, he distinctly saw a letter half-written, and every evidence of an eagerness to hide it from observation. The second informant, Priquet, swore that while on duty as morning sentinel on the gallery between the two towers, he saw, through the window of the central chamber, a female writing with great earnestness and alarm during the whole time he was on guard.

All the ladies were immediately summoned before the authorities. The hour of the separation between the Princess and her royal friend accorded with the solemnity of the circumstance. It was nearly midnight when they were torn asunder, and they never met again.

The examinations were all separate. That of the Princess Lamballe was as follows:

Q. Your name?

A. Marie-Thérèse-Louise de Savoy, Bourbon Lamballe.

Q. What do you know of the events which occurred on the 10th of August?

A. Nothing.

Q. Where did you pass that day?

A. As a relative I followed the King to the national assembly.

Q. Were you in bed on the night of the 9th and 10th?

A. No.

Q. Where were you then?

A. In my apartments at the *château.*

Q. Did you not go to the apartments of the King in the course of that night?

A. Finding there was a likelihood of a commotion, I went thither toward one in the morning.

Q. You were aware then that the people had arisen?

A. I learnt it, from hearing the tocsin.

Q. Did you see the Swiss and national guards, who passed the night on the terrace?

A. I was at the window, but saw neither.

Q. Was the King in his apartment when you went thither?

A. There were a great number of persons in the room, but not the King.

Q. Did you know of the Mayor of Paris being at the Tuileries?

A. I heard he was there.

Q. At what hour did the King go to the national assembly?

A. Seven.

Q. Did he not, before he went, review the troops? Do you know the oath he made them swear?

A. I never heard of any oath.

Q. Have you any knowledge of cannon being mounted and pointed in the apartments?

A. No.

Q. Have you ever seen Messrs. Mandat and d'Affry in the *château?*

A. No.

Q. Do you know the secret doors of the Tuileries?

A. I know of no such doors.

Q. Have you not, since you have been in the Temple, received and written letters, which you sought to send away secretly?

A. I have never received or written any letters, excepting such as have been delivered to the municipal officer.

Q. Do you know anything of an article of furniture which is making for Madame Elizabeth?

A. No.

Q. Have you not recently received some devotional books?

A. No.

Q. What are the books which you have at the Temple?

A. I have none.

Q.   Do you know anything of a barred staircase?

A.   No.

Q.   What general officers did you see at the Tuileries, on the night of the 9th and 10th?

A.   I saw no general officers; I only saw M. Rœderer.

For thirteen hours was her highness, with her female companions in misfortune, exposed to these absurd forms, and to the gaze of insulting and malignant curiosity. At length, about the middle of the day, they were told that it was decreed that they should be detained till further orders, leaving them the choice of prisons, between that of la Force and of la Sulpétrière.

Her highness immediately decided on the former. It was at first determined that she should be separated from Madame de Tourzel, but humanity so far prevailed as to permit the consolation of her society, with that of others of her friends and fellow-sufferers, and for a moment the Princess enjoyed the only comfort left to her, that of exchanging sympathy with her partners in affliction. But the cell to which she was doomed proved her last habitation upon earth.

On the 1st of September the Marseillois began their murderous operations. Three hundred persons in two days massacred upward of a thousand defenseless prisoners, confined under the pretext of malpractices against the state, or rather devotedness to the royal cause. The spirit which produced the massacres of the prisons at Paris extended them through the principal towns and cities all over France.

Even the universal interest felt for the Princess Lamballe was of no avail against this frenzy. I remember once (as if it were from a presentiment of what was to occur) the King observing to her, "I never knew any but fools and sycophants who could keep themselves clear from the lash of public censure. How is it, then, that you, my dear Princess, who are neither, contrive to steer your bark on this dangerous coast without running against the rocks on which so many good vessels like your own have been dashed to pieces?" "Oh, sire," replied her highness, "my time is not yet come — I am not dead yet!" Too soon, and too horribly, her hour did come!

The butchery of the prisons was now commenced. The Duke de Penthièvre set every engine in operation to save his beloved daughter-in-law. He sent for Manuel, who was then *Procureur* of Paris. The Duke declared that half his fortune should be Manuel's if he could but save the Princess Lamballe and the ladies who were in the same prison with her from the general massacre. Manuel promised the Duke that he would instantly set about removing them all from the reach of the blood hunters. He began with those whose removal was least likely to attract attention, leaving the Princess Lamballe, from motives of policy, to the last.

Meanwhile, other messengers had been dispatched to different quarters for fear of failure with Manuel. It was discovered by one of these that the atrocious tribunal* who sat in mock judgment upon the tenants of these gloomy abodes, after satiating themselves with every studied insult they could devise, were to pronounce the word "*libre!*" It was naturally presumed that the predestined victims, on hearing this tempting sound, and seeing the doors at the same moment set open by the clerks of the infamous court, would dart off in exultation, and, fancying themselves liberated, rush upon the knives of the barbarians, who were outside, in waiting for their blood! Hundreds were thus slaughtered.

To save the Princess from such a sacrifice, it was projected to prevent her from appearing before the tribunal, and a belief was encouraged, that means would be devised to elude the necessity. The person who interested himself for her safety contrived to convey a letter containing these words : "Let what will happen, for God's sake do not quit your cell. You will be spared. Adieu."

Manuel, however, who knew not of this cross arrangement, was better informed than its projector. He was aware it would be impossible for her highness to escape

* Thibaudeau, Hebert, Simonier, etc.

from appearing before the tribunal. He had already removed her companions. The Princess Tarente, the Marchioness Tourzel, her daughter, and others, were in safety. But when, true to his promise, he went to the Princess Lamballe, she would not be prevailed upon to quit her cell. There was no time to parley. The letter prevailed, and her fate was inevitable.

The massacre had begun at daybreak. The fiends had been some hours busy in the work of death. The piercing shrieks of the dying victims brought the Princess and her remaining companion upon their knees, in fervent prayer for the souls of the departed. The messengers of the tribunal now appeared. The Princess was compelled to attend the summons. She went, accompanied by her faithful female attendant.

A glance at the seas of blood, of which she caught a glimpse upon her way to the court, had nearly shocked her even to sudden death. Would it had! She staggered, but was sustained by her companion. Her courage triumphed. She appeared before the gore-stained tribunes.

After some questions of mere form, her highness was commanded to swear to be faithful to the new form of government, and to hate the King, the Queen, and royalty.

"To the first," replied her highness, "I willingly submit. To the second, how can I accede? There is nothing of which I can accuse the Royal Family. To hate them is against my nature. They are my sovereigns. They are my friends and relations. I have served them for many years, and never have I found reason for the slightest complaint."

The princess could no longer articulate. She fell into the arms of her attendant. The fatal signal was pronounced. She recovered, and crossing the court of the prison, which was bathed with the blood of mutilated victims, involuntarily exclaimed, "Gracious Heaven! What a sight is this?" and fell into a fit.

Nearest to her in the mob stood a mulatto, whom she had caused to be baptized, educated, and maintained, but whom, from ill-conduct, she had latterly excluded from her presence. This miscreant struck at her with his halbert. The blow removed her cap. Her luxuriant hair (as if to hide her angelic beauty from the sight of the murderers, pressing tigerlike around to pollute that form, the virtues of which equaled its physical perfection), her luxuriant hair fell around and veiled her a moment from view.* An individual, to whom I was nearly allied, seeing the miscreants somewhat staggered, sprang forward to the rescue; but the mulatto wounded him.† The Princess was lost to all feeling from the moment the monster first struck at her. But the demons would not quit their prey. She expired, gashed with wounds.

Scarcely was the breath out of her body, when the murderers cut off her head.‡ One party of them fixed it, like that of the vilest traitor, on an immense pole, and

* This circumstance was related to me by a person, who knew the Princess from her childhood, long before she left Turin.

† This person followed her remains for a considerable distance, but the loss of blood prevented him from seeing the horrors which ensued. He left France very soon after, and died at Naples. He himself related these particulars to Sir William Hamilton, from whom I had them in 1793.

‡ It may not be uninteresting to my readers to learn the peculiar circumstances under which I became possessed of the details which are here recorded.

When I was residing in Paris, in 1803, I felt a vacuum, I thought something seemed wanting or wrong, whenever I let a day pass without paying my devotions to the Cemetery de la Madeleine, which contained the remains of some of the royal martyrs.

One day, when I was in this sacred retreat, I was much surprised at being accosted by two men. They asked me what I was doing there.

I at first looked at them in silence, but with that contemptuous sternness which spoke more plainly than any language could utter. They repeated their question in a tone of more authority.

It was just at the time when Bonaparte had compelled the Italians to offer him the Consulship of Italy.

I answered that I did not know what right they had to interrupt the living, who was only seeking a quiet retreat among the dead.

"Yes," said they, "but you are seeking curiously among the dead,

bore it in triumph all over Paris; while another division
of the outrageous cannibals were occupied in tearing her
clothes piecemeal from her mangled corpse. The beauty
of that form, though headless, mutilated and reeking with
the hot blood of their foul crime — how shall I describe
it ? — excited that atrocious excess of lust, which impelled

which induces us to think all is not as it should be. Who are you?
What is your business in Paris ?"

I told them that I wished to know, before I satisfied their imper·
tinent curiosity, what right they had thus to interrogate me.

"The right of fathoming suspicious appearances," replied they.
"We have observed you, madam, often and often. You always
come hither alone. Your head and face are invariably concealed."

"For that very reason you should not have disturbed my privacy.
Being alone, what can you fear from me? My being veiled is to
avoid impertinent curiosity, like that which you now exercise."

Seeing that I was not to be intimidated, they became more tract-
able, and said, "We do not come here without orders. We have
long watched your motions. You always stand over a particular
grave. What do you seek there ? Time has destroyed every vestige;
why, when she was put into the ground, God rest her poor soul!
there was a hundredweight of lime cast upon her body, that it
might the more rapidly consume itself."

"Whose body do you mean?" exclaimed I.—"Whose ?" answered
one of the men. "Why, do you think me so ignorant as not to
know? Ah," continued he, putting a handkerchief to his face to dry
the tears that were falling. "Ah, I knew that unfortunate Queen!
and I knew also her unfortunate friend ——"

"The Princess Lamballe ?" cried I.

"To be sure I did!"

"Can you give me any information, by which I may be enabled to
pay that deplored victim the same tribute of devotion which I have
offered to this ?"

"Ah! madam!" answered the man, "if I had been able to have
found her precious body, I should not now be a police officer. The
Duke de Penthièvre offered any money for it, if it could have been
found and brought to the curate of the parish, or his chaplain, for
burial; but it was impossible to ascertain it from the number of victims that were heaped confusedly one upon another. Manuel, rough
as he was, not having succeeded in saving her alive, though the Duke had
paid him munificently to do so, exerted all his authority to bring the
corpse to burial; and having, by his anxiety for its recovery, nearly
committed himself to the bloody tribunal of his companions, he was
obliged to give up the pursuit. If the murderers had not stripped her

these hordes of assassins to satiate their demoniac passions upon the remains of this virtuous angel!

Is there a deed in the history of the most savage nations, which bears a parallel in brutality?

This incredible crime being perpetrated, the wretches fastened ropes round the body, arms, and legs, and dragged it naked through the streets of Paris, till no

of all her clothes, we should have been able to have identified the body from some part of her linen, but not a rag was left by which she could be distinguished from her fellow-martyrs."

I was chilled with horror at this description, when one of the men said, "Madam, I was one of the late King's gamekeepers, and afterward employed by that unfortunate Queen in the grounds of Trianon. Often, very often, have I had the honor of presenting Her Majesty and the Princess of Lamballe with bunches of roses and myrtle!"

"Ah!" interrupted the other, the tears standing in his eyes, "God rest their poor souls! There are no such women now in France!"

"Do you indeed think so?"

"Yes, yes," said his companion, "you may believe him, madam. He also was an old servant of the Royal Family."

While I was thus interestingly engaged with these two men, who had completely overcome my first unfavorable impression, the Duke Serbelloni's carriage drew up, and set that nobleman down at the door of the church.

I should explain that the Duke was a particular friend. I had been indebted to the unfortunate Princess for my introduction to His Grace at Milan, on my first being commissioned to go to Italy. To him, also, I owe the first knowledge of my present husband, to whose family he recommended me, when I visited Venice, on the way to Naples, where I had been thrown into a dangerous illness by the fatal intelligence of her highness's murder. But for this event, by which all my future prospects were annihilated, I should never have changed my condition without her consent, though I have never known aught but happiness in the union for which I asked no sanction but my own.

But to quit this digression. The Duke, whom I had not long left with my husband and some others at my lodging in the Hotel Boston, Rue Vivienne, seemed surprised to find me at such a place, and especially in such company.

"*Cosa mai fatte qui?*" "What are you doing here?" cried he in Italian.

I told him it was one of my daily haunts; when the two men, who knew the Duke, asked, "Sir, will you be answerable for this lady's appearance to-morrow at the office of the police?"

The Duke answered in the affirmative; and we left the place and the vestige remained by which it could be distinguished as belonging to the human species; and then left it among the hundreds of innocent victims of that awful day, who were heaped up to putrify in one confused and disgusting mass.

The head was reserved for other purposes of cruelty and horror. It was first borne to the Temple, beneath the windows of the royal prisoners. The wretches who were hired daily to insult them in their dens of misery, by proclaiming all the horrors vomited from the national Vesuvius, were commissioned to redouble their howls of what had befallen the Princess Lamballe.* The Queen sprang up at the name of her friend. She heard subjoined to it, "*la voilà en triomphe*," and then came shouts and laughter. She looked out. At a distance she perceived something like a Bacchanalian procession, and thought, as she hoped, that the Princess was coming to her in triumph

men, with whom I should have been happy to have had a longer conversation.

This wish was gratified in a few days. Fouché, being satisfied with the Duke Serbelloni's explanation of my churchyard adventure, sent these very men back to me, with a note, signifying that I had no occasion to appear at his office; but at the same time advising me to abstain from visiting *la Madeleine;* an advice which, *malgré moi*, I attended to.

From this second interview with the men, I gleaned the above details of horror. I fainted during the shocking narrative. I could not listen to learn how this most infamous, most atrocious scene ended; and it has too deeply affected me ever since to allow of my making any further inquiries, as to where the insulted form of this transcendent loveliness and purity had been deposited. But I have every reason to believe that no inquiries could have been of the least avail.

* These horrid circumstances I had from the Chevalier Cléry, who was the only attendant allowed to assist Louis XVI. and his unhappy family, during their last captivity; but who was banished from the Temple as soon as his royal master was beheaded, and never permitted to return. Cléry told me all this when I met him at Pyrmont, in Germany. He was then in attendance upon the late Countess de Lisle, wife of Louis XVIII., at whose musical parties I had often the honor of assisting, when on a visit to the beautiful Duchess de Guiche. On returning to Paris from Germany, on my way back to Italy, I met the wife of Cléry, and her friend M. Beaumond, both old

from her prison, and her heart rejoiced in the anticipation of once more being blessed with her society. But the King, who had seen and heard more distinctly from his apartment, flew to that of the Queen. That the horrid object might not escape observation, the monsters had mounted upon each other's shoulders so as to lift the bleeding head quite up to the prison bars. The King came just in time to snatch Her Majesty from the spot, and thus she was prevented from seeing it. He took her up in his arms and carried her to a distant part of the Temple, but the mob pursued her in her retreat, and howled the fatal truth even at her very door, adding that HER head would be the next the nation would require. Her Majesty fell into violent hysterics. The butchers of human flesh continued in the interior of the Temple, parading the triumph of their assassination, until the shrieks of the Princess Elizabeth at the state in which she saw the Queen, and serious fears for the safety of the royal prisoners, aroused the commandant to treble the national guard and chase the barbarians to the outside, where they remained for hours.

The head was then taken through the streets. By a singular circumstance it became the cause of immediate death to one who had been in my employ. The strange event happened as follows:

My English man servant and the young girl who had accompanied me from France to Italy were both taken very ill from the violent heat we had suffered from traveling night and day in the month of August, 1792. I was, therefore, obliged to send them both back for the benefit of their native air. They reached Paris on the

friends of mine, who confirmed Cléry's statement, and assured me they were all for two years in hourly expectation of being sent to the Place de Grève, for execution. The death of Robespierre saved their lives.

Madame Cléry taught Maria Antoinette to play upon the harp. Madame Beaumond was a natural daughter of Louis XV. I had often occasion to be in their agreeable society; and, as might be expected, their minds were stored with the most authentic anecdotes and information upon the topics of the day.

very day of the massacre. The first thing the girl saw, on alighting from the diligence, was the head of the well-known benefactress of her mistress. The fellow who was bearing it thrust it so near their faces that the long hair of the victim entangled itself on the button of my man servant's coat, who took a knife and cut the locks to disentangle himself from the head. On his return to Italy he gave me the hair which he thus cut off. I have kept it by me ever since. The poor girl, at sight of the horrid spectacle, gave but a shriek, and died in six hours after she reached the inn!

The horrid spectacle was next exhibited within the Palais Royal. Madame Buffons, the avowed mistress of its royal occupier, was dining with him. They both started up and ran to the window. On discovering the cause of the tumult, Madame Buffons fainted. The Duke of Orleans, it is said, remarked, "Oh, it is Lamballe's head — I know it by the long hair." Madame Buffons reviving, exclaimed, "Heaven knows how soon mine may be struck off and paraded in the same manner! Send it out of sight. Send it out of the palace, or I shall expire!"

What further became of these precious remains has never transpired. The probability is that, amid the sanguinary cannibal drunkenness, they were cast among the remains of the other victims; for though immense sums were offered, and repeated efforts made to regain them, no traces ever could be discovered.

Ah me! What have I lost in this ill-starred Princess! More, more than even a mother! Oh, that I could but strew flowers over her grave! But even this little consolation has been rendered impossible.*

* It was reported that Napoleon, when he became Emperor of France, respecting the virtues of this illustrious sufferer, ordered, in commemoration of this event, the funeral rites to be performed in the parish where she had been butchered, on the 3d day of every September. Her birthday would have been on the 8th of the same month. It was certainly doing honor to himself, to cause so just a tribute to be paid to the memory of one who had been the pride and blessing of the country he was called to govern.

Words cannot express what a void I felt on returning some years after these horrible calamities to Paris, to find that no trace of the angelic form of my beloved benefactress had been suffered to remain; that no clue had ever been discovered to the sod which enwraps her mutilated body; that there was not even a tombstone to point out the resting place of her mangled frame. There would have been a happiness even in communing with her spirit over her burial place. Nothing is more calculated to discipline the human heart than the midnight haunts of the churchyard. What a school for royalty and earthly grandeur! Every sense is there tempered and intellectualized. Love, friendship, paternal and filial sympathies, are all awakened into rational activity by the reflections excited by such a scene. Grief on the green sod knows no deception. How often have I left the sons of mirth and gayety paying libations to Bacchus to pass an hour at the grave of Maria Antoinette, lamenting I could not enjoy the same consolation, and unburden the anguish of my soul in solemn prayer, over her martyred friend. But she is above the reach of mortals. She is in Heaven; she dwells where virtues like those of a Lamballe can alone find refuge against earthly venom. I well know I shall be harshly dealt with for my weakness in thus pining after the remains of those who exist no longer; and I anticipate the lash of the literary rod. Yet I cannot withhold the tears of grateful recollection. Often have they lifted a load of oppression from my bosom; the scalding drops which parched my cheeks, as they fell tributary to her cruel fate, have given me as much relief as those which, at other times, have dimmed my eyes with laughter at her repartees.

But away, busy, intruding memory! Lead me no further into the fields of melancholy and despair. Long have I trodden on the icy, chilling paths of the neglected tomb — the only remaining solace to my bereavements. Let me withdraw from these dejecting solitudes — if not for my own sake, at least for that of others!

CHAPTER XXVIII.

IT NOW only remains for me to complete my record by a few facts and observations relating to the illustrious victims who a short time survived the Princess Lamballe. I shall add to this painful narrative some details which have been mentioned to me concerning their remorseless persecutors, who were not long left unpursued by just and awful retribution. Having done this, I shall dismiss the subject.

The execrable and sacrilegious modern French Pharisees, who butchered, on the 1st, 2d, and 3d of September, 1792, all the prisoners at Paris, by these massacres only gave the signal for the more diabolical machinations, which led to the destruction of the still more sacred victims of the 21st of January, and the 16th of October, 1793, and the myriads who followed.

The King himself never had a doubt with regard to his ultimate fate. His only wish was to make it the means of emancipation for the Queen and Royal Family. It was his intention to have appealed to the national assembly upon the subject, after his trial. Such also was the particular wish of his saintlike sister, the Princess Elizabeth, who imagined that an appeal under such circumstances could not be resisted. But the Queen strongly opposed the measure; and His Majesty said he should be loath, in the last moments of his painful existence, in anything to thwart one whom he loved so tenderly.

He had long accustomed himself, when he spoke of the Queen and royal infants, in deference to the temper of the times, only to say, "my wife and children." They, as he told Cléry, formed a tie, and the only one remaining, which still bound him to earth. Their last embraces, he said, went so to his aching heart, that he could even yet feel their little hands clinging about him, and see their streaming eyes, and hear their agonized and broken voices. The day previous to the fatal catastrophe, when permitted for the last time to see his family, the Princess Elizabeth whispered him, not for herself, but for the Queen and his helpless innocents, to remember his intentions. He said he should not feel himself happy if, in his last hour, he did not give them a proof of his paternal affection, in obtaining an assurance that the sacrifice of his life should be the guarantee of theirs. So intent was his mind upon this purpose, said Cléry to me, that when his assassins came to take him to the slaughtering place, he said, "I hope my death will appease the nation, and that my innocent family, who have suffered on my account, will now be released."

The ruffians answered, "The nation, always magnanimous, only seeks to punish the guilty. You may be assured your family will be respected." Events have proved how well they kept their word.

It was to fulfill the intention of recommending his family to the people with his dying breath that he commenced his address upon the scaffold when Santerre* ordered the drums to drown his last accents, and the axe to fall!

* In the year 1803, the highroads from Italy and Germany to France were in such a horrid state that some parts of the French territory were absolutely impassable. The toll-keepers had most of them fled from their gates, having been repeatedly beaten by the carters, wagoners, postboys, and diligence-drivers, for making them pay, though the roads were so bad that vehicles were upset, limbs broken, carriages crashed, and lives lost. Having experienced some very rough traveling, and not wishing to ruin a very handsome carriage, we determined to leave it to be conducted slowly by our servants, and took our seats in one of the diligences to Rheims. We

The Princess Elizabeth, and perhaps others of the royal prisoners, hoped he would have been reprieved, till Herbert, that real *Père du chêne*, with a smile upon his countenance, came triumphantly to announce to the disconsolate family that Louis was no more!

Perhaps there never was a king more misrepresented and less understood, especially by the immediate age in which he lived, than Louis XVI. He was the victim of natural timidity, increased by the horror of bloodshed, which the exigencies of the times rendered indispensable to his safety. He appeared weak in intellect, when he was only so from circumstances. An overwrought anxiety to be just made him hesitate about the mode of overcoming the abuses, until its procrastination had destroyed the object of his wishes. He had courage sufficient, as well as decision, where others were not menaced and the danger confined to himself; but where his family or his people were involved, he was utterly unfit to give direction. The want of self-sufficiency in his own faculties has been his and his throne's ruin. He consulted those who caused him to swerve from the path his own better reason had dictated, and, in seeking the best course, he often chose the worst.

The same fatal timidity which pervaded his character extended to his manners. From being merely awkward,

had only traveled a few paces when the diligence stopped and took up an outside passenger. A very heavy storm came on, and the master of the diligence opened the carriage door to let the outside passenger get in. Two gentlemen, who were seated between us, the moment they saw the stranger's face, started, drew their pistols, jumped out, called the coachman, and swore the passenger should not enter, and that if he even attempted again to take his place in the same vehicle, they would blow out his brains. When the fellow found all resistance vain, he contented himself, after a good drubbing, to be left behind, and walked to his journey's end. The gentlemen having resumed their places in the carriage, we naturally inquired into the cause of all this bustle. We then learned that the man who had been expelled from the coach was the wretch Santerre, who commanded the troops at Paris on the occasion above mentioned, and who so cruelly ordered the drums to beat, to hasten the execution and prevent his dying King's last words from being heard.

he at last became uncouth; but from the natural goodness of his heart, the nearest to him soon lost sight of
his ungentleness from the rectitude of his intentions,
and, to parody the poet, saw his deportment in his feelings.

Previous to the Revolution, Louis XVI. was generally
considered gentle and affable, though never polished.
But the numberless outrages suffered by his Queen, his
family, his friends, and himself, especially toward the
close of his career, soured him to an air of rudeness, utterly foreign to his nature and to his intention.

It must not be forgotten that he had lived in a time
of unprecedented difficulty. He was a lamb governing
tigers. So far as his own personal bearing is concerned,
who is there among his predecessors, that, replaced upon
the throne, would have resisted the vicissitudes brought
about by internal discord, rebellion, and riot, like himself? What said he when one of the heterogeneous, plebeian, revolutionary assemblies not only insulted him, but
added to the insult a laugh? "If you think you can
govern better, I am ready to resign," was the mild but
firm reply of Louis. How glorious would have been the
triumph for the most civilized nation in the center of
Europe had the insulter taken him at his word. When
the experimentalists DID attempt to govern, we all know,
and have too severely felt, the consequences. Yet this
unfortunate monarch has been represented to the world
as imbecile, and taxed with wanting character, firmness,
and fortitude, because he has been vanquished! The
despot conqueror has been vanquished since! Let the indulgent father and affectionate husband put his hand
upon his heart and say, were he now to choose a monarch
between the two, whether he would not feel himself safer
and happier under a king like Louis?

His acquirements were considerable. His memory * was
remarkably retentive and well stored; a quality, I should

* The memories of kings are, like those of players, always in action
and vigorous from hard exercise. This faculty in both cases may be
independent of the higher powers of intellect. Actors, though they

infer from all I have observed, common to most sovereigns. By the multiplicity of persons they are in the
habit of seeing, and the vast variety of objects continually passing through their minds, this faculty is kept in
perpetual exercise.

But the circumstance which probably injured Louis
XVI. more than any other was his familiarity with the
locksmith, Gamin. Innocent as was the motive whence it
arose, this low connection lessened him more with the
whole nation than if he had been the most vicious of
princes. How careful sovereigns ought to be, with re-
pect to the attentions they bestow on men in humble
life; especially those whose principles may have been de-
moralized by the meanness of the associations consequent
upon their occupation, and whose low origin may have
denied them opportunities of intellectual cultivation.

This observation may even be extended to the liberal
arts. It does not follow because a monarch is fond of
these that he should so far forget himself as to make
their professors his boon companions. He loses ground
whenever he places his inferiors on a level with himself.
Men are estimated from the deference they pay to their
own stations in society. The great Frederic of Prussia
used to say, "I must show myself a king, because my
trade is royalty." *

know not the difference between topography and geography, and
cannot tell whether Spain be in Europe or Africa, yet have memories so flexible that they can study a part from morning to night.
This makes me fancy the power of retention quite mechanical. The
application of memory must, of course, depend on genius and education; to further prove this, my humble opinion, in the year 1790
I had the honor to be in company with the Prince Maximilian, at
Paris, then in the French service; when I came to Munich in the
year 1819, His Majesty, then King of Bavaria, did me the honor to
recollect even a part of the conversation, as well as remember my
person.

    * Though Frederic was so passionately fond of music and distinguished
performers, yet he was very particular as to whom he admitted to his
private concerts, and even those who obtained the honor were never received upon terms of personal familiarity. The highest celebrity was
the only passport even to an introduction. From this he refused to

It was only in destitution and anguish that the real character of Louis developed itself. He was firm and patient, utterly regardless of himself, but wrung to the heart for others, not even excepting his deluded murderers. Nothing could swerve him from his trust in Heaven, and he left a glorious example of how far religion can triumph over every calamity and every insult this world has power to inflict.*

allow Mademoiselle Schemelling, afterward the famous Madame Mara, to become a candidate, until one of her patrons, piqued at the denial, caused her to sing to the wind instruments in the King's antechamber. Frederic, much surprised at her voice and execution, asked some one of the band if she understood music. Being answered in the affirmative, he ordered her to be brought into the concert room. There he set before her one of his flute concertos, which he knew she had never seen before. She sung it offhand. He instantly engaged her ; and she became afterward that great Mara, whom so many have imitated, but scarcely any have equaled, and certainly none have surpassed.

* I would not wish to be understood as underrating the claims of genius, or as wishing to dissuade anyone from conferring the high rewards to which it has a right to aspire. I am only speaking of state policy. Talents can never be too much appreciated and patronized. When a proper distinction is observed between the artist and his protector, the patronage confers honor on the one, and advantages on the other; and great men of rank and birth seldom lavish such attentions, without calculating upon an equivalent, either in amusement or in public approbation; but how paltry is the compliment of a dinner, a supper, or wine, for the delight received from superior ability ! Therefore let me rather denounce than encourage reserve in the rewards of merit. Any sovereign can draw his sword over the head of an individual and say, " Rise, Cousin Prince! Cousin Duke! Lord! Knight!"—but he cannot with equal facility say, "Rise, Cousin Homer! Cousin Virgil! Cousin Horace!" He would be COZENED in the attempt. God only can impart those gifts. If the great Creator has thought proper, in His divine wisdom, to distinguish a small class of men from the great mass of speaking animals, surely mortals cannot dispense with admiring those whom Providence has so eminently marked out for their models. But it seldom happens that political and literary distinctions can be reconciled, and thence the inexpediency of potentates making companions and confidants of those whom they admire. Besides, it is rare that the highest desert attains the highest notice. Too often does merit in an humble garb feel the bleak winter in a garret, while the superficial impostor, for a song and a laugh, is gorgeously fed in the sunshine of royal favor, especially if of foreign import.

There was a national guard, who, at the time of the imprisonment of the Royal Family, was looked upon as the most violent of Jacobins, and the sworn enemy of royalty. On that account the sanguinary agents of the self-created assembly employed him to frequent the Temple. His special commission was to stimulate the King and Royal Family by every possible argument to self-destruction.

But this man was a friend in disguise. He undertook the hateful office merely to render every service in his power, and convey regular information of the plots of the assembly against those whom he was deputed to persecute. The better to deceive his companions, he would read aloud to the Royal Family all the debates of the regicides, which those who were with him encouraged, believing it meant to torture and insult, when the real motive was to prepare them to meet every accusation, by communicating to them each charge as it occurred. So thoroughly were the assembly deceived, that the friendly guard was allowed free access to the apartments, in order to facilitate, as was imagined, his wish to agonize and annoy. By this means, he was enabled to caution the illustrious prisoners never to betray any emotion at what he read, and to rely upon his doing his best to soften the rigor of their fate.

The individual of whom I speak communicated these circumstances to me himself. He declared also, that the Duke of Orleans came frequently to the Temple during the imprisonment of Louis XVI., but always in disguise; and never till within a few days after the murder of the poor King, did he disclose himself. On that occasion he had bribed the men who were accustomed to light the fires, to admit him in their stead to the apartment of the Princess Elizabeth. He found her on her knees, in fervent prayer for the departed soul of her beloved brother. He performed this office, totally unperceived by this predestined victim; but his courage was subdued by her piety. He dared not extend the stratagem to the apartment of the Queen. On leaving the angelic Princess, he was so overcome by remorse, that he requested my informant to give him a glass of water, saying, "that woman has unmanned me." It was by this circumstance he was discovered.

The Queen was immediately apprized by the good man of the occurrence.

"Gracious God!" exclaimed Her Majesty, "I thought once or twice that I had seen him at our miserable dinner hours, occupied with the other jailers at the outside door. I even mentioned the circumstance to Elizabeth, and she replied, "I also have observed a man resembling Orleans, but it cannot be him, for the man I noticed had a wooden leg."

"That was the very disguise he was discovered in this morning, when preparing, or pretending to prepare, the fire in the Princess Elizabeth's apartment," replied the national guard.

"Merciful Heaven!" said the Queen, "is he not yet satisfied? Must he even satiate his barbarous brutality with being an eyewitness of the horrid state into which he has thrown us? Save me," continued Her Majesty, "Oh, save me from contaminating my feeble sight, which is almost exhausted, nearly parched up for the loss of my dear husband, by looking on him! — Oh, death! come, come and release me from such a sight!"

"Luckily," observed the guard to me, "it was the hour of the general jail dinner, and we were alone; otherwise, I should infallibly have been discovered, as my tears fell faster than those of the Queen, for really her's seemed to be nearly exhausted. However," pursued he, "that Orleans did see the Queen, and that the Queen saw him, I am very sure. From what passed between them in the month of July, 1793, she was hurried off from the Temple to the common prison, to take her trial." This circumstance combined, with other motives, to make the assembly hasten the Duke's trial soon after, who had in the meantime been sent with his young son to Marseilles, there being no doubt that he wished to rescue the Queen, so as to have her in his own power.

On the 16th of October, Her Majesty was beheaded.

Her death was consistent with her life. She met her fate like a Christian, but still like a queen.

Perhaps, had Maria Antoinette been uncontrolled in the exercise of her judgment, she would have shown a spirit in emergency better adapted to wrestle with the times than had been discovered by His Majesty. Certain it is she was generally esteemed the most proper to be consulted of the two. From the imperfect idea which many of the persons in office entertained of the King's capacity, few of them ever made any communication of importance but to the Queen. Her Majesty never kept a single circumstance from her husband's knowledge, and scarcely decided on the smallest trifle without his consent; but so thorough was his confidence in the correctness of her judgment that he seldom, if ever, opposed her decisions. The Princess Lamballe used to say, "Though Maria Antoinette is not a woman of great or uncommon talents, yet her long practical knowledge gave her an insight into matters of moment which she turned to advantage with so much coolness and address amid difficulties, that I am convinced she only wanted free scope to have shone in the history of princes as a great queen. Her natural tendencies were perfectly domestic. Had she been kept in countenance by the manners of the times or favored earlier by circumstances, she would have sought her only pleasures in the family circle, and, far from Court intrigue, have become the model of her sex and age."

It is by no means to be wondered at that, in her peculiar situation, surrounded by a thoughtless and dissipated Court, long denied the natural ties so necessary to such a heart, in the heyday of youth and beauty, and possessing an animated and lively spirit, she should have given way in the earlier part of her career to gayety, and been pleased with a round of amusements. The sincere friendship which she afterward formed for the Duchess Polignac encouraged this predilection. The plot to destoy her had already been formed, and her enemies were too sharp-sighted and adroit not to profit and take advantage of the opportunities afforded by this weakness. The miscreants had murdered her character long, long before they assailed her person.

The charge against her of extravagance has been already refuted. Her private palace was furnished from the state lumber rooms, and what was purchased, paid for out of her savings. As for her favorites, she never had but two, and these were no supernumerary expense or encumbrance to the state.

Perhaps it would have been better had she been more thoroughly directed by the Princess Lamballe. She was perfectly conscious of her good qualities, but Polignac dazzled and humored her love of amusement and display of splendor. Though this favorite was the image of her royal mistress in her amiable characteristics, the resemblance unfortunately extended to her weaknesses. This was not the case with the Princess Lamballe; she possessed steadiness, and was governed by the cool foresight of her father-in-law, the Duke de Penthièvre, which both the other friends wanted.

The unshaken attachment of the Princess Lamballe to the Queen, notwithstanding the slight at which she at one time had reason to feel piqued, is one of the strongest evidences against the slanderers of Her Majesty. The moral conduct of the Princess has never been called in question. Amid the millions of infamous falsehoods invented to vilify and degrade every other individual connected with the Court, no imputation, from the moment of her arrival in France, up to the fatal one of her massacre, ever tarnished her character. To her opinion, then, the most prejudiced might look with confidence. Certainly no one had a greater opportunity of knowing the real character of Maria Antoinette. She was an eyewitness to her conduct during the most brilliant and luxurious portion of her reign; she saw her from the meridian of her magnificence down to her dejection to the depths of unparalleled misery. If the unfortunate Queen had ever been guilty of the slightest of those glaring vices of which she was so generally accused, the Princess must have been aware of them: and it was not in her nature to have remained the friend and advocate, even unto death, of one capable of depravity. Yet not a breath of discord ever arose between them on that score. Virtue and vice can never harmonize; and even had policy kept her highness from avowing a change of sentiments, it never could have continued her enthusiasm, which was augmented, and not diminished, by the fall of her royal friend. An attachment which holds through every vicissitude must be deeply rooted from conviction of the integrity of its object.

The friendship that subsisted between this illustrious pair is an everlasting monument that honors their sex. The Queen used to say of her, that she was the only female she had ever known without gall. "Like the blessed land of Ireland," observed Her Majesty, "exempt from the reptiles elsewhere so dangerous to mankind, so was she freed by Providence from the venom by which the finest form in others is empoisoned. No envy, no ambition, no desire, but to contribute to the welfare and happiness of her fellow-creatures — and yet, with all these estimable virtues, these angelic qualities, she is doomed, from her virtuous attachment to our persons, to sink under the weight of that affliction, which, sooner or later, must bury us all in one common ruin — a ruin which is threatening hourly."

These presentiments of the awful result of impending storms were mutual. From frequent conversations with the Princess Lamballe, from the evidence of her letters and her private papers, and from many remarks which have been repeated to me personally by her highness, and from persons in her confidence, there is abundant evidence of the forebodings she constantly had of her own and the Queen's untimely end.*

* A very remarkable circumstance was related to me when I was at Vienna, after this horrid murder. The Princess of Lobkowitz, sister to the Princess Lamballe, received a box, with an anonymous letter, telling her to conceal the box carefully till further notice. After the riots had subsided a little in France, she was apprised that the box contained all, or the greater part, of the jewels belong-

There was no friend of the Queen to whom the King showed any deference or rather anything like the deference he paid to the Princess Lamballe. When the Duchess de Polignac, the Countess Diana Polignac, the Count d'Artois, the Duchess of Guiche, her husband, the present Duke de Grammonte, the Prince of Hesse-Darmstadt, etc., fled from Paris, he and the Queen, as if they had foreseen the awful catastrophe which was to destroy her so horribly, entreated her to leave the Court, and take refuge in Italy. So also did her father-in-law, the Duke de Penthièvre; but all in vain. She saw her friend deprived of Polignac, and all those near and dear to her heart, and became deaf to every solicitation. Could such constancy, which looked death in its worst form in the face unshrinking, have existed without great and estimable qualities in its possessor?

The brother-in-law of the Princess Lamballe, the Duke of Orleans, was her declared enemy merely from her attachment to the Queen. These three great victims have been persecuted to the tomb, which had no sooner closed over the last than the hand of Heaven fell upon their destroyer. That Louis XVI. was not the friend of this member of his family can excite no surprise, but must rather challenge admiration. He had been seduced by his artful and designing regicide companions to expend millions to undermine the throne, and shake it to pieces under the feet of his relative, his sovereign, the friend of his earliest youth, who was aware of the treason, and who held the thunderbolt, but would not crush him. But they have been foiled in their hope of building a throne for him upon the ruin they had made, and placed an axe where they flattered him he would find a diadem.

The Prince of Conti told me at Barcelona, that the

ing to the Princess, and had been taken from the Tuileries on the 10th of August.

It is supposed that the jewels had been packed by the Princess in anticipation of her doom, and forwarded to her sister through her agency or desire.

Duchess of Orleans had assured him that even had the
Duke of Orleans survived, he never could have attained
his object. The immense sums he had lavished upon the
horde of his revolutionary satellites, had, previous to his
death, thrown him into embarrassment. The avarice of
his party increased as his resources diminished. The
evil, as evil generally does, would have wrought its own
punishment in either way. He must have lived suspected and miserable, had he not died. But his reckless
character did not desert him at the scaffold. It is said
that before he arrived at the Place de Grêve he ate a
very rich ragoût, and drank a bottle of champagne, and
left the world as he had gone through it.

The supernumerary, the uncalled-for martyr, the last
of the four devoted royal sufferers, was beheaded the
following spring. For this murder there could not have
been the shadow of a pretext. The virtues of this victim
were sufficient to redeem the name of Elizabeth * from
the stain with which the two of England and Russia,
who had already borne it, had clouded its immortality.
She had never, in any way, interfered in political events.
Malice itself had never whispered a circumstance to her
dispraise. After this wanton assassination, it is scarcely to
be expected that the innocent and candid looks and streaming azure eyes of that angelic infant, the dauphin, though
raised in humble supplication to his brutal assassins,
with an eloquence which would have disarmed the savage
tiger, could have won wretches so much more pitiless
than the most ferocious beasts of the wilderness, or saved
him from THEIR slow but sure poison, whose breath was
worse than the upas tree to all who came within its influence.

The Duchess d'Angoulême, the only survivor of these

* The eighteen years' imprisonment and final murder of Mary, Queen
of Scots, by Elizabeth of England, is enough to stigmatize her forever,
independently of the many other acts of tyranny, which stain her
memory. The dethronement by Elizabeth of Russia of the innocent
Prince Ivan, her near relation, while yet in the cradle, gives the Northern
Empress a claim to a similar character to the British Queen.

wretched captives, is a living proof of the baleful influence of that contaminated prison, the infectious tomb of the royal martyrs. That once lovely countenance, which, with the goodness and amiableness of her royal father, whose mildness hung on her lips like the milk and honey of human kindness — blended the dignity, grace, elegance, and innocent vivacity, which were the acknowledged characteristics of her beautiful mother — lost for some time all traces of its original attractions. The lines of deep-seated sorrow are not easily obliterated. If the sanguinary republic had not wished to obtain by exchange the Generals La Fayette, Bournonville, Lameth, etc., whom Dumourier had treacherously consigned into the hands of Austria, there is little doubt but that, from the prison in which she was so long doomed to vegetate only to make life a burden, she would have been sent to share the fate of her murdered family.*

How can the Parisians complain that they found her royal highness, on her return to France, by no means what they required in a princess ? Can it be wondered at that her marked grief should be visible when amid the murderers of her family ? It should rather be a wonder that she can at all bear the scenes in which she moves, and not abhor the very name of Paris, when every step must remind her of some outrage to herself, or those most dear to her, or of some beloved relative or friend destroyed! Her return can only be accounted for by the spell of that all-powerful *amor patriæ*, which sometimes prevails over every other influence.

That this passion was paramount in the breast of the Duchess d'Angoulême I am persuaded, from a story related to me of her by her royal highness's aunt, the late Archduchess Maria Christiana, Governess of the Low Countries. "My niece," said the archduchess, "has noth-

---

* It is no less singular than true that the wretch Gamin, the King's blacksmith, who had been in the habit of working with Louis XVI., and afterward betrayed him so infamously to the national assembly, was chosen by that assembly, or some of its regicide members, to prepare the locks and other things necessary for his daughter's departure.

ing in her of the House of Austria.   She is her father's child — a Frenchwoman every inch of her"; and, to confirm the remark, she mentioned the following circumstance.

The change from the horrible situation from which her royal highness had been so miraculously saved, and the narrow escape, perhaps, from an untimely and ignominious death, to the midst of her mother's imperial relations,* and all the splendors of palaces, would, it was imagined, have lighted up her mind with a rapture, like that which must fill the wearied and woe-worn spirit that suddenly awakes in Paradise.   To make the transition still more impressive, every device to amuse a youthful mind was put in action; and even the Emperor has been seen gamboling for her diversion, and himself drawing her in a little garden chair round the gardens of Schoubrunn.

But all was in vain.   She was never seen to laugh or even smile during the whole time of her residence there. In her room she kept an urn, with the emblems of death, and much of her time was devoted in prayers before it, to the departed souls of her murdered family.

When Madame de Mackau, who had brought her into Germany, was obliged to leave her and return to France, the young Duchess was literally inconsolable, and would fain have gone back with her.   She was remonstrated with, respecting such superabundant patriotism toward the ungrateful country on which she could only look with execration, upon which she answered: "True, it has been cruel and ungrateful, but still it is my country; and I do not deny that I feel the most poignant grief at having left it, and am overwhelmed at the idea of perhaps never more being able to return to it!"

Fate has since decreed that she SHOULD return to it; and may her native land, to which she has preserved such constancy, through so many cruelties, remember it, and endeavor to atone for what it has inflicted on her.

---

* The Emperor and Empress were her first cousins: one the son of Leopold, Grand Duke of Tuscany, the other daughter of the late Queen Carolina of Naples, and both brother and sister of Maria Antionette.

Before I dismiss this subject, it may not be uninteresting to my readers to receive some desultory anecdotes that I have heard concerning one or two of the leading monsters, by whom the horrors upon which I have expatiated were occasioned.

David, the famous painter, was a member of the sanguinary tribunal which condemned the King. On this account he has been banished from France since the restoration.

If anyone deserved this severity, it was David. It was at the expense of the Court of Louis XVI. that this ungrateful being was sent to Rome, to perfect himself in his sublime art. His studies finished, he was pensioned from the same patrons, and upheld as an artist by the special protection of every member of the Royal Family.

And yet this man, if he may be dignified by the name, had the baseness to say in the hearing of the unfortunate Louis XVI., when on trial, " Well! when are we to have his head dressed *à la guillotine?* "

At another time, being deputed to visit the Temple, as one of the committee of public safety, as he held out his snuffbox before the Princess Elizabeth, she, conceiving he meant to offer it, took a pinch. The monster, observing what she had done, darting a look of contempt at her, instantly threw away the snuff, and dashed the box to pieces on the floor.

Robespierre had a confidential physician, who attended him almost to the period when he ascended the scaffold, and who was very often obliged, *malgré-lui*, to dine *tête-à-tête* with this monopolizer of human flesh and blood. One day he happened to be with him, after a very extraordinary number had been executed, and among the rest, some of the physician's most intimate acquaintances.

The unwilling guest was naturally very downcast, and ill at ease, and could not dissemble his anguish. He tried to stammer out excuses and get away from the table.

Robespierre, perceiving his distress, interrogated him as to the cause.

The physician, putting his hand to his head, discovered some reluctance to explain.

Robespierre took him by the hand, assured him he had nothing to fear, and added, " Come doctor, you, as a professional man, must be well informed as to the sentiments of the major part of the Parisians respecting me. I entreat you, my dear friend, frankly to avow their opinion. It may perhaps serve me for the future, as a guide for governing them."

The physician answered, " I can no longer resist the impulse of nature. I know I shall thereby oppose myself to your power, but I must tell you, you are generally abhorred — considered the Attila, the Sylla, of the age. The two-footed plague, that walks about to fill peaceful abodes with miseries and family mournings. The myriads you are daily sending to the slaughter at the *Place de Grève*, who have committed no crime, the carts of a certain description you have ordered daily to bear a stated number to be sacrificed, directing they should be taken from the prisons, and, if enough are not in the prisons, seized, indiscriminately in the streets, that no place in the deadly vehicle may be left unoccupied, and all this without a trial, without even an accusation, and without any sanction but your own mandate — these things call the public curse upon you, which is not the less bitter for not being audible."

"Ah!" said Robespierre, laughing. "This puts me in mind of a story told of the cruelty and tyranny of Pope Sextus the Fifth, who, having, one night, after he had enjoyed himself at a Bacchanalian supper, when heated with wine, by way of a *bonne bouche*, ordered the first man that should come through the gate of the *Strada del popolo* at Rome, to be immediately hanged. Every person at this drunken conclave — nay, all Rome — considered the pope a tyrant, the most cruel of tyrants, till it was made known and proved, after his death, that the wretch so executed had murdered his father and mother ten years previously. I know whom I send to the *Place de Grève*. All who go there are guilty, though they may not seem so. Go on, what else have you heard?"

"Why, that you have so terrified all descriptions of persons, that they fear even your very breath, and look upon you as worse than the plague; and I should not be surprised, if you persist in this course of conduct, if something serious to yourself should be the consequence, and that ere long."

Not the least extraordinary part of the story is that this dialogue between the devil and the doctor took place but a very few hours previous to Robespierre's being denounced by Tallien and Carrière to the national convention, as a conspirator against the republican cause. In defending himself from being arrested by the guard, he attempted to shoot himself, but the ball missed, broke the monster's jawbone only, and nearly impeded his speaking.

Singularly enough, it was this physician who was sent for to assist and dress his wounds. Robespierre replied to the doctor's observations, laughing, and in the following language:

"Oh, poor devils! they do not know their own interest. But my plan of exterminating the evil will soon teach them   This is the only thing for the good of the nation, for, before you can reform a thousand Frenchmen, you must first lop off half a million of these vagabonds, and, if God spare my life, in a few months there will be so many the less to breed internal commotions, and disturb the general peace of Europe.*

* When Bonaparte was contriving the Consulship for life, and, in the Irish way, forced the Italian Republic to volunteer an offer of the Consulship of Italy, by a deputation to him at Paris, I happened to be there. Many Italians, besides the deputies, went on the occasion, and among them, we had the good fortune to meet the Abbé Fortis, the celebrated naturalist, a gentleman of first-rate abilities, who had traveled three-fourths of the globe in mineralogical research. The Abbé chanced one day to be in company with my husband, who was an old acquaintance of his, where many of the chop-fallen deputies like themselves, true lovers of their country, could not help declaring their indignation at its degraded state, and reprobating

The same physician observed that from the immense number of executions during the sanguinary reign of that monster, the *Place de Grève* became so complete a swamp of human blood that it would scarcely hold the scaffolding of the instrument of death, which, in consequence, was obliged to be continually moved from one side of the square to the other. Many of the soldiers and officers, who were obliged to attend these horrible executions, had constantly their half boots and stockings filled with the blood of the poor sufferers; and as, whenever there was any national festival to be given, it generally followed one of the most sanguinary of these massacres, the public places, the theaters especially, all bore the tracks of blood throughout the saloons and lobbies.

The infamous Carrière, who was the execrable agent of his still more execrable employer, Robespierre, was left afterward to join Tallien in a conspiracy against him, merely to save himself; but did not long survive his atrocious crimes or his perfidy. It is impossible to calculate the vast number of private assassinations committed

Bonaparte for rendering it so ridiculous in the face of Europe and the world. The Abbé Fortis, with the voice of a Stentor, and spreading his gigantic form, which exceeded six feet in height, exclaimed: "This would not have been the case had that just and wise man Robespierre lived but a little longer."

Everyone present was struck with horror at the observation. Noticing the effect of his words, the Abbé resumed:

"I knew well I should frighten you in showing any partiality for that bloody monopolizer of human heads. But you do not know the perfidy of the French nation so well as I do. I have lived among them many years. France is the sink of human deception. A Frenchman will deceive his father, wife, and child; for deception is his element. Robespierre knew this, and acted upon it, as you shall hear."

The Abbé then related to us the story I have detailed above, *verbatim*, as he had it from the son of Esculapius, who himself confirmed it afterward in a conversation with the Abbé in our presence.

Having completed his anecdote, "Well," said the Abbé, "was I not right in my opinion of this great philosopher and foreseer of evils, when I observed that had he but lived a few months longer, there would have been so many less in the world to disturb its tranquillity?"

in the dead of the night, by order of this cannibal, on persons of every rank and description. I knew a daughter of this Carrière very well, who was educated by Madame Campan. She is married to an Italian, and if ever the hand of God marked "Beware of the descendants of the guilty!" she, poor woman, and her children, are woeful living examples. Her bodily infirmities, though a young and well-looking woman, are of the most disgusting nature, and have baffled the art of all the physicians in France and Italy. When attacked, she is distorted in the most frightful and hideous manner. Her children, every one of them, are disgustingly deformed, with scarcely the resemblance of human features.

My task is now ended. Nothing remains for me but the reflections which these sad and shocking remembrances cannot fail to awaken in all minds, and especially in mine. Is it not astonishing, that in an age so refined, so free from the enormous and flagitious crimes which were the common stains of barbarous centuries, and at an epoch peculiarly enlightened by liberal views — the French nation, by all deemed the most polished since the Christian era, should have given an example of such wanton, brutal, and coarse depravity to the world, under pretenses altogether chimerical, and after unprecedented bloodshed and horror, ending at the point where it began.

The organized system of plunder and anarchy, exercised under different forms more or less sanguinary, produced no permanent result beyond an incontestible proof that the versatility of the French nation and its puny suppleness of character utterly incapacitate it for that energetic enterprize without which there can be no hope of permanent emancipation from national slavery. It is my unalterable conviction, that the French will never know how to enjoy an independent and free constitution.

The tree of liberty unavoidably in all nations has been sprinkled with human blood; but when bathed by INNOCENT victims, like the foul weed, though it spring up, it rots in its infancy, and becomes loathsome and infectious.

Such has been the case in France; and the result justifies the Italian satire:

> " *Un albero senza fruta*
> *Baretta senza testa*
> *Governo che non resta.*"

O France! for what misdeeds hast thou to atone, for
what execrable crimes! Within thy cities the earliest
rudiments of my education and my first permanent impressions were received. Thou art almost my country,
the scene of my first interests and attachments. But
thy enormities overshadowed my youth, blighted and
neutralized my prospects, steeped my riper age in grief,
and harassed my maturity with disappointment. Thou
hast left me nothing but reminiscences of wrong and insult to those to whom thou and I both owed so much;
and my present condition amid thy rapacious children
convinces me that thou art devoid of liberality, incapable of justice, saturated with the dregs of the worst
species of barbarism, and art only subdued somewhat in
thy infernal propensities by the uplifted arm of the
nations that surround thee!

Pardon me, generous reader, if, when I touch on this
cruel, cruel subject, I raise a voice too clamorous for the
common ear. Grant me your indulgence should I chance
to be overswayed by the impetuosity of emotions, necessarily kindled by recollections of the dreadful misrule of
a lawless horde of plunderers. It were impossible to
touch unmoved upon scenes which rise around me in
colors of blood and forms of havoc, the most terrific
that ever sickened the human mind with deadly horror,
even were they DISCONNECTED with the angelic Princess,
whose condescensions for me began to assume more of
the mother than the friend; but when gratitude mingles
with the natural excitement of recollections so overwhelming, language can afford no expressions adequate
to what I feel.

But I must endeavor to calm this anguish. I think I
hear some one expostulating with me thus: "Oh! after a

lapse of so many years, surely your good sense — the philosophy for which you have been so much prized — the preservation of your health — the duty you owe to a beloved husband and family — ought in some degree to efface these impressions, and restore you to resignation and tranquillity."

The remonstrance is just. Yet I cannot always exercise that fortitude within myself to which I might counsel others. To dwell on such events in terms of calm serenity is a task beyond my forbearance, and I trust my fervor will be forgiven. I have no interest in what I have transcribed or stated. I can never be blessed in this world with a sight of the august queen who forms the leading subject of my narrative, and can expect nothing from her relations, who did so little for her during the last moments of her miserable life. But I have undertaken the task of vindicating her, as far as my humble abilities and authentic information would allow; and posterity will judge between her and the foul wretches who have steeped themselves in her blood, after having so relentlessly persecuted her before they took her life, and pursued her name with villainous slanders when they had no longer power over her person.

Of that part of my work which belongs to my illustrious patroness and most deplored friend, it would be presumptuous in me to speak. Concerning what I myself have written, I have but one word to say. Accuracy has been my sole ambition. I do not court a place in the Temple of Fame, and shall be more than satisfied by being thought worthy of the glorious distinction of admittance into the Temple of Truth.

Printed in the United States
100130LV00003B/124/A

9 781410 204127